Wisdom's Daughters
How Women Can Change The World

Cathy Pagano

BALBOA.
PRESS

A DIVISION OF HAY HOUSE

Balboa Press books may be ordered through booksellers or by contacting:
Balboa Press
A Division of Hay House
1663 Liberty Drive
Bloomington, IN 47403
www.balboapress.com
1-(877) 407-4847

Because of the dynamic nature of the Internet, any web addresses or links contained in
this book may have changed since publication and may no longer be valid. The views
expressed in this work are solely those of the author and do not necessarily reflect the
views of the publisher, and the publisher hereby disclaims any responsibility for them.

The author of this book does not dispense medical advice or prescribe the use
of any technique as a form of treatment for physical, emotional, or medical
problems without the advice of a physician, either directly or indirectly. The
intent of the author is only to offer information of a general nature to help you
in your quest for emotional and spiritual well-being. In the event you use any
of the information in this book for yourself, which is your constitutional right,
the author and the publisher assume no responsibility for your actions.

Keepers of the Earth: Native American Stories and Environmental
Activities for Children, by Michael J. Caduto and Joseph Bruchac.
Fulcrum Publishing: Golden, CO. Copyright 1988, 1989, 1997
Michael J. Caduto and Joseph Bruchac. Used by permission.
Story Water by Rumi, with kind permission from Coleman Barks, translator.
Cover Art: Kerstin Zettmar, "Aphrodite with Stars" Kerstin is a marvelous artist
and healer from Rhode Island. Please check out her work @ www.zettmar.com

Any people depicted in stock imagery provided by Thinkstock are models,
and such images are being used for illustrative purposes only.
Certain stock imagery © Thinkstock.
Printed in the United States of America

ISBN: 978-1-4525-6582-8 (sc)
ISBN: 978-1-4525-6583-5 (e)
ISBN: 978-1-4525-6584-2 (hc)
Library of Congress Control Number: 2012923877
Balboa Press rev. date: 1/21/2013

Table of Contents

Wisdom's Daughters

When woman is lost, so is man. The truth is,
woman is the window to a man's heart and a
man's heart is the gateway to his soul.

JADA PINKETT SMITH

To Lady Wisdom,
for calling me to her path.

And with love and gratitude to friends and family
who made publishing this book possible.

Forward

Wisdom's Daughters is my youngest child, and I've been pregnant with it for a long while now. You can imagine how delighted I am to finally give birth! It makes *Wisdom's Daughters* my 5th child, and it brings to mind a dream I had while I was studying at the C. G. Jung Institute in Zurich, Switzerland. I dreamed that I gave birth to my *quintessence*. I later found out the *quintessence* is the fifth element, the union of the above and below, the true essence of a thing.

In the dream, my *quintessence* was a beautiful girl named Megan, which means *the pearl*. *Wisdom's Daughters* is also *my pearl of great price*. It has certainly grown luminous through the many obstacles I've faced birthing it into the world. But each of those obstacles slowed me down and forced me to relearn and refine Lady Wisdom's lessons. I had to learn to do the work, not just understand it. I had to become a whole and free woman to guide other women to finding their wholeness and freedom.

Wisdom's Daughters is about women waking up to our feminine powers and real inner freedom. And it is about women's power to change the world. The stories, dreams and visions in it help us understand Lady Wisdom's voice, because she speaks in the symbolic language of the Unconscious. I learned that to find our wisdom we have to be open to the imagination. We have to balance our left and right brain perceptions so we can see with new eyes. I hope this book feeds both sides of the brain: our masculine-oriented left brain that wants to understand things and our feminine-oriented right brain which gives us knowledge of life through the voice of the imagination.

First and foremost, I want to thank my four children: Jennifer, Michael, Gregory and Jonathan. As I began to listen to Lady Wisdom, they were there testing me every step of the way. They challenged me to become a better person, and I learned to understand them through the eyes of Lady Wisdom. I also want to thank my women friends for exploring the unknown with me. When I first began learning about the Goddess back in the 70s, I never would have believed that women would still be under attack in the early decades of the 21st Century. Patriarchy has always disregarded women and our wisdom. But the Cosmic Story of our times is saying that a new day is dawning. Women are stepping forward with great wisdom to help solve the world's problems. As we enter this new age, women will no longer be pressured to think and act like men, but as conscious women we will have the opportunity to show men the way to integrate the heart and mind, the spirit and soul of humanity.

May that day come soon!

Cathy Pagano
St. Nicholas Day, December 6, 2012

King Solomon and Lady Wisdom

There was once a king in Israel named Solomon, a son of King David, the shepherd boy who slew a giant, and Bathsheba, the beautiful one who stole a king's heart. After David died, his son Solomon became king of Israel.

The first thing Solomon did after he was crowned was to go to the sanctuary of Gibeon, a holy place where the Hebrew god, Yahweh, spoke to a seeker in dreams.

And that night, Yahweh came to Solomon in a dream and said: "Ask of me what you will and I will grant it to you."

And in the dream, Solomon said: "You showed great mercy and kindness to my father David while he was king, for he loved you. And now you have shown him even greater love by letting his son sit on his throne after his death."

"You, O Lord, have now made me king over a great people, and I feel like a little child. How can I rule over them if I don't know how?"

"Therefore, I ask you for an understanding heart to judge your people, so I can discern between good and bad. I ask you for the Wisdom to judge your people and be a good king."

And Yahweh was pleased with Solomon for asking for this gift. And Yahweh said: "Because you have asked for Wisdom and have not asked for a long life for yourself, or riches, or power over your enemies, but instead seek Wisdom, I will give you what you ask for. I will give you a wise and understanding heart. And no one before or after you will be remembered as you are – the wise king."

And then Yahweh added: "And I will give you the things you have not asked me for, both riches and honor, and there will be no other king like you in all your days. Just promise that you will walk in my ways, and keep my commandments as your father David did, and I will give you a long life."

Then Solomon awoke, and remembered his dream. And went back to Jerusalem and stood before the Ark of the Covenant of the Lord and gave thanks.

Now soon after, two women came to Solomon for judgment, for he sat in his judgment hall and his people could come before him to ask for justice.

And one of the women said: "Oh great King, this other woman and I live together in one house. Not long ago, I gave birth to a child and three days after, this woman also gave birth to a son. And in the night, this woman must have mistakenly smothered her child, for she came to my bed and stole my living child, while she left her dead son with me. And when I awoke in the morning and saw that the child was dead, I thought at first that was my son, but when I looked closely, I saw that it was not. This woman took my son and left me her dead son."

Now the other mother spoke up: "No, great King, this is not the truth. The living child is mine, and this woman speaks out of her grief and guilt. This is my son."

And the first mother cried out that it was not true. And so the mothers argued before the king over the living child.

Now Solomon looked at the women and said: "Both of you say that this is your son. How will we find the truth?"

And Wisdom whispered in Solomon's heart and he listened. Then Solomon called for his sword. And he stood with the sword in his hand and said to his guard: "Divide the living child in half, and give one half to one woman and the other half to the other woman."

Now, when the true mother heard this, she cried out in pain. "No, no. Do not kill the boy. Give him to this woman. Only let him live." And Solomon asked the other mother what should be done. And she said: "Divide him in two."

Then Solomon looked at the women and took the boy in his arms and gave the child to his true mother. "I will not slay this child, but I give him back to the mother who loves him."

And the people of Israel heard of this judgment and understood that Solomon's wisdom came from their great god, Yahweh, and they feared and honored him.

Introduction

Wisdom's Daughters

*In this crucial time of our Earth walk, it is essential that we women
reclaim our ability to nurture, create, and renew life. It is our responsibility
to heal ourselves, reclaim the healing power that is ours, and thus
form a solid foundation for transformation on other levels of life.*
—Brooke Medicine Eagle

The world will be saved by the western woman.
—The Dalai Lama

Wisdom is a Lady

What would you ask for if your God promised you anything you
wanted? Who amongst us would pick Wisdom, as Solomon did, when
offered that miraculous gift? How many of our leaders have asked for
a wise and understanding heart above all else? Perhaps we don't ask
for Wisdom because we don't feel the burden of responsibility that
Solomon felt for his people. But in this time of great transitions, if we
don't take responsibility for ourselves and our world, who will? Freedom
implies responsibility.

If there was ever a time in our human history when we need Wisdom,
it is now. We are living in extraordinary times, a moment of collective
destiny where the human race can and must participate consciously in our

own evolution. This evolution is both personal and collective, opening us to new capacities for co-creation and offering us new possibilities for cultural transformation. For the cultural paradigm that we live in is dying, but it is not going gracefully. We need a new way to understand our world and our place in it. And then we have to create a new and more viable way of living here on our beautiful planet, Earth.

It's true we live in chaotic and changing times, and so people live in fear of war, disease, poverty, death, violence and the unknown. Because the human psyche processes life through stories and images, our unconscious is bringing up ancient images of apocalypse, earth changes and *End Time* scenarios. People have been content to remain unconscious of the damage done to our environment, but we are already living with the results of these misguided policies. But to allow ourselves to fall into more unconsciousness and despair is unimaginative and lazy. We have been given the supreme gift of free will and so our choices do matter. What if, by choosing to follow Lady Wisdom's call, we learn to turn our god-like Creative Imagination to transforming our society and re-creating the world rather than continuing our wars and our conspicuous consumption? We do have it in our power to create a heaven on earth if we so choose. It seems we might only have a small window of time to accomplish this. As of now, the patriarchal paradigm that has shaped our worldview and brought us to this crisis point does not want to transfer its power to the children who will have to live in the future world.

We who are living in these most interesting times have a challenge before us—will we be strong enough and committed enough to use our free will to create peace here on this beautiful Earth of ours? Or will we continue to allow the death and destruction that is rampant in our present world to rage on until we are all lost. If we are all really interconnect, perhaps the fires that raged in Arizona during the early summer of 2011 were caused by humanity's rage at the state of our world. Each of us holds the world in our hands through our choices. Isn't it time to take responsibility for those choices and evolve into a greater vision of who we might become?

If we choose to take up our responsibility to all of life, then we absolutely have to be *'wise as serpents and harmless as doves'* (Matthew 10:16). Unfortunately, the mystics know that Lady Wisdom cries out in the streets for us to come to her so she can give us her gifts, but most people ignore her. Could it be because Wisdom is a Lady?

While we haven't seen great wisdom in society's leaders, more and more ordinary people are looking for meaning in their lives, and that's when Lady Wisdom begins to be sought after. My experience as a counselor is that women search for wisdom as they search to understand themselves. And that fact gives me hope that we will, indeed, create the right kind of change in our world. Like Solomon's judgment, most women would know who that baby's mother was.

With the complex issues facing the world today, I believe that women's freedom and equality is the most important challenge we face, because it is not only a social issue but a *soul* issue. Our world is facing tremendous challenges that will force us to change our worldview, and it is women, who so often champion the soul's perspective on life, who will help find the right solutions to those issues. If women and our unique ways of perceiving life are not respected and granted equal validity on the world stage, perhaps we won't make the absolutely necessary changes we need to make so life can continue to evolve here on our home, the Earth. Women will shift the balance of power, and the old power structures do not want to give up power. Perhaps that's why women's rights are under attack again.

Social and economic equality between the sexes is not enough though, if by equality we mean what we find in America and the West today. As women entered the workplace, we were expected to act like men, and so we have learned the masculine qualities of indivivuality, rationality and focus. But for true equality to blossom, women must discover our unique feminine standpoint and own our unique feminine voice. When we feel confident in our standpoint, our new social structures will respect and value what we discover.

Women, in ever larger numbers, are searching for our lost wisdom. Don't forget, western women have only *been given* the right to vote in the last century, while there are large numbers of women who still don't have that right. While our Islamic sisters are being pushed back into virtual slavery by fundamentalist Islam, western women and our rights are under attack in the United States. Women have learned that we have to act in the appropriate, patriarchal-approved ways to be listened to and valued. We all know that outer freedom does not guarantee inner freedom just as outer tyranny does not invariably block inner freedom.

Many women are working hard to claim our inner freedom from old complexes, beliefs and fears that have been passed on from mother to daughter for generations. These beliefs developed from a patriarchal view of women, one that believed that women and our wisdom were not only irrelevant, but sinful. And so women's wisdom has been ruthlessly repressed. Until now.

The first thing women discover as we search for our feminine Self is how to let go of these patriarchal (rule by the Fathers) projections and expectations that have constrained us for the past 4,000 years. C.G. Jung defined the Self as the archetype of wholeness, the unique and individual spark of Spirit that is our truest nature. To really become relevant in these changing times, women must search for our wholeness, for that is where our native wisdom will be found. We do this when we trust our own instincts, listen to our intuitions and are honest with our feeling and then use our rational mind to make the right choices. Women have to step outside the box of collective convention (the Father's House) and learn to be free. Our still-patriarchal culture wants all of us to believe in its version of reality, a way of understanding the world which subjugates our feminine gifts to its service, gifts that are used, but often not valued.

These gifts of feminine consciousness are still viewed as less important than the masculine gifts of rationality and focus, individuality and scientific facts. When are feelings taken into account when deciding on issues of war and peace? When is intuition honored? Why are psychic abilities still characterized as witchcraft or worse? Where are patience and endurance valued? When do we value the whole instead of the separate parts? When I was growing up, I wanted to have a man's freedom and power to affect change in the world. My heroes were mostly male, since there weren't very many powerful women in my life. They inspired me and I worked hard to become a good Father's Daughter, sharpening the sword of my intellect, striving to live the values that both church and state promoted, getting my degrees so I could become a *useful* member of society.

But I soon realized that I hadn't been given the equal respect for my own deep feminine wisdom in my personal life, nor did I see any feminine wisdom respected and used in decision-making by our cultural institutions. Women's wisdom, which springs from compassion, feeling, cooperation, endurance and intuition, is still too often disregarded in personal relationships as well as in cultural settings, and so we all lose out on valuable opportunities to change our world for the better.

Our Lost Wisdom

What is Wisdom, you might ask? How can I possibly possess it? An ancient writer spoke of her this way.

> *For in her is the Spirit of understanding;… loving that which is good, quick, beneficent, gentle, kind, steadfast, assured, secure,… intelligible, pure, subtle: for Wisdom is more active than all active things;… For she is the brightness of eternal light, and the unspotted mirror of God's majesty, and the image of his goodness… For she is more beautiful than the Sun, and above all the order of the stars: being compared with the light, she is found before it. For after this cometh night, but no evil can overcome Wisdom.* Wisdom 7:22-30

My five-year-old friend Ava explained wisdom this way to her father when asked about loving her slightly older brother. *"Wisdom is when you know you love them in your heart, but you haven't figured it out on the outside yet."*

I believe we are all searching for our lost wisdom.

For a long time now, Lady Wisdom, adorning our public buildings as the Greco-Roman Wisdom-goddesses, Minerva and Pallas Athena, could only be channeled through a masculine, left-brained mode of perception if women wanted to be taken seriously in our culture. Women who go into politics, law, medicine, science and finance— considered masculine professions—find they have to toe the patriarchal line every day. While they use their intuition and feeling whenever possible, they have to fit their feminine perceptions into an already structured reality.

But the world is changing. Women are healing our inner wounds, and learning to express our feminine being without fear or shame. Women have a need to get to know ourselves, after long centuries of being subjugated and twisted by patriarchal expectations. When women look within and acknowledge our strengths and recognize our weaknesses and wounds, we begin to untwist ourselves. We stand up for ourselves, our feelings and our beliefs. We stop trying to become a man's perfect fantasy. *We become our own fantasy! The woman we always wanted to be.* We stop being afraid to excel, and since we've learned to listen within to our own wisdom, we find solutions to our problems. We remember that we are here on Earth to be whole, not perfect, as is so often expected of each of us.

As women heal the wounds inflicted on our feminine being, we become living examples of new ways of being for our children and men. Feminine consciousness within men is just as twisted and wounded – maybe even more so, since the patriarchy looks down on men who are in touch with their feminine soul. While there are many women who still uphold the values of patriarchy and will defend them to their deaths, there are also men who have reclaimed their feminine consciousness and are examples of the new masculine King who works in harmony with Feminine Spirit.

Our culture has not served us well. By devaluing the feminine aspects of life, we created an out-of-control life-style that is killing the Earth, and killing us. And so, it is most especially women's purpose, our unique purpose, to achieve our inner freedom and learn to embody Wisdom, helping to create a new society that equally values and respects both women and men, feminine and masculine consciousness and most especially Soul and Spirit.

As women regain and express our feminine powers, and become wise women, we need an archetypal image that allows us our shadows as well as our light. Women have learned to understand the bright light of the Sun, for we have been Father's Daughters, daughters of the patriarchy, for a long time now. We are unique individuals as much as any man. But still... We sense that we can be more.

There are many ancient forms of the Divine Feminine, goddesses that women can learn from, and in turning to these ancient powers, women have become more comfortable with our innate feminine powers. But these ancient goddesses are just that—ancient. Their images come from different times and different cultures. We need to discover an image of the Divine Feminine that can help us find our unique purpose in these tumultuous times of change, one that embodies the returning Goddess-energy that so many people are feeling.

The Woman Clothed with the Sun

In the many cultural stories that speak about the changing of the ages, it is always Feminine Spirit that brings about the transition to new life, for Feminine Spirit knows the rhythms of life, death and rebirth and is the 'opener of the way'. Living in a world of duality, we must allow masculine and feminine energies to inhabit their unique attributes. Our job is to understand how these different energies work together and how to best use them. In times of cultural transformation, our right-brain, feminine consciousness is our best guide, for it opens us to the Creative Imagination, the realm of possibility.

The return of the Goddess awakens the transformative energy that births the changing of the ages. While other cultures understand this Divine Feminine energy through their own mythological traditions, we westerners have lost touch with our mythological roots. Largely ignored in the western religious story of the changing of the ages is an image of Lady Wisdom, who mediates this transformation to a new world age.

In this story of world-wide spiritual transformation, there is a powerful image of *conscious woman*, an image of the archetypal Feminine Spirit who transforms the old world and gives birth to this new age. I am drawn to this archetypal image because I believe it speaks to our modern sensibilities. And I know that this archetypal image gives us instructions for opening to and incarnating Wisdom.

This image of the awakening Feminine Spirit is an image of the Cosmic Woman: *A Woman, clothed with the Sun, standing on the Moon, crowned with Stars, who is in labor, giving birth to a Savior.* In earlier times and different traditions, this archetypal image was understood as Lady Wisdom. Today I feel this Goddess image of *conscious woman* can be incarnated by women everywhere. This *Woman clothed with the Sun* is Lady Wisdom, who calls all women to become her daughters.

Our times are the forerunner of a new world age, and the times call on us to honor Lady Wisdom, who in Gnostic Christianity is the equal partner of Christ. But Lady Wisdom is not associated with any one religion. We find her in all traditions. Lady Wisdom is the image of the Anima Mundi, the World Soul (Earth's consciousness) and the source of the Collective Unconscious, the library of our collective memories and skills. As such, she belongs to all of us and is within all of us. I believe she is calling women out of the Father's House so we can give birth to a new collective paradigm, a new *way of doing* to match her *deep being* that embraces partnership over domination, love over power, unity over divisiveness, peace over war, and our collective benefit over individual profit.

In leaving the Father's House, women are not rejecting the masculine energies of life, but by re-connecting to our own unique feminine gifts, we are re-integrating both feminine and masculine energies at a newer, higher level of consciousness. Women are learning to re-balance the two lights in our sky: Earth's bi-polar consciousness—the Sun and Moon. Perhaps we will entrain with the Earth once we learn to use both sides of the brain fully. We are becoming this *Woman clothed with the Sun*, finally able to access our feminine wisdom freely and consciously. This wisdom gives us the insight to make life-enhancing decisions, to understand complex situations and to consciously co-create new directions for our culture. This wisdom gives us spiritual insights into life.

We are called to be social artists, people who use our creative vision to enhance and strengthen our common lives, our one world. Our job now is to bring this knowledge and wisdom into the public arena. But we have to face the fact that our womanly wisdom is still viewed with suspicion by the patriarchy. We have only to look at the reaction to Chief Justice Sotomayor calling herself a 'wise Latina woman' to realize how deeply afraid patriarchal men are of sharing their power and privilege. Our most powerful institutions, which control our civilization, are still solidly entrenched in this kind of patriarchal thinking. We live with an unbalanced perspective on life, one that often disregards feminine qualities and values, or else uses them to support our culture's masculine values. We live in a dying paradigm that disregards the Soul and therefore also the Feminine Spirit. And it has led us to the brink of global annihilation.

What the World Needs Now is Wisdom

The truth is: *Wisdom is what we most need right now in our world.*

Women, in breaking away from the patriarchal structures and strictures of life, are recognizing our gifts and re-discovering our wisdom. Wisdom itself is encoded in both our physical and soulful DNA, and as you will see, is available to us within our own bodies, minds, souls and spirit. Wisdom belongs to all humanity, and yet the truth is that women and feminine consciousness connect most easily to it. That is why I believe it is women's gift to the world. That is why it is so important for women to *leave the Father's House*--leave behind the rules and expectations of being a proper wife, worker, mother, friend, as well as the rebellious roles we play out against those rules—being wild, irresponsible, addicted, promiscuous, stupid, angry, or crazy. We need to step outside our collective expectations and heal ourselves, so that we can learn Lady Wisdom's ways and incarnate it in our lives.

To leave the Father's House means to leave behind the old rules and perspective of patriarchy, to take responsibility for our own life and find meaning in what we do; to learn to understand our feelings instead of being overwhelmed by them or repressing them; to learn to listen to and trust our intuitions instead of ignoring them; to search for our personal visions and meaning in life instead of buying into the prevailing collective story of desire, power and consumption; to open ourselves to love in whatever form it comes to us, instead of continuing to get lost in the misery and need to possess and control love; to rediscover our creativity and give it to the world, whether it is our children who grow into conscious adults or our artistic creations that open others to healing and consciousness.

These are the gifts women find once we leave the Father's House behind. We find our own talents, our own patterns of life; we find the source of the wisdom we need to live securely with our Mother, the Earth. The *yin* and *yang* of cosmic interchange is Earth's bi-polar energy, and we all need to bring them into balance within and without. Coupled with the masculine values of action, rationality, individuality, creative genesis and discipline, feminine values empower the imagination, love and compassion, endurance and compromise. Wisdom encourages intelligent and fruitful dialogue over issues and opens us to think with our hearts, to love in a way that allows for our imperfections while demanding greater consciousness, to use our imaginations for life rather than profit. Wisdom takes the *whole* into account, while still honoring individuality. What wonders could we achieve here on Earth if we all asked for the gifts of Lady Wisdom?

Wisdom is not a word we use very often anymore in our society, just as Lady Wisdom is so often ignored by the world. But it's not because there isn't plenty of wisdom around. I hear it flowing out of women all the time. The older woman walking her dog is secure in what she knows and isn't afraid to say it. Mothers who listen to their instincts know it. Women who are turning to the ancient goddesses find it. But we have to name it to own it. Yes, we are wise.

The truth is that men also go in search of Lady Wisdom. These are men who have engaged in deep soul work and who have integrated their feminine and masculine consciousness. They have created the best of our western culture. And of course, Lady Wisdom shows herself to children who see the world through Spirit's eyes. But there are still so many Father's Daughters who do not even know there are other possibilities, as well as men who don't realize wisdom is even there to be found. And the power structures of religion, government, finance and industry—the Fathers—too often denounce and disrespect feminine wisdom, and so our people are not taught about this vital aspect of life.

Lady Wisdom cries out in the marketplace, but no one listens.

In most traditions, the archetype of Wisdom is female. It is not only the Hebraic Wisdom that is feminine, but also the Gnostic, the Greek, the Native American, the Celtic. Men and gods desired Lady Wisdom, just as King Solomon desired the Queen of Sheba, who was the incarnation of Lady Wisdom for him. So it makes sense that when women search for our life's purpose, we discover our connection to Lady Wisdom within ourselves.

My Connection to Lady Wisdom

Some are called by Lady Wisdom early in life. I was, even though I didn't know her name at the time. The truth is, I loved the ancient and the fantastic; the ancient archetypal stories found in fairy tales, myths and modern fantasy inspired me more than our modern cultural stories. And the truth is these archetypal stories contain so much ancient wisdom. After I learned astrology, I came to understand why I was drawn to them. The Sun in my birth chart, which symbolizes my sense of individuality and purpose, is located in the House of the Collective Unconscious. This part of a birth chart symbolizes the Piscean ocean of mystical union, indicating that my life's purpose is to dive deeply into the spiritual mysteries of life and bring back something new.

My Jungian studies helped me understand that my archetypal dreams were messages about my life's purpose. I had to re-awaken certain archetypal energies within myself, so I could re-member and re-awaken my feminine powers. So I could hear the voice of Lady Wisdom.

Lady Wisdom came to me in dreams throughout the years. Dreams carry messages from Spirit; dreams show us the condition of our soul. They come to educate our conscious ego, showing us the things that ego doesn't see. They come to us to transform our feelings. They show us the future, or perhaps other worlds. And maybe they even literally take us to other dimensions. We can't yet say for sure. But I know that dreams have meaning. C. G. Jung believed that dreams come from different levels of our unconscious psyche. Some are from the personal Unconscious, and show us our shadows and our complexes at work. Some dreams come from our cultural Unconscious, where we work out our family lineage and any psychological complexes that are generational. Then there are the Big Dreams, the dreams that come from the Collective Unconscious, the World Soul, which entail multiple dimensions of reality. These dreams are archetypal because some basic principle of life is involved, some deep wisdom must be sought for and integrated into life. While archetypal dreams are unexpected and numinous, they are meant to instruct and guide the soul. So these are some of my formative dreams that I believe are the voice of Lady Wisdom.

The first two dreams I can remember from early childhood were recurring dreams. The first took me deep into the Collective Unconscious, into the waters that give birth to all of us, showing me its ancient beginnings.

> I am under the ocean in a bathysphere. I am so cold, for this ocean is ancient beyond measure and it feels like the cold of outer space. I feel so ALONE. I look through the porthole and see giant, ancient whale-like creatures, swimming back and forth around me in the dark waters.

The second dream presented me with a fairy tale motif of finding the magical doll, which helps me with its wisdom and caring. This motif of the magical doll is found in many fairy tales, especially in different versions of *Cinderella*, which is a story about Lady Wisdom being rejected and devalued. By the way, *Cinderella* isn't waiting for a prince to marry her; she is waiting for the new cultural dominant (the prince) to recognize her wisdom.

My family and I are visiting with friends of the family. I go off by myself and climb a secret staircase that nobody knows of except me, and I find a secret room. In that room is a beautiful doll that belongs to me. It is a magical doll and I know it is special. And I can come to this room often to be with my doll.

In the fairy tales where the doll is left with the daughter at her mother's death, the doll represents the mother's wisdom passed down to her daughter. And because it is woman's wisdom it bears the stamp of Lady Wisdom.

These dreams were only the beginning of my journey in search of Lady Wisdom. I first started in Jungian analysis when I was 29 years old, and I dreamed that I had to understand that the *Unconscious* has its own consciousness and treasures, and I had to engage my masculine intelligence and beliefs to work to understand it. And finally, I had to learn to let the Crone, who is Lady Wisdom, lead me on my journey to wholeness.

I am in the maternity ward of the hospital. I am trying to get out of the hospital and my husband and father have come to help me. As we go past the nursery, I see through the glass a beautiful golden dragon instead of babies. I am filled with joy at the sight. I know that it will disappear in 69 seconds, the time it takes for one heartbeat of the Earth.

Then I'm walking down to the front of my high school auditorium where the principle is waiting to give me the silver sword of the king.

Then I am journeying down a country road, and an old woman is showing me the way.

The dragon can symbolize both the highest consciousness as well as the most reptilian primeval unconsciousness. Of course, like any symbol, its power will come through each person according to their character. But for me, the dragon holds deep Earth Wisdom, just as it guards the treasures of the Collective Unconscious, Lady Wisdom's glittering horde. A golden dragon is even more special and I immediately associated it with the queen dragons in Anne McCaffrey's stories of *The Dragon Riders of Pern*, stories about a world where dragons bond with humans to save the planet from destruction.

The golden queen dragons are especially conscious and intelligent, for they are the mothers of all the dragons. Later I learned to associate gold with spiritual consciousness, like the aura we see around the heads of saints. So to me, the golden dragon meant that I was seeing the birth of a conscious Unconscious, the birth of a connection to Earth's Wisdom. And since big dreams influence us all our lives, I see this golden dragon, this golden consciousness, connected to the *Woman clothed with the Sun*.

Like Arthur's sword *Excalibur*, the silver sword I receive from my high school was the training of my mind, my ability to use my mind to discern truth, as well as my love of knowledge. I love to learn and that love keeps opening my mind to new and different perspectives. My sword is sourced in my values and my curiosity and my will. It is my ability to discern the Truth.

The word Crone means *the crown*, symbolizing a state of sovereignty and completeness. The Crone is associated with the radiant crown of energy surrounding the head when the body's seven chakras are aligned with the crown chakra. The Crone who leads the way in my dream journey is another aspect of Lady Wisdom.

Wisdom does not come all at once, nor does it come easily, but is gained through hard work and responsibility, and these dreams indicated that I was called to this work. Later, while I was training at the C.G. Jung Institute, I had this amazing dream that set me on the road to discovering the *Woman clothed with the Sun*:

> I am hurrying my daughter and her friends along the streets of my hometown, trying to get them home because there is a lion loose in the streets. I meet an old friend and he is going to try to stop the lion before it hurts anyone. I don't know if he'll be able to do it or if he's just being foolish to think he can.
>
> Then I am at the triple-crossroads in my small village in Rhode Island. Everyone is gathered there so we can fight off the lion. I am sitting in an old-fashioned buckboard wagon. Suddenly it gets dark and I see that a giant wave is about to descend on all of us. I see a waning crescent moon in the sky and I think, 'this is it'. Then it seems like the wave has gone past and I see a beautiful waxing crescent moon in the sky.

I hear a voice that says, "You will be the mother of a savior." Then I look around and see that everyone is putting things back to normal. And I think, "Just like the Swiss!"

The lion is an ancient symbol of royalty and power. A wounded lion can be dangerous. To understand this dream, I explored the astrological sign of Leo, the Lion. I'm one of the baby-boomers, born when the planet Pluto was in the sign of Leo from 1938 to 1958. Pluto's archetypal energy brings the urge for evolution, the need to release what is dead and regenerate the energy on a deep level. My generation's evolutionary task is to let go of our old understanding of Leo and heal the lion's wound: our innate entitlement, our ridiculous sense of fun, our outrageous drama-making, our childish creativity that we usually waste on irrelevancies. My generation is called upon to give birth once again to the archetypal power of kingship and queenship, where our creativity is at the service of humanity. We need to learn how to use our creative power for life, rather than the death-in-life that our culture has become.

I was also born with Saturn, the archetypal reality principle, in Leo. Saturn presents us with the wound of not being good at a certain part of life, and its healing becomes our initiation into a deeper, richer life. Saturn in Leo tests our ability to love and feel loved, to have self-confidence without bravado and to use our creativity. Saturn in Leo can fill us with pride and a refusal to see our faults. When Saturn (which can be crystallized, limiting and fear-bound) and Pluto (which destroys what will not die naturally) unite in a sign, evolution can be severely repressed and that energy can turn to violence and destruction. Change is hard work and many of my generation just refused the call to initiation. But Saturn can also focus our attention on Pluto's evolution, giving us the discipline to do the hard work of transformation. Working with these energies, I got the chance to heal my wounded lion in Zurich.

The part of me that decided to go on this journey to stop the wound from being passed on to the next generation is reminiscent of The Fool in the Tarot, setting off on an impossible journey with all the innocence of youth. My wounded Leo self-confidence specifically came from my family heritage and I didn't want to pass it on to my children. A mother's love is the strongest power on Earth, and I would not pass on pain if I could help it. So I knew I had to confront it and transform it, for my children's sake.

The next part of the dream is Lady Wisdom giving me my instructions, if you will. She shows me that transformation is a natural process (the waning and waxing moon), even though it's also overwhelming (the tidal wave of change)! And she sets me on my journey to discover who the *Woman clothed with the Sun* is.

This dream called to me through the years, especially when I went to live in that town with the triple-crossroads to raise my children there. As you can see, Lady Wisdom came to me in my dreams, calling me out of the collective sleep we call reality and into a place that is more real and full than I could ever imagine.

Another dream that seemed to mark me as one of Wisdom's Daughters was a dream in which, to save my family, I was held captive while someone nailed eagle feathers—another symbol of Lady Wisdom—into my 3rd Eye. While this image might seem extreme, ancient shamans had to go through terrifying ordeals to gain their power. It was obviously very important that I learn to use my connection to the imagination (the 3rd Eye) with reverence, responsibility and wisdom.

One last dream showed me how to dance with the mystery of life:

> I am flying into Egypt. While the plane re-fuels, I decide to quickly go see the pyramids. I look at my plane ticket to make sure I can get back on the plane and see that it says my name is Star. As I walk down the road, I see someone coming toward me. As I get closer, I see that it is a baby Sphinx. It comes to me and takes my hands and it dances with me on the road. It is golden, with a human face, a lion's body and small wings. We are both full of joy as we dance.

These archetypal dreams are products of the Creative Imagination, the realm of co-creation. The Sphinx has always symbolized the mystery of life, and here was a living Sphinx, young and dancing and full of joy! What a wonderful symbol to give me hope on my journey to greater consciousness. Working with these dreams has brought me some of the wisdom I do possess. They gave me a new understanding of life, not only my life but also the way life works. It is through working with these images that I have discovered my inner truth, my inner creativity and great love. This wisdom helped me creatively and consciously raise my children, counsel people through crisis and have grown-up, loving relationships. It is through believing in these and other dream images that I have re-discovered my own feminine standpoint and my own connection to Lady Wisdom.

Recovering our Wisdom Traditions

Because we have lost touch with our wisdom traditions, I did not realize that Lady Wisdom was calling to me. But my generation began to explore and search for wisdom in the 60s and we continue to explore still. We sometimes use other words like consciousness and spiritual awakening to explain a wisdom experience. Perhaps we realize the root cause of a psychological complex: why we are insecure, or rebellious, or even why we are too comfortable in our discomfort. Or we suddenly understand the meaning of a relationship or a conflict, and finally know what to do. How do we explain those elusive times when we momentarily understand the meaning of life? Like my dream of the baby Sphinx, the riddle of life demands that we dance with life. All of these awakenings are wisdom experiences. When we chose to look for meaning in life, we are gifted with the wisdom to understand what is really going on and to make the life-giving choice. Lady Wisdom attunes us to our deepest Self, so we make the right choices.

When women's intuitive, feeling way of knowing is respected and valued by the male establishment, the changes are, and will continue to be, remarkable. Give a woman equal say in how to manage the world, and we'll work with men to come up with solutions to our many problems. When women and our feminine wisdom are respected and valued by men and their masculine know-how, decision-making takes on a whole new dimension. Once we learn to balance masculine and feminine consciousness, we can consciously co-create a peaceful, loving world. We need a new vision of life, and it is this image of Lady Wisdom as the *Woman clothed with the Sun,* who is giving birth to that new vision, that can guide us into the future.

People have been working with this new feminine consciousness since the 60s, especially women who are getting in touch with many aspects of the ancient goddesses. But why has the Goddess returned right now in our history? Is it just so women can regain our powers of feeling and imagination so we can imagine ourselves into health, love, money and happiness? If this is the only reason women search for the Goddess, then how does that differ from men's goals and who we were in the Father's House? Are we really only here to make use of everything, even spiritual powers, to gain material and personal possessions?

Lady Wisdom wants us to discover meaning in life, and if there is a meaning for the return of the Goddess, it is this: Women need to reclaim our connection to Lady Wisdom so we can give her gifts to the world. The Goddess, through women, has returned to transform the world during this shift in world ages. Lady Wisdom can guide us as we dis-mantle the patriarchy and give birth to a world of partnership, compassion and peace.

The Path to Wisdom

Wisdom implies knowing how to live in harmony with the world. When I was young, I got initiated by an Indian guru. I was told he knew everything about me by just being in my presence. I always wondered how he did it. Now I know. Being in the moment, fully present, he could pick up the information from my *being*.

That's what wisdom does—it gives us the invisible information we need to freely choose the right path in any situation. Back in the 60s, I thought I would have to become a saint to achieve this kind of *knowing*. But we don't have to be saints to acquire wisdom. We have to become self-aware and use both masculine and feminine consciousness. Or we could say use both sides of our brains.

Of course, the problem is how to open ourselves to hear the voice of Lady Wisdom. *This opening must happen on four levels of awareness: the physical, the psychological, the imaginal and the spiritual.* We have to learn to think holistically, which means listening to our hearts as well as our minds, opening to our imagination as well as looking at the facts. As we integrate these four aspects of our life, Lady Wisdom's voice will become clearer and clearer to us, until we speak with her own voice.

To begin to understand how to ask for wisdom, first we need to know about the many different stories of the ending of the Age, for whether we acknowledge it consciously or not, these stories are alive and well and gestating in our Collective Unconscious. Everyone is feeling the pressure of change. While many people live in fear that the challenges facing us will kill us, I believe that's just a lack of imagination.

The image of the *Woman clothed with the Sun* found in the Christian *Book of Revelation* shows us the key to understanding how to bring about this great collective transformation. Next we look at the importance of understanding symbolic language, which opens us to the Creative Imagination, the realm of inspiration and co-creation. Lady Wisdom speaks in symbolic language, so understanding how the imagination works is of primary importance. By learning to understand symbolic language, which is the feminine language of the soul, we have access to the rich storehouse of wisdom within the Collective Unconscious.

Then we'll discover how to reclaim our true feminine standpoint. Since it is so important to learn how to interpret symbolic language, we'll explore a fairy tale about the Father's Daughter who got away and became a wise woman. Then, working with images from this story as well as the image of the Cosmic Woman, we will explore the archetypal realms of Earth, Sun, Moon and Stars. The Earth is the womb of our becoming; the Sun, which is both life-giving and death-dealing, is our conscious awareness; the Moon, whose beauty and mystery calls to us, provides the timing rhythm of unfolding our unique life and purpose, while the Stars reflect the spiritual and archetypal principles that guide us on our journey through life.

I have deliberately filled this book with images and stories that can awaken you to your own knowledge of symbolic language, the language of the Creative Imagination. If you want to learn a new language, you have to practice. The stories, dreams, quotes and concepts I fill the chapters with are intended to help you understand symbolic language. Then we have to go beyond *understanding* what this image of the Cosmic Woman means and embody her. We have to work with the energies contained in the images to expand our awareness of ourselves, our life's purpose and our society.

Once we re-connect with these realms of being, we will see that Lady Wisdom is indeed still calling out to us to come and claim our heritage, which is to make a paradise of our world. In the past, we have called that a utopian ideal, implying that it's *pie-in-the-sky* and won't work. But we live in a society with the consciousness, intelligence and resources to finally create a peaceful, prosperous world if only we can develop the wisdom and the will to do it.

The truth is, the Kingdom of Heaven is here, within us and within our reach. But our Mother Earth is waiting for us to wake up. It is our choice. Once we incarnate the energies of the *Woman clothed with the Sun*, we can share Lady Wisdom's resources with the each other and with the world. So let us all become lovers of Lady Wisdom like Solomon, and learn to use our creativity to re-create our world. This is our destiny and our responsibility at this time in Earth's story.

Are you ready to answer Lady Wisdom's call?

The Woman Clothed with the Sun

A great portent appeared in heaven, a woman clothed with the sun, with the moon under her feet, and on her head a crown of twelve stars; she was with child and she cried out in her pangs of birth, in anguish for delivery.

And another portent appeared in heaven; behold, a great red dragon... And the dragon stood before the woman who was about to bear a child, that he might devour her child when she brought it forth; she brought forth a male child,... but her child was caught up to God and to his throne, and the woman fled into the wilderness, where she has a place prepared by God...

And when the dragon saw that he had been thrown down to the earth, he pursued the woman who had borne the child. But the woman was given the two wings of the great eagle that she might fly from the serpent...

Book of Revelation 12: 1-6, 7-9, 13-14

Chapter One
Women Will Change the World

Sometimes, it takes one woman; sometimes, it takes many. Almost always, I've found, when there are enough women in the room so that everyone stops counting, women become free to act like women.

It's then that we can eliminate double standards, and accept that men and women are different – and that they bring a different range of experiences, skills, and strengths to public life... .

It's then that we can take advantage of all that each of us has to offer. And it is then that women will rule the world. And when women rule, we will have changed the very definition of power. We will have changed the world.[1]

—*DEE DEE MYERS*

The Unveiling

The Unveiling: the unveiling of the code that describes how to understand Lady Wisdom, thereby transforming ourselves and our world.

As we begin the 21st Century, humanity is confronted with the need for fundamental transformation at all levels of life. The old ways of living in and perceiving the world are no longer capable of dealing with the rapid changes and global scope of the complex problems that face us. We must evolve to meet the new needs of the times. We will have to adjust to a paradigm shift in our core beliefs and in the way we understand the world and our place it in, for we can no longer ignore our responsibility for creating the problems that face us nor can we be easily absolved of our guilt in creating them. Like God and the Devil, we have become creators, both of great good and of great evil.

The human psyche naturally looks for unifying images to make sense of chaos. Since these fundamental changes will involve a psychological death before new life can grow, our collective psyche has reanimated the apocalyptic images of western culture, as well as Native and Eastern images, to try to make sense of current world events. The *Book of Revelation* is sometimes called *The Apocalypse*, but we have to remember that an apocalypse is *an unveiling*, an opening into the hidden dimensions of the Divine reality behind our mortal reality. Many people are trying to see beyond the veil, trying to understand the meaning of these times through these apocalyptic images.

The events of September 11, 2001 have become a marker for this unveiling. The Fundamentalist Christians believe it is a sign of the Second Coming, a marker on the Rapture Index. Jungian psychologist Randy Morris believes that the events of 9/11 can be seen as a revelatory experience, a visitation from "beyond the veil" to enlighten us about the state of our national consciousness and shadow.[2] After September 11th, the world's heart chakra was blown open, and for a moment, we became one world. Unfortunately, September 11th soon became the rallying point for the patriarchal forces of war and exploitation, symbolized by the great dragon of *Revelations*. But it also became a call for people of goodwill and conscience to unite in spirit and dedication to create a world of peace and prosperity and freedom for the whole world. That one moment of unity gave us a glimpse of our future.

The 2004 Tsunami in South Asia overwhelmed our psyches just as surely as the waves overwhelmed their victims, for we had never before seen such devastation from a natural disaster. It made us feel our vulnerability in the face of nature's destructive power. It also proved that modern people are so far removed from their instincts that they actually stood on the beach and let their children play as the waters pulled back before the waves came crashing to shore. Only ancient tribal people and animals were in touch with their internal warning system, removing themselves from danger.

The April 20, 2010 BP Gulf Oil Spill and the devastating March 11, 2011 earthquake in Japan with its subsequent nuclear meltdown at Fukushima, have poisoned the land and water. They are both urgent reminders that our technology is not going to save us but rather destroy us if used irresponsibly. And yet, the powers-that-be refuse to take action to change the way we live and do business. Their attitude is 'business as usual'—an attitude that is so wrong-headed that it leaves me speechless. So now it is up to each of us to take a stand for life and use our gifts to re-create the world.

In the past century, uncounted people have dreamed of giant tidal waves sweeping through the land or hanging suspended in the sky. R.J.J. Tolkien called these his Atlantean dreams, feeling they were past life memories. C. G. Jung saw these dreams as harbingers of the Aquarian Age, an age in which there will be a great upsurge in the Collective Unconscious (symbolized by the ocean) so that the archetypal patterns that make us human can be lived out consciously. All stories point to an age of conscious humanity. From ancient times, the image of the Age of Aquarius was seen as a deluge, an upwelling of the waters of life that brings freedom from tyranny. Like the giant tidal wave, this energy will destroy those aspects of civilization that cannot or will not give way to individual freedom and creative collaboration. We have now experienced the reality of these dream images, and yet the archetypal image opens us to a deeper understanding of the transformations our world must undergo; not just physical changes, but the transformation of the hearts and minds and bodies of humanity. But just as these newest disasters created fear and vulnerability, they also engendered compassion and a clearer vision of reality. A global consciousness is forming.

Many people live in fear of such disasters, while others call upon their bravery and determination to deal with these disasters in a courageous way. Hurricane Katrina in 2005 saw New Orleans overwhelmed by the waters, except this time, nature was abetted by human neglect of the levees that were to protect the city. Sandy, the northeast Super Storm of 2012, devastated the East Coast shoreline, finally convincing us of the truth of climate change. Natural disasters have become commonplace, or rather, they have become common knowledge. Before our modern era, we might never have found out about the devastating tsunami in Asia, which caused more deaths than many wars. Because of modern media, we have come to realize that floods, earthquakes, volcanic eruptions, devastating fires, mudslides, tornadoes and hurricanes have all occurred with startling regularity in the last decades of the 20th and first years of the 21st Century. Climate change is accelerating at an alarming rate, and yet our governments are slow to impose restrictions on corporate violators and individuals have been slow to take personal responsibility for conservation. Our old paradigm, which cannot encompass this emergency, makes it hard for people to take action. Only a new paradigm can. We have to recognize the dangers of climate change and *name it* so the world can join together to do something about its human causes. The Earth's ecosystem is breaking down. Mother Earth is getting sick. If we let this continue, we will destroy ourselves as well as everything else on Earth. Good stewardship of the Earth must become part of our spiritual lives.

Then there are the equally devastating results of our failed western economic policies that have ravaged the environment and caused a widening rift between the rich and the poor. The wars of the 20th Century and the war on terrorism that has begun the 21st Century have shown us that hatred and intolerance are still viable rallying cries to men who would rather dominate than love. Cancer and AIDS have reached epidemic proportions. Corporate scandals of corruption, vast public and private debt, violence and addictions are pervasive in western society. The world appears to be descending into chaos. Our ego-centric western consciousness, which tried to transcend the human condition and transform this planet into a *safe* place, has instead brought us to the edge of destruction, both in war and in peace.

Our world is literally dying, and our corporate philosophy of conspicuous consumption, the materialistic shadow side of the Christian belief that this world is unimportant compared to our heavenly home, is the major cause. Where once religion and philosophy steered humanity towards its purpose, we now have the corporate media pounding out our glorious new purpose: to consume! After the tragedy of 9/11, President Bush called on Americans to *go shopping*! It only got us into more debt and now we see the bankruptcy of these policies. Our economic policies are killing off species at cataclysmic rates. We are destroying forests which might contain cures for many of our diseases and which certainly clean our polluted air. We are poisoning our waters, which is *Life* to everything on this planet. We are depleting the topsoil that grows our food. We are poisoning the land with our toxic wastes and causing mutations and birth defects in ourselves and the other species we share this planet with. We are killing ourselves! And yet, while American supermarkets, fully stocked with food that we finally realize is killing us, spring up every mile or two, millions around the world are starving to death. Yes, we are killing ourselves, but it seems that western culture intends to kill off everyone else before it has to die itself.

The Cosmic Story of Our Times

Many people feel there is nothing we can do to change course, sure that we are headed for destruction. They turn to the *Book of Revelation* or the prophecies of Nostradamus, Edgar Cayce and the Mayan calendar. Unfortunately, many people believe that the end of the world is upon us. At the same time, other people are turning to a personal spiritual path for answers to the pressing concerns in their lives. Whether people turn to non-traditional or fundamentalist religions, tarot readers or E. T. channelings, Native American, Wiccan, Western or Eastern mysticism, there is a feeling that we are approaching a crisis point and the world as we know it will never be the same. If movies are any indication of collective apocalyptic fantasies, then we are projecting vast destruction coming at us from the rest of the universe.

Aside from older movies such as *E.T.* and *Star Trek*, these new stories tell us that either space rocks or exploding stars are about to destroy us or that aliens from outer space want to overwhelm us for some diabolical end. Or that 2012 will bring the total destruction of our world. But this lack of imagination cannot be overcome until we become conscious that we are caught up in fears. We see on the movie screen the projections of the fears of our primitive, reptilian brain, which is trying to overwhelm our fragile civilized consciousness. These reptilian fears—fight or flight, them or us, life or death—are also represented by the dragon of *Revelation,* the regressive pull of human unconsciousness and fear, which tries to devour the heavenly woman and her child. The old order is aggressively trying to keep the new life that is being born from growing to maturity, because it does not want to let go of its power.

But the natural laws of the Earth say that all things must die, so new life can grow. All of us have a chance to look at our beliefs about life and the future of our world, for it is our beliefs that control our behavior and allow for new possibilities... or not. Before we begin to create the future, we have to look at what unconscious story is shaping our present consciousness and our world, for it is always the story going on behind the scenes that shapes reality.

What stories are giving shape to the chaos of our times?

End Time Prophecies

Many people believe we are living in the *End Times*, and this belief is shaping personal values and world events. Many other people don't know what to believe because they don't have a story to frame what's going on in their lives. But our ancestors went through their own chaotic times and left a memory of it within the Collective Unconscious, and so within each of us. Whatever our conscious beliefs, this story of the *End Times* affects all of us, because it has been percolating in the Collective Unconscious for thousands of years, lodged deep within the human psyche. There is an unconscious archetypal *end time* framework that will use whatever kinds of energies we lend it. That's why it's so important for each of us to use our life energies in a conscious, loving way. This is how we create the future, because the archetypes are awake and alive within the chaos. How the energy forms around them will determine what our future looks like. We have a choice about the outcome.

We seem to be at the in-between time, a time when the old tide is pulling out and the new is beginning to flow and surge in. So there are tidal eddies. As we shift out of the perspective of the religious Piscean Age and into the more secular Age of Aquarius, the still powerful influence of the old religious myths have to be understood if we want to come through this time of chaos and change to create a new reality. Perhaps this test of getting through the end of the Age is the only way for us to grow up and realize we are meant to be conscious spiritual beings, and that we can either create heaven here on Earth or destroy life on this planet.

The Hopi Prophecies

There are *End Time* stories from many different cultures. The Hopi prophecies speak of the emergence of a new world. The Hopi Nation is the Record Keeper of the Native Americans. The Hopis call this time in history *The Fourth Age of Man*. According to them, the Earth has been wiped clean three times already. The first time was by Fire; the second time was by Ice; the third, most recent, time was by the Flood, approximately 11,000-12,000 years ago. According to the Hopis, we are about to enter *The Fifth Age* called *The World of Illumination*. But before this world can emerge, we will have to go through a purification in which we will be tested to see if we can make a leap in consciousness. This purification is meant to bring us into balance and peace. We will all be asked to choose our path: the path of greed and comfort and profit, or the path of love and strength and balance. The Hopi Prophecy Rock at Oraibi shows the 'two-hearted' people, people who think with their heads instead of their hearts. It is talking about us! Many native prophecies call for the rebirth of Feminine Spirit to heal the land, and many Native elders point to the birth of two white buffaloes in the last decade as an indication that White Buffalo Woman, the Great Mother Goddess, is watching over us in this time of purification. If our left-brain society, which is oriented to a masculine consciousness of individuality and rationality, and lives in the head, continues to reject the heart, which is feminine and knows by intuition and feeling, then the purification will become self-destruction. But if we heal ourselves and think with our hearts, the *World of Illumination* will be born.[3]

2012 and the Mayan Prophecies

There are other prophecies that speak of the changing of the Ages. The one people are talking about is based on the Mayan calendar.[4] The Maya had an incredible understanding of time. Many westerns have heard that the Mayan calendar is coming to an end. There is a perception that this means that the end of the world is coming in the year 2012, but this is misleading and once again shows a very western perception of the ending of things. Westerners don't value cycles.

The Mayans tracked cycles within cycles within cycles of time. Their calendar acted as a harmonic calibrator, linking and coordinating the earthly, lunar, solar and galactic seasons. The calendar says that a rare astronomical and mythical event will occur on the Winter Solstice of 2012. On that day, there will be a cosmic alignment between the Earth, Sun, the Pleiades star cluster and the center of the Milky Way Galaxy, called by the Maya the Sacred Tree. On December 21, 2012, the Sun will rise at the center of this Sacred Tree, the womb of the Milky Way Galaxy, which represents the World Tree and the Tree of Life.

On that day, the Maya predict that all the diverse cycles of time-keeping will simultaneously turn over and start again, vibrating to a new era. It might even symbolize the end of a Great Year, the 26,000 year cycle that spans the whole zodiac. This alignment with the center of the Milky Way Galaxy will supposedly align Earth with the spiritual intentions of the rest of the galaxy, as well as bringing these placements into alignment with the constellation of the Pleiades, the crown chakra of the galaxy. While some people believe world-shattering destruction awaits us, the symbolism also tells us that we will receive divine guidance and wisdom. While this myth does not relieve us of the duty to solve the problems we have created for ourselves, it does say that we will have the help of cosmic energy to create a new world. As Gregg Braden says:

> To know in advance where our choices can have the greatest impact tips the scales in our favor as we complete the cycle that holds our well-being and, ultimately our survival, in the balance. And that is the beauty of Fractal Time. Because the rhythms and patterns of nature tell us precisely when we can expect the repeating cycles of the past, they also tell us when we have the greatest opportunity to change the hurtful and destructive patterns of the past—the choice points—that create the new cycles of life![5]

The Precession of the Astrological Ages

The ancient Greeks believed in the changing of the Aion, a change that is brought about by the precession of the zodiac, which is caused by the wobble of the Earth's axis. This precession causes the vernal (Spring) equinox point to slightly shift against the backdrop of the constellations through time: this point, which moves backwards through the constellations, is now at the beginning of the constellation of Pisces and is moving into the constellation of Aquarius, the water-bearer, who pours out a stream of water into a fish's mouth. Each age, a period of about 2100 years, brings in a different vibration and energy, reflecting the evolution of human consciousness. As one age ends and another begins, there is a transition, when the energies of both ages mix, causing confusion until things settle down. According to this theory, we are living in such a time.

Ray Grasse, in his book on the astrological ages, *Signs of the Times*[6], gives examples of these astrological Ages, past, present and future.

The Age of Taurus (an Earth sign) 4200-2100 BCE, was the age of monumental earthworks and construction. These Taurean builders achieved an astonishing mastery of matter that has proved durable (like Taurus) down through the ages. We are still in awe of the Great Pyramid and Stonehenge, which date from this age. During the age of Taurus the bull was symbolically worshiped as the Egyptian bull-god Apis, as the golden calf of Moses, and by Poseidon's white bull who fathered the Minotaur in Crete. The Great Goddess was worshiped in Egypt as Hathor the Golden Cow. Mother Earth was sacred and people knew that their prosperity, fertility and very life depended on her.

The Age of Aries (a Fire sign) 2100BCE-1AD, was the age of the warriors from Greece, Persia, India and Israel. The Great Ram was worshiped in Egypt as well as in Israel. The Golden Fleece was sought by Jason and the Argonauts. This was the age of the hero, and of the awakening of patriarchal self-awareness that gave form to individual ego consciousness (just like the sign of Aries, which represents the search for self-identity). As the inner consolidation of the human ego took place, outer empires rose and fell. This was the beginning of the rise of monotheistic religions. Aries' cry of "I am" is echoed in the name of the Jewish God Yahweh, "I am that I am".

We are now at the end of the Age of Pisces (a Water sign), 1-2100AD, called the Age of Faith, which uses the symbolism of water in its religious beliefs: baptism, walking on water, changing water into wine. The symbolism of the fishes of Pisces was taken over by the early Christians when they used the sign of the fish to indicate Christ, the fishermen who became apostles, and the eating of fish (the sacred food) on Friday. Jesus Christ became the god-image of the Piscean Age. At its best, this Age taught humanity to relate to the divine and to the world in a more emotional way, adding a new element of compassion and faith to society. The world of the imagination also became important, both in religious experience and in art. Since the sign consists of two fishes swimming in opposite directions, the negative side of the Piscean Age ushered in dogmatism and persecution in religion. As a sign concerned with matters of faith, this was an age of religious extremes and intolerance. Many believed the Piscean qualities of suffering and guilt were synonymous with spirituality. It was an age of neurosis, martyrdom and sado-masochism as well as an age in which humanity was learning to transcend the ego and surrender personal desires in service to higher ideals. The water element at its most refined is concerned with the principles of sacrifice (to make sacred), nurturing, worship and devotion. *Not my will but Thine.* The Piscean Age brought a sense of inwardness, a sense of personal conscience and moral responsibility to the human experience.

The Age of Aquarius, (an Air Sign) 2100-4200AD, is upon us. Aquarius will be more concerned with Ideals than feelings—an age of the awakening of the Mind and its vast potentials, as well as the urge for true freedom. We experienced a preview of what this new age will be like when Uranus, the planet that rules Aquarius, transited through Aquarius from 1996-2003. The giant advances in technology and research, especially in the fields of information and communication, are the first step to creating a unified world. The idea of a global village springs from it. The brilliance of the Aquarian mind reflects the working of the Cosmic Mind. Mental telepathy and other unexplored talents of the human mind will probably be at our disposal. In terms of religious beliefs, there will hopefully be tolerance and the knowledge that diverse paths lead to Divine Spirit. Hopefully too, science and spirituality will work together to bring us to our human potential. Carl Jung saw the Age of Aquarius as an age when the archetypes are lived consciously by humanity. There is the possibility that if we can stand up for our ideals now when the world seems so dark, we might usher in a golden age of consciousness, of equality and creativity, of law and justice, unseen in these previous ages. But there is always a shadow side to everything, and so our ideals must be grounded in reality and never taken to extremes, such as forcing our ideals on others or trying to 'create' perfect human beings. Aquarius' shadow can turn idealism into fanaticism and judgment.

The End: A Final Death or a Chance for Rebirth

These stories of the *End Times* speak of a great change that is somehow pre-ordained. The question is: do we have to go through a time of literal suffering, physical death and destruction, or can we make the transition easier by changing ourselves? If we are indeed at the *End Times*, we are in the death aspect of the cycle of life. When we study nature, we can see this cycle at work: gestation, birth, growth, maturity, producing new seeds and death, so new seeds have space to grow. Our western perception of life is that death is The End.

But endings are deceiving, because even though something is dying, a transformation is going on, and you can be sure that something else is being born. It appears that humanity is being called upon to *die* to an old order, an old consciousness. As would be expected in such a materialistic culture as our own, we have projected that death outside ourselves. It is being *embodied*—both in our own bodies and in the Earth's body. What we haven't understood is that this death has to happen on a deep psychological level within each person. If it is true that the inner and outer worlds are reflections of each other, than what we are seeing is how destitute western culture and consciousness have become. It is a killing mentality and it is killing itself. If we are to get through this death to new life, we must face these *End Times* with the knowledge that it is a call to action, not despair. Only in facing this death honestly and openly will we be able to bring about transformation and new life for ourselves and for our world.

The chaos of this death can give birth to a leap in consciousness, the awareness that we are all one, and that we have the source of our being here on our mother, the Earth. Our individual and collective purpose has to be to get through these *End Times* and to become the cornerstone for a new age of peace. As has happened in the past, those voices of our culture that are devalued by our collective consciousness—women, people of color, the trees, the waters, the air, the children—will be the foundation stone of this new vision of life. We need to learn the lessons of compassion and a loving heart before we can bring about peace and change in the world, for in the most essential ways, we are truly all one, which is the ultimate lesson of the Piscean Age. We have the seeds of this new life within us.

Before we can go out to colonize the starry heavens, we must become a responsible race here on earth. If we cannot face and clean up our own toxicity, both individually and collectively, perhaps we will not be permitted to go beyond the borders of our own solar system. C.S. Lewis once wrote about Earth as *The Silent Planet*[7], the one planet in the solar system that was barred from communication with the rest of creation because our *Eldil* or ruling Spirit, Lucifer the fallen one, refused to recognize his place in the cosmic order. Before we can know our place in the cosmic order, before we can truly know that we are all one and that we are part of one world, we have to deal with our demons, we have to look at our shadows. We have to face death, if we are to go on to new life. We have to come up against the *End Times* and discover a new cosmology, a new story about creation and our place in it.

Other cultures view the *End Times* as a time of purification and rebirth. These same themes can be found in the *End Time* visions of the three major western Religions of the Book (Judaism, Christianity, and Islam), which also have many things in common. The Jews wait for their Messiah, who will lead them to victory over their oppressors and set up a kingdom of justice. Islam believes that the Mahdi, their Messiah figure, will return and bring about the final judgment at the last day: those who are sinful will suffer in a physical fire, while the blessed will have physical pleasure and happiness. Christians also believe in a last battle between good and evil and a last judgment, when the evil ones will be cast into Hell for eternity and the Chosen Ones will be given their New Jerusalem. There is a common theme in these beliefs that (1) some people will be *chosen*, and that (2) there will be a battle between good and evil. *To be chosen* implies that others are not chosen. And there is an innate cruelty in the battles between good and evil; the *chosen* people come out looking just as vicious as the evil people. These stories are very much male visions of the world. It is interesting that in most apocalyptic visions, women play such a small part. My guess is that women didn't have much of a say in passing on those visions.

Christianity's *End Time* Story: *Book of Revelation*

Christianity has given us its own vision of these *End Times* in the *Book of Revelation*. *The Revelation of St. John the Divine*[8] is written in the tradition of Jewish apocalyptic thought, which has its roots in the conquest of the Israelites in 586 B.C, when the Babylonians under King Nebuchadnezzar, conquered the city of Jerusalem and destroyed

Solomon's Temple. This Babylonian Exile made the Jewish people rethink their religious and political history for all time. Following in this tradition, both Jesus and John the Baptist believed they were living in the *End Times* and expected the manifestation of the Kingdom of God. The *Book of Revelation*, the last book of the Christian Bible, speaks to that belief.

Believed to have been written by Jesus' disciple, John, the son of Zebedee, while he was exiled by the Romans on the island of Patmos in the last years of the 1st Century, it is a visionary book full of astrological symbols and Jewish apocalyptic prophecies that speaks of the end of the age and God's judgment of the world. The images and symbols have fascinated and terrified people throughout the ages. The images of the Four Horsemen of the Apocalypse are well known to most of us, for war, plague, famine and death are most definitely part of our world. A literal reading of the book shows a vision of judgment and punishments and destruction except for the chosen few. A symbolic reading can be a guide to self-understanding and transformation, for this book can be understood as a story of our collective Christian shadow as well as the possibility of evolving to a higher state of consciousness.

The American Christian fundamentalist version of the *End Times* has a very powerful influence on American politics today. Besides a literal belief in the events described in the *Book of Revelation,* these fundamentalists believe in a doctrine called *dispensationalism*, formulated by two 19th Century American preachers. This doctrine states that Israel must exist as a nation to play a key role in bringing about the end of the present age, the 'rapture' of the chosen ones and the second coming of Christ. Bill Moyers, in a January 30, 2005[9] article, describes the essence of their beliefs. "Once Israel has occupied the rest of its "biblical lands," legions of the antichrist will attack it, triggering a final showdown in the valley of Armageddon. As the Jews who have not been converted are burned, the Messiah will return for the rapture. True believers will be lifted out of their clothes and transported to Heaven, where, seated next to the right hand of God, they will watch their political and religious opponents suffer plagues of boils, sores, locusts and frogs during the several years of tribulation that follow." Mr. Moyers has reported that these Christian fundamentalists "are sincere, serious and polite as they tell you they feel called to help bring the rapture on as fulfillment of biblical prophecy. That's why they have declared solidarity with Israel and the Jewish settlements and backed up their support with money and volunteers. It's why the invasion of Iraq for them was a warm-up act, predicted in the *Book of Revelation* where four angels "which are bound in the great river Euphrates will be released to slay the third part of man." A war with Islam in the Middle East is not something to be feared but welcomed—an essential conflagration on the road to redemption. The last time I googled it, the rapture index stood at 144-just one point below the critical threshold when the whole thing will blow, the Son of God will return, the righteous will enter Heaven and sinners will be condemned to eternal hellfire."

The Christian *End Time* story can give rise to fanaticism, for not everyone is called to be one of the *righteous remnant*, those who are chosen to live in the New Jerusalem with God as their constant companion. In other *End Time* stories, everyone goes through the change together. To avert disaster, people have to take responsibility for saving the world. In the Christian version, if you are not one of the saved, you will die painfully and burn in Hell for eternity. Is it any wonder that after all these centuries of hearing this story we fear death? And yet, other cultures have not feared death as we do.

Other cultures saw death as a doorway to new life. Jesus Christ showed us this truth with his Resurrection—the promise that we are more than our bodies and that our souls live on. Nature also shows us that the cycle of life includes death, which in turn leads to a rebirth. We are the children of Mother Earth and therefore subject to her laws. This is the knowledge that Lady Wisdom offers us. Just look at the turning of the seasons or the cycle of the moon. Rebirth is part of our DNA coding. It must be, for we are children of the Earth, and Earth herself has not cut us off from her blessings, even if we imagine we have left her far behind.

The Return of Wisdom: The Woman Clothed With the Sun

There is an image in the *Book of Revelation,* often ignored by Christian fundamentalists, which I consider very important to this issue of the *End Times.* It is the image of the *Woman clothed with the Sun.* She is the pivot point, the crux of the matter. For she gives birth to the Divine Child, and afterwards, the war in heaven against the dragon and his legions brings about a new heaven and a new Earth. Amidst death and destruction, a new birth! A birth which is not without peril, for the dragon, the deadly pull of the old order, the inertia of unconsciousness that is so much a part of human nature, will be waiting to swallow up this new being. It is this image of conscious femininity that speaks to me when I imagine the purpose and power of women today.

> Now a great portent appeared in heaven: a Woman clothed with the sun, with the moon under her feet, and on her head a crown of twelve stars. She was pregnant, and in labor, crying aloud in the pangs of childbirth. Revelation, 12: 1-2.

This is the image of a Goddess, yet she is also a woman. It is also an image we first saw in July 1969 when men first landed on the Moon and sent us pictures of Earth, hanging above the Moon, surrounded by the Stars. We saw another version of this image in the heavens on both June 8, 2004 and June 5, 2012, when the planet Venus passed in front of the Sun. Venus/ Aphrodite, the planet that symbolizes the powers of love, sexuality, connection and wisdom, made herself known to the world.

This *Woman* is Goddess, Earth and woman, and all three are laboring to bring new life to the planet. She is clothed in the light of consciousness, for light banishes the darkness of injustice, unconsciousness and ignorance. She has her standpoint on the Moon, the regulator of earthly rhythms and tides and the eye of the Unconscious. And she is crowned with twelve Stars, which represent the twelve astrological signs that symbolize the archetypal human journey toward consciousness, wholeness and wisdom. It is a most painful and dangerous journey, yet like labor, once begun it will not stop until it has run its course. The *Woman* cries out in anguish, for the convulsions of birth are overwhelming. The child she is giving birth to wants to be born. And she is birthing something awesome and something new, otherwise the regressive energy of unconsciousness would not try to destroy her and her child.

This child is what the Christian theologian Matthew Fox calls the Cosmic Christ, the awakening to our own divinity, as well as the honoring of our humanity. Meister Eckhart, one of the great creation-centered mystics of our own western spiritual tradition, celebrates the divine presence in all of creation.

There is only one birth—and this birth takes place in the being and in the ground and core of the soul… Not only is the Son of the heavenly Creator born in this darkness—but you too are born there as a child of the same heavenly Creator and none other. And the Creator extends this same power to you out of the divine maternity bed located in the Godhead to eternally give birth….The fruitful person gives birth out of the very same foundation from which the Creator begets the eternal Word. It is from this core that one becomes fruitfully pregnant. [10]

This is the child being birthed by the *Woman* in these times by every conscious individual. This is the child of our creative vision for a different future, the archetype of the possible human. It is said that this child will rule with a rod of iron. Iron can represent fetters and hardness, or it can represent strength and firmness. Originally the child was taken up to heaven because humanity was not ready to incarnate him. But now we are, and the new world he represents will use the gifts of both feminine and masculine Spirit equally.

This *Woman* calls all women to our purpose and destiny. It is a time for women to reclaim our ancient powers and wisdom as we deal with the anxieties of these apocalyptic times. These are the powers of inner sight and vision, of empathy and healing. These powers have always come from women's connection with the Earth, and as women re-discover our own spiritual power, it is not surprising that we return to an Earth-based, body-based spirituality. Feminine Spirit is the archetypal energy of the incarnation of Spirit. It is concerned with the spiritualization of matter, with the knowledge that all created things and beings partake of Spirit, just as quantum physicists are proving. We cannot afford to believe that this world is an illusion and that our true rewards lie in some heavenly paradise reserved for the elect. It is this very idea that has led us into the trouble we now find ourselves in.

The Heavenly Woman

So who is this *Woman* and why is she important? For Roman Catholics, the appearances of Mary in the past few centuries have led church officials to proclaim this the 'Marian Age'. Mary, the Mother of God, has reappeared to remind our rational age that we need to turn to

Feminine Spirit if we are to get through this *End Time*. One of Mary's first appearances was as the Virgin of Guadalupe in 1531, who is the very image of the *Woman*, standing on the Moon, surrounded by the golden rays of the Sun and crowned with Stars. She is the patroness of Mexico.

Then there was an appearance of Our Lady to a French nun in 1830. Her visions were of Mary standing on the globe of the world with stars surrounding her head. A great light shone from her, and rays of many-colored lights came from many rings on her hands. These were the graces that she promised to shower on anyone who asked for her help.[11] This image of Mary, so similar to the *Woman* from *Revelation*, has connected many Catholics to a deep spirituality. The Church also believes that this next age will be the Age of the Holy Spirit, when divine blessings flow to humanity. The Holy Spirit is a manifestation of Lady Wisdom.

The Virgin Mary as Mother of God is the form the Goddess has taken during the Christian era. Many women who are trying to reconnect with their inner goddess have rejected Mary as 'nothing but' a patriarchal image of the perfect mother and obedient servant. But throughout the history of the Catholic Church, Mary has taken on most of the aspects of the ancient Goddess. As the Queen of Heaven, she became the Co-Redemptress with her Son, and served as a mediator between God and humanity.

> Deathless, pure, and by inference, without sin of any kind; at home in the courts of heaven, no mere spirit but body and soul complete; an ever-active intercessor and comforter; a friend of individual mortals, close at hand in their earthly pilgrimage...[12]

Such is the Virgin Mary, the merciful and sorrowing mother of all humanity. In many ways, Mary symbolizes the crone aspect of the Goddess, the spiritual mother and virgin who mediates between life and death. And yet, she is most truly a human woman. The Church took away her human sexuality, and that is a split that women have to heal, for to be 'no mere spirit but body and soul complete' entails the reclaiming of our bodies as temples of Spirit.

Throughout the ages, men seem to have had a great lust for and yet a fear of the body's instincts and they have created religions to help them tame those instincts. Unfortunately, they have projected their fears onto women, who are much more in touch with the body's instincts. Since Christianity split the Divine Feminine into Virgin Mother and Scarlet Whore, we now have to heal the virgin/whore split in the western psyche. The image of the *Woman clothed with the Sun* heals this split by making the instincts of the body, and Earth's natural laws, conscious. To be *clothed with the Sun* is to make the natural rhythms of the lunar life of the body/Earth conscious; to be *clothed with the Sun* is to be *crowned with the Stars* of spiritual consciousness.

Wisdom's Daughters: The Conscious Feminine

I believe women are being called to a great destiny. As we inhabit the image of the *Woman clothed with the Sun,* we take up the powers of Feminine Spirit. And I believe that if one woman gave birth to the *Son of God*, then all women have the potential to be the Mother of the Savior. It is this potential that I want to explore.

My dream of the wounded lion, the tidal wave and the voice that spoke to me of a new birth of the Savior has been a guiding light to me through the years. The images created order out of the chaos of my changing life. I go back to these images again and again, and I always find that they have something new to teach me. Soon after that dream, I moved to that town by the sea, and I experienced the ebb and flow of the tides and the Moon, and I was called upon to nurture and mother the creative potential of many people there. That's where I learned to become one of Wisdom's Daughters.

Like my dream of giving birth to the Savior, women are dreaming and then manifesting great wisdom in their lives. Feminine Spirit is appearing with great power in the dreams of modern women and men. These ancient archetypal images are alive and well and living in the Collective Unconscious. They want to incarnate in us, visiting us in dreams and visions.

This *Woman* is an image of conscious Feminine Spirit. She redeems and births a new consciousness on a collective human level. She is an image of Lady Wisdom, a consciousness of the sacredness of life and of our essential place as stewards of our Mother Earth. The Earth is also this *Woman*, and we, her human children, are embodiments of her consciousness. She calls upon us to know ourselves, to become conscious of our instincts and emotions, to understand ourselves as earthly beings as well as spiritual beings. It is time to stop rejecting this earthly life out of shame and guilt. It is time to let our *knowing* support our *being*.

Joseph Campbell spoke of the power of myth to give us "clues to the spiritual potentialities of the human life."[13] Myths are the big stories that help us understand our experience of being alive, by opening our imaginations and moving us forward in our lives. We can use these mythic stories to help us find new identities outside the patriarchal paradigm, identities that recognize our unique destiny. When we look to something greater than ourselves, we experience a change of perspective. When we look to the stories of the ancient Goddess, who was the guardian of the transformative mysteries of birth, death and rebirth, we understand that we share in her powers. We women are mediators of transformation.

It is time to live as responsible adults, freely choosing our life, not moving through it at the mercy of unconscious patriarchal beliefs. It is time for us to acknowledge the Goddess as the equal partner to God; not as the ancient Great Mother or Heavenly Father, but as the divine man and woman, the Christ and Sophia, united in partnership.

Looking Back to The Future

Because women's experiences differ from men's, it is important that we define our own understanding of Feminine Spirit. Just as our external forms are different and yet complementary, our inner wisdom will complement men's knowledge. So while I speak of women's wisdom, it does not mean that it is foreign to men, for the feminine soul in men is developing and speaking to them. But this new vision of the world springs from feminine consciousness and a woman's experience.

Because we are at a major cultural turning point, we are standing at a frontier, a boundary we must cross over in the hope of finding something new, something unknown. We look to see what being a free and conscious woman will entail. Many women have turned to the ancient images of the Goddess to reclaim a sense of their wholeness. This Goddess wears many faces and she tells women that we can be many things and take on many shapes. It is never 'either...or' with her, but 'this and also that.'

And yet, we really can't go back and worship these ancient images as our fore-mothers did. We can reclaim them, though, by understanding how their powers unconsciously affect our lives. C. G. Jung said that the god-images that spoke to our ancestors have been reduced to psychological processes in our modern psyches. Because our patriarchal culture suppressed the Goddess and our feminine gifts, women often don't realize that we are empathic or that we are seers or healers. Instead, we are confused by what we're feeling or intuiting or sensing.

With the repression of the Goddess and its effect on the status of women came a devaluation of the feminine, symbolic mode of consciousness. In accepting the domination of rational consciousness, we have all been deprived of the wisdom that an imaginal, intuitive consciousness brings to our lives. This type of consciousness is a way of perceiving through images and stories, dreams and visions. It speaks to the heart, not to the head. Matthew Fox calls it our *mystical brain* and believes that its suppression is the underlying cause of unbalance in western civilization.

> A crucial dimension of this imbalance in the West is the stunted growth of our mystical awareness and the under-development of our mystical brain. Our brains are amazingly complex creations of time, nature, and divinity. Part of what we know about the brain is that the right and left hemispheres perform different tasks. The left lobe accomplishes analytic and verbal processes for us, and the right lobe accomplishes the synthetic, sensual, and mystical tasks. Western civilization, which dominates the globe today, has invested almost exclusively in left-lobe processes in education, politics, economics, and religion.[14]

Right-brain thinking is associated with feminine consciousness. By exploring the image of the *Woman clothed with the Sun* through images and stories, we can begin to understand this consciousness and how it works. As women incarnate this new vision of Feminine Spirit, walking the path of Wisdom, we will shine in this area of human consciousness. It is time for the *feminine imagination* to come alive again.

Birthing a New Heaven and a New Earth

The *Woman clothed with the Sun* is an image of Feminine Spirit that is embodied, conscious, imaginative and spiritual. Women have to be willing to take the journey to claim her gifts. Self-knowledge will lead us to the purpose of this labor we've undertaken—the birth of the Divine Child. All things are born of women. The *Woman* of *Revelation* brings lasting values and a cosmology that can unite us to ourselves and to the rest of the universe. We are her daughters and our task is her task. She calls us to our true Selves, to our wisdom, and offers us an image of who we might become, just as Christ, the Buddha and Quetzalcoatl have been images of Masculine Spirit which have shaped the very best character in men.

This archetypal image of Feminine Spirit expresses the power and purpose of women in these transformational times. She shows women who we might become and the reason for our quest for freedom and consciousness at this time in our human history. The fact that this figure is found in a story of the *End Times* places women front and center in the mythic story of our times. As women come to understand and incarnate the gifts Lady Wisdom bestows, we will foster change in society as well as help men come to trust these same gifts within themselves.

In re-imagining the Feminine Spirit for our times, new pathways open up for women to explore. Understanding feminine consciousness can help us own our innermost feelings and intuitions. I feel that women should own our feminine potentials, potentials that are rooted in our womanly bodies. Our capacity for literal childbearing does not necessarily tie us down to a biological function. The wisdom that our bodies incarnate is the basis of other types of creativity and consciousness. We are daughters of Mother Earth as well as Lady Wisdom, and we have a share in her gifts of creativity and diversity. We need to look to her as our guide.

This Cosmic Woman, clothed with the Sun, standing on the Moon, and crowned with Stars, bestows on us the powers of transformation. The new consciousness which is birthed can lead us to create a more balanced civilization. The millennial fears people are caught up in are the projections of our own shadows. The horrors of war, disease and earth changes have to be faced by people working together. But they also have to be face by each individual.

For many Christians, the most horrifying image in their *End Time* story is the image of the Anti-Christ. We can look for a specific person to be this Anti-Christ, or we can look within ourselves and at our own culture. Perhaps the real Anti-Christ is our corporate culture. It has created a culture that has lost touch with the soulful aspects of life. As our scientific and economic world-view took over the cosmology of Christianity, it left us a life without meaning. As the Church condemned the sinfulness of the body and the Earth, it created the Anti-Christ of rampant materialism and loss of soul. It is the other side, or Dark Twin, of Christianity, the second fish of the Piscean spiritual duality.

As we deal with this *loss of soul* in our individual lives, we are dealing with Anti-Christ, a consciousness that is against Christ consciousness, which is Love. As we reclaim our connection with the Feminine Spirit, we are re-awakening our human potential to receive grace and blessings and that love which Christ preached. The truth is each of us can embody the Second Coming of Christ. With the help of Feminine Spirit, we can give birth to a truly new world order, one blessed by the partnership and creativity of conscious men and women. It is time to see that our fears of annihilation are really a lack of imagination. Once we understand the divine laws of nature, and of our feminine natures, the power of the Creative Imagination can give us the answers to our most pressing problems. Then we can create a world of peace and unity where all of us can partake of the blessings and grace of human life here on Earth.

Ask yourself what you intend to do to birth a new world that values Feminine Spirit and the feminine dimension of life.

Scheherazade

Once, there lived a Sultan who discovered that his wife was betraying him by taking as her lover a black slave. After killing them both, he vowed that, since no woman could be trusted, he would wed one every day and have her strangled the next morning. The Sultan ordered his Vizier to provide him with a new wife every day.

This the Vizier did reluctantly, but dutifully. The people of the kingdom grew more sorrowful every day, as more of their daughters were taken from them and put to death. The Sultan, who was once much loved by his people, was now hated.

Finally, the Vizier's own daughter, Scheherazade, a woman of surpassing knowledge, wit and beauty, determined to find a way to stop the slaughter. She demanded that her father give her as a bride to the Sultan. For the Sultan had exempted the Vizier's daughters from his edict. Her father was horrified, but she insisted and he finally relented. Before the wedding, Scheherazade told her sister to come to her bedchamber in the night and ask her to tell one last story before she died.

This she did, and with the Sultan's permission, Scheherazade began to tell a story, but with the coming of the dawn, stopped at just such a place that the Sultan wished to hear what was coming next. Therefore, he let her live for one more day. And each night, her stories were never completely told and the Sultan let Scheherazade live one more day so he could hear her stories. And so for 1,001 nights, Scheherazade told stories of love and betrayal, innocence and duplicity, wonder and intrigue, secret dreams and amazing discoveries until the dawn came when she had no more stories to tell.

As she waited for her husband's decision – for now he could kill her despite their three children - the Sultan realized how loyal Scheherazade had proved to be, and he saw the injustice of his vow, because he finally understood how fragile our human consciousness is and how we all fail at some point in our lives and have to face the consequences. However horrible the price had been, the Sultan wisely chose to learn from his mistakes because of Scheherazade and her stories. He understood something more about love than he had before, and after this always gave Scheherazade respect for her wisdom and honor for her valor.[1]

Chapter Two
The Rebirth of Feminine Language: Reclaiming Our Imagination

The intuitive mind is a sacred gift, and the rational mind is a faithful servant. We have created a world that honors the servant, but has forgotten the gift.
—*Albert Einstein*

I do not know what bounds may be placed on the power of the imagination. It can heal the body, reveal the secrets of divine truth, transform the personality, incarnate God, and open up worlds of infinite diversity and potential.
—*Jeffrey Raff*

Albert Einstein said, "Imagination is more important than knowledge." If imagination is so important to our lives, why aren't we trained in its use?

What is the power of the imagination that it can move us to tears, to action, to love, to surrender, to death, to transformation? Both mystics and quantum physicists know that the human imagination is the most creative faculty we possess. Imagination is involved in magical workings as well as the transformation of consciousness. Imagination is the source of manifestation. And imagination is sourced in feminine consciousness.

Imagination is the Language of the Feminine Spirit

Imagination is foremost the language of the feminine, of the heart, of life itself. It is a soul language of images and symbols, of music and art, myth and spirituality: a language that has the ability to move us at the deepest levels of our being. It is also the universal language of our species, the one language we all share—the language of dreams and visions. We tend to relegate imagination to children, but it is too powerful a tool to leave behind once we leave childhood. Women also tend to have wonderful imaginations. But through centuries of persecution and denigration, women have abandoned this intuitive way of knowing when we wanted to make our way in a man's world.

In his intriguing book *The Alphabet Versus The Goddess*[2], the brain surgeon, Dr. Leonard Shlain, believes that we are just now beginning to relearn what he calls the language of the Goddess, the language of images, through the medium of films and television as well as through our use of the Internet. It seems we are depending more and more on images for information. It is a fascinating study that explores the different ways human beings perceive and integrate the world into their consciousness. His thesis is that once people and cultures learn to read and write and abandon their oral and pictorial traditions, their culture goes through tremendous changes which develop the left side of the brain and cause that culture to become predominantly masculine in orientation, valuing linear, sequential, reductionist, abstract thinking. It also downplays feminine values and ultimately women's power in the culture. "Literacy has promoted the subjugation of women by men throughout all but the very recent history of the West. Misogyny and patriarchy rise and fall with the fortunes of the alphabetic written word."[3] Whether this is the whole truth or not, it is an interesting theory about how our brains change the culture we live in.

We know much more about the complementarity of the two polarities or modes of consciousness through the work of neurologists on the functions of the right and left hemispheres of the brain. The left side of the cerebral cortex of the brain controls the right side of the body, and the right side of the cortex controls the left side of the body. The structure and function of these two hemispheres is related to two different types of consciousness that exist simultaneously within each of us. The left hemisphere is predominantly involved with analytical, logical thinking, whose method of operation is primarily linear and sequential. We associate these concepts with the left side of the brain: the masculine, day, doing, the active, the rational, light, time, intellect, linear, sequential, heaven and cause & effect. The right hemisphere is primarily responsible for our orientation in space, artistic endeavors, body image and recognition of faces. We associate these concepts with the right side of the brain: the feminine, night, being, intuitive, dark space, sensuous, eternity, nonlinear simultaneous the receptive and synchronicity. The right brain is more holistic, simultaneous and integrative than the left hemisphere.[4]

Brain studies show us that women's brains are different from men's. In her beautiful book, *An Alchemy of Mind*, Diane Ackerman explains the differences between how men and women process the world.

A woman's brain has a larger corpus callosum, the sparkling bridge between the hemispheres, and also a larger anterior commissure, which links the unconscious realms of the hemispheres. This may allow the emotional right side to contribute more intensely to the left side's conversation, thought and other doings. Men more often focus on a problem with the hemisphere that specializes in it, while women tend to recruit both sides of the brain.

Girls emphasize what they have in common, and boys roughhouse with each other, talk competitively and avoid eye contact. Males do better on math reasoning, figure-ground and spatial tests and have better aim. Girls excel at language, social and empathy skills and spotting similarities between objects. They are more sensitive at hearing and smelling. In rhyming, both girls and boys are equally skilled, but boys use only one side of their brain, while girls use both.

Men have a harder time reading facial expressions than women. Men have more activity in the limbic brain and so react to emotional situations through actions. If angry, they attack. If fearful, they run away. Women's brains show more activity in the cingulate gyrus, adjacent to the language areas. They deal with emotions in a more symbolic fashion — they talk about them.

Women tend to worry more about losing attachments while men worry more about losing face. Men become more jealous over sexual infidelity, while women become jealous over emotional infidelity.[5]

The feminine outlook values a holistic, simultaneous, synthetic and concrete view of the world. Images form the natural language of feminine consciousness, which connects us to the sensual world of appearances. Jung believed that *psyche/soul* entails the imaginative possibilities of our human nature. The right side of the brain perceives all parts of the picture simultaneously, creating a whole gestalt. This is what a symbolic image does—it expresses the whole meaning of the idea.

Feminine consciousness is an inner vision first and foremost, the inner vision of Feminine Spirit. It is the language of images that is the mother tongue of Lady Wisdom. For the past few centuries, western culture marginalized this vision until we invented the moving picture and saw our inner images projected out into the world.

We have to understand how the power of images affects *psyche*, since we've deluded ourselves into thinking that they have no affect at all. The biggest delusion is that our dreams are meaningless, when in fact they are the royal road to our inner wisdom. We have to question how movies and television affect us and our children and our beliefs. We know from what the Nazis did in Germany that people can be manipulated by the use of archetypal images and symbols. And look at how our corporate media misuses the power of images to influence people into thinking they need to buy and consume their products.

It is up to our artists and writers, our teachers and visionaries, and women who are the caretakers of life, to make sure that we don't twist the meaning of images or use them to manipulate our beliefs. If we let this happen, we kill the imagination, the source of our creativity and wisdom. We can learn to use the imagination wisely once we understand its true value, and it will help us solve the overwhelming problems of creating a free and just society, here and around the world. It is only through balancing and valuing both masculine and feminine perspectives that we can create real change in our attitudes and beliefs about what is possible, what is life-giving, what is needed to heal the world.

If what Dr. Shlain says is true, it seems we all learned a masculine vision of life through the process of learning to read and write. While the eye scans the linear sequence of letters in words to discover their meaning in a one-at-a-time fashion, we are learning to think abstractly and see separation rather than wholeness. I'm not proposing we stop reading and writing. I don't know a single woman who doesn't love to read! We just need to learn how to put our wonderful imaginations to work in solving life's problems.

Imagination Is More Important Than Knowledge

So what is the imagination and how it is more important than knowledge? The first thing you need to know about imagination is that you need to use it to understand it—a very concrete, feminine way of learning! Then you have to understand how humans have related to it through the ages.

When was the last time you sat around a campfire in the woods, listening to a breeze moving through the leaves overhead, and then looking up, been amazed by the brilliant stars playing hide and seek beyond the treetops? The night, the fire, the stars and the breeze in the trees all evoke a response in you, a response of joy and wonder. Before long, you might find yourself telling stories, to others if they are with you, or to yourself if you are alone. Your imagination is awake, and you find yourself meeting the universe face to face. This is how children feel. This is also how our ancestors felt in the face of the majesty of life, before our modern rationality and our modern conveniences blinded us. Often it is only at night or in nature that we are able to come close to this ancient mystery once again.

The Native Americans lived close to this mystery day and night as did the Celts and other aboriginal peoples. They lived with hearts opened to the mysteries of the Earth and they were able to penetrate the veils between the worlds. The Aborigines of Australia can still walk in the Dreamtime; Celts might vanish into the Hollow Hills where the Fairy Folk still dance. Is our modern life so full of joy that we dare banish these other realms forever as *just so* stories? I think not, since joy is one of the things that is singularly lacking in most people's lives today.

We once had joy. Not so very long ago, we still believed in a cosmos that was friendly and awesome and full of mystery. Nature was alive with Spirit and we humans were part of nature. We had a sense of place; we belonged here. Then in the sixteenth century at the beginning of our modern era with its new scientific worldview, we lost our inheritance- we no longer saw ourselves as a part of nature. Unlike such scientists as Galileo, Newton and Kepler, who combined a deep reverence for the cosmos as God's creation and a need to understand and prove how that creation worked, this new scientific philosophy viewed matter as dead. They taught us that Earth is only dead matter, animals have no feelings and plants have no consciousness. This belief itself sprang from a religious viewpoint that believed that life on Earth was inherently evil. Science slowly gave us a new view of ourselves and suddenly we don't fit into this picture of a dead world that has to be conquered at all costs. We lost our true home when we stopped honoring this beautiful Earth as our Mother and Sustainer and instead rushed to own, rape and abuse her.

Corporations, fictional entities that now have the same rights as human beings, and governments have used this philosophic *carte blanche* to conquer nature and turn it into commodities that keep the global economic machinery running. This philosophy of life not only alienates us from our environment, but ultimately, from ourselves. This philosophy says the world is a machine, there is no God; therefore there is no meaning in life. If the laws of the universe are just mechanical, then goodness and justice and mercy play no part in life. This has developed into a philosophy of greed that is pervasive in companies that destroy the environment as well as in people's lives in their pursuit of the almighty dollar. This worldview says that since there is no ultimate meaning in life, why be responsible for my life? Is it any wonder that there is so little joy in our modern world since we are taught that these are the rules of the game?

The riddle we are faced with is: how do we bring new life into this death-in-life that most modern people are living? Modern life demands that we work more, consume more, and are in more debt than ever before. There is a *too-muchness* about modern western culture that speaks of a hidden dissatisfaction with the glories of the capitalist system. Wanting so many things indicates that nothing is satisfying. We are like little children on the day after Christmas who discard their new toys before they ever become beloved.

The Swiss psychologist Carl G. Jung once described a psychoneurosis as "the suffering of a soul which has not discovered its meaning." Jung saw this suffering as the symptom of spiritual stagnation and believed it to be the major symptom of western culture. And look at how these symptoms have spread around the world, giving rise to rampant consumerism as well as religious fanaticism. We have created a world out of balance, over-valuing a dead-end masculine perspective at the expense of a feminine perspective that understands the cycles of life and death. We won't be able to relieve the immense suffering of poor and outcast peoples from the dangers of war, disease and hunger until we reconnect to our spiritual nature and honor such basic human values as truth, love, sacrifice and honor.

And in America we have to look at the violence that is so prevalent in a society that prides itself on goodness and freedom and ask how we've helped to create it. According to a Senate Judiciary Report, "The United States is the most violent and self-destructive nation on Earth." The U.S. leads the world in violent crimes, most especially in violent crimes against women. There is more violence, more homelessness, more sickness, more toxic pollution, more addiction and more useless consumption and waste than in any other society that we know of. These symptoms surely suggest that something about the way we live is hurtful and destructive. If we have nothing that feeds our souls, we languish and die. So we create death all around us.

The Passion of Matter

A soulless society feeds on ignorance, violence and poverty. It has nothing to teach its citizens. Americans take pride in the fact that we're free, but real freedom is earned by responsibility and choice. It is time to set aside childish things and grow up if we want to take up the burden of freedom and choice. It is time to take up our service to the world. For what good is served when politics and our media culture fosters fragmentation and ignorance, rather than enlightened choice?

An ancient alchemical text, the *Corpus Hermeticum*, explains why people remain in ignorance.

Wickedness remains among the many, since learning concerning the things which are ordained does not exist among them. For the knowledge of the things which are ordained is truly the healing of the passion of matter. [6]

Healing the passion of matter! How can we do this? By taking responsibility to learn, to grow, to deal with the constant longing in our souls, because our souls know the answers to the questions of our life and can give us the knowledge we need to live consciously and well

One of the meanings of the word *passion* is *to suffer*. Matter, or our human nature, is suffering through a lack of understanding of the things that are ordained in our lives, that is, the natural laws of our human nature. We have lost our connection to what it means to be fully human – body, mind and spirit. We need to listen to our bodies, our minds, our emotions and our spiritual understanding so that we make good choices in our lives.

What we have been told is that matter is dead, and that our human bodies are corruptible and ultimately evil. This philosophy gave rise to crass materialism and compulsive consumerism. But *healing the passion of matter* entails seeing that matter is full of spirit; that life itself is sacred. For the alchemist, the transformation of matter through the alchemical process was such a healing, for it entailed the spiritualization of matter. While the Enlightenment scientific community rejected alchemy and astrology, scientists such as Galileo, Kepler, Francis Bacon and Isaac Newton were alchemists and astrologers, because they viewed matter as full of spirit. And of course, our physicists now tell us that matter is most definitely alive and full of consciousness!

Perhaps we are suffering through our problems as a labor that gives birth to a new consciousness that can heal the fragmentation of the western ego. This seems to be our ultimate purpose this lifetime, for our world is at a turning point. We are being forced into consciousness by the suffering of our *matter*—both our personal bodies and the Earth's body.

Any sacrifice on our part can now be seen as a *making sacred* or giving meaning to our lives. We are beginning to understand that we have to suffer through a situation to find its meaning. Ask anyone who's gone through the pain of divorce or disease about the suffering that brings consciousness. Although the suffering is bitter, no one comes away from the experience without coming into a conscious relationship with themselves for the first time in their lives. Through all the emotional suffering people have learned that there is meaning in everything we do in life. We just have to find a context for our suffering, a context that is the healing of the passion of matter. That context is a cosmology, a sacred story that helps us understand the things that are ordained for us (i.e., living a joyous, conscious life). We need to re-discover a sacred story about Life.

Our New Sacred Story

New stories are being told about our times, stories told by alternative healers, seekers, pagans, traditionalists. Over a quarter of the people in our country, about 50 million people, are what sociologist Paul Ray calls *cultural creatives*, people who are active in transforming our political, social and spiritual heritage. Many of these people are women, and all of them believe in the feminine principles of love, peace, service and interdependence.[7] They are working to understand and bring about the 'things that are ordained', the necessary changes we all have to make if we are to continue living here on Mother Earth. Many people believe that when a critical mass of these creative people is reached, (really only a small percentage of the entire population) then a new consciousness will become available to anyone who tries to access and ultimately understand and use the gifts of the imagination for its true purpose.

We need to find our place in the universe once more. We need to come home. The search for meaning was ignored when our modern scientific worldview focused on *how things work* rather than *why things are*. This is what happens when we separate spirit from matter. But the search for meaning has always been the work of our poets, artists, musicians, mystics, alchemists, great teachers, pure scientists, storytellers, psychologists and women. So there is hope that we'll re-discover those stories and begin to live within them again.

We are all being called upon to be the healers of our times, and we are seeing this happen. It seems there is a growing movement among baby boomers (an estimated 1.1 million already) to move out of the corporate world and go to work in non-profit organizations, with millions more to follow in the coming years. About one half of the 78 million boomers are interested in jobs that help others, putting their talents to work for the group.

Those of us who lived through the 60s or were born in the 60s came to renew our consciousness, our sense of what it means to be human and our responsibilities to each other. We do this by discovering our own individuality and talents, and then contributing them to the greater life of the community. Many people have had to face their own wounding and heal themselves, heal the passion of their matter, and in that healing have discovered their ability to heal others. The idea of the wounded healer is a very ancient belief, and is at the root of shamanic lore. To see this happening on a collective, cultural level is exciting, because it means that we have a chance to create the change that will heal the passion of matter. For we are remembering that matter, our physical world, is alive and intelligent and knows the things that are ordained for the health of life on this Earth.

People are healing themselves by listening to the voices of the Earth's imagination—the winds, the waters, crystals, plants, the stars, the body, the soul. For only by going through the darkness ourselves can we become true guides for others who still reside there. The great Western mystic, Hildegard of Bingen, said that "God has arranged everything in the universe in consideration of everything else."[8] Perhaps the inner suffering and loneliness of many people has been Spirit arranging for the new creativity that our times so desperately need.

We are living in a defining moment. The times are calling upon us to envision the future life of this planet. Ours is an age of rapid change and chaos; the violence of our culture reflects the violence of this chaos. The transition of the ages always involves a return to chaos so new forms can arise. These times give rise to great spiritual awakenings, and many people are opening up to the gifts of Feminine Spirit. Once again, medicine people, visionaries and mystics are being heard and honored. But it is a spiritual awakening that must take place within the heart of each individual, and each individual has to do the hard work to gain self-knowledge, which precedes the true gifts of Spirit. This self-knowledge is not only one of *criticism of self* but also of the *acceptance of self.* We have to name ourselves and our wounds for them to heal. And we have to gather the tools for healing that can be passed on to others who are still suffering.

The Power of the Imagination

An important tool we ignore to our detriment is the element of human imagination, the voice of Feminine Spirit. We misuse our modern media, and over-stress left-brain thinking in our schools, and so our imaginations stagnate. Our quest for scientific objectivity has taken a wrong turn, because we have rejected the place of imagination in the search for truth. William Irwin Thompson speaks of imagination as the awareness of the unseen (feminine) part of life.

Imagination is needed to shape a theory or a hypothesis, and Whitehead argued a long time ago that pure induction could never produce a scientific view of the world. A heap of facts was useless, and neither a Homeric epic nor a scientific theory of evolution could ever be produced from mere facts. For people in a pre-scientific culture, people endowed with acute powers of observation and remarkable sensitivity, there was no way to imagine the life at one's feet except through the poetic imagination which made the little creatures half human. And in a way, this poetic imagination of the ancients is more sensitive to humanity's embeddedness in the biosphere, for in seeing "the little people" as half human the ancient Irish "fairy faith" recognized that there is no "us" and "them," that we are in them, and they are in us.

The imagination is, therefore, not a source of deception and delusion, but a capacity to sense what you do not know, to intuit what you cannot understand, to be more than you can know.[9]

Most of us don't take responsibility for our imaginations, and so we engage in daydreams that have little meaning other than childish wish-fulfillment. But Jane Roberts, in her *Seth* books, shows that imagination is much more than that.

Imagination also plays an important part in your subjective life, as it gives mobility to your beliefs. It is one of the motivating agencies that helps transform your beliefs into physical experience. It is vital therefore that you understand the interrelationship between ideas and imagination. In order to dislodge unsuitable beliefs and establish new ones, you must learn to use your imagination to move concepts in and out of your mind. The proper use of imagination can then propel ideas in the directions you desire.[10]

If we don't acknowledge and use our creative imaginations, we are ignoring a psychic reality that operates on us according to its own laws and patterns. We become blind to the unknown parts of ourselves. We forget soul.

"For the creative imagination is not so named with some metaphorical intent, nor in a spirit of fiction, but in the full sense of the term: the imagination creates, and is universal creation itself. Every reality is imaginal, because it is able to present itself as a reality."[11]

Along with a rejection of a deep spiritual nature within ourselves, we have rejected this feminine mode of consciousness which is imaginative, playful and mysterious. It is time for women to re-discover our feminine wisdom. Men have always been fearful of and yet attracted to this aspect of the feminine imagination. Why else would they have such a love-hate relationship with the *enchantress* in women? This is also why most men have always projected their souls onto women, for they just don't understand how to use imagination like women do. That is another reason to learn it. Women have to teach men its proper use and function, because right now, the masculine mind uses the imagination to dominate and manipulate people.

Our rational, scientific world-view has flattened out our lives into a two-dimensional, spiritless travesty of what we might become. It narrows our options and imprisons our vision. The inner mystery is ignored until it sends us symptoms, like gifts, to enlarge our vision of the meaning of our lives. That is why so many people have started down the spiritual path through the psychologist's office. The word *psyche* and the word *soul* are related. The Oxford English Dictionary explains the word psyche thus:

"...breath or to breathe; hence life; the animating principle in man and other living beings, the source of all vital activities, rational or irrational, the soul or spirit in distinction to the body. It is also considered the animating principle of the universe as a whole, the anima mundi or world soul."[12]

Psychology itself deals with the logos of psyche - the meaning of soul. The Greek philosopher Heraclitus said: "You could not discover the limits of soul (psyche) even if you traveled every road to do so; such is the depth (bathun) of its meaning (logos)."[13] To go into the depths, to deepen events into experience, to look for many layers of meaning in our lives, to engage in imaginal work; this is something to be desired if we are to fill our lives with something more than addictions and mindless entertainments.

When we entertain the notion of soul, we once again get back in touch with the vital activities of life, the rational, thinking activities and the irrational, imaginative ones. It is the imaginative function of psyche, or soul, which entices us to dive into the depths of life's mysteries. And it is through psyche that we transcend our human isolation and become a part of the whole, a part of the world soul. It is the knowledge that each one of us is a part of this larger whole, that we each contain a spark of Divinity, which gives us the courage to confront the mysteries of life. Like Jacob wrestling with the angel all night, we each must wrestle with this angel of mystery until we claim the gift of our individual lives and names.

To enter the mysteries (which is one meaning of the word *mysticism*), we must go into the place of mystery; we must go into the place of soul or psyche. We must encounter the Unconscious within and discover for ourselves the reality of the human psyche. It is there that we will discover the repressed Feminine Spirit and reclaim our native ability to understand symbolic language. There we can reclaim our ancestral roots and our ties to ancient feminine wisdom. It is through the imagination that we begin to reclaim the gifts of the Feminine Spirit, and the first of these gifts is joy.

Stories Are the Language of the Unconscious

Everything that we know and feel is derived from the images of the psyche. These fantasy images run through our daydreams and night dreams, and they are constantly taking shape even when we are busy working and thinking. For the most part, we are unconscious of them, and even though everyone is fascinated by their dreams, not many people are willing to take them seriously: even though researchers have found that dreams play an essential role in keeping us both physically and psychologically healthy. Most people do not understand the language of dreams because it is non-directed and free-floating, and we have forgotten the deeper meanings that images point to and symbolize. We have forgotten because of our one-sided dependence on rational, left-brain processing.

Ancient cultures, Egyptian, Native American and Celtic, preferred a more imaginative, non-directed type of thinking. These cultures accepted that dreams and visions have a meaning, and they found ways to bring these gifts into the community, either through rituals or through stories, music and poetry. In their acceptance of this more imaginal consciousness, they established cultures that lived in harmony with the world around them. Each tribe and each person knew his/her/its place in the cosmos and this made for the harmony and balance that is so sorely lacking in our violent culture.

There is an old Seneca story that speaks to the heart of this matter, for the Native American tribes lived constantly in the presence of stories.

Long ago, there were no stories in the world. Life was not easy for the people, especially during the long winters when the wind blew hard and the snow piled high about the longhouse.

One winter day a boy went hunting. He was a good hunter and managed to shoot several partridge. As he made his way back home through the snow, he grew tired and rested near a great rock which was shaped almost like the head of a person. No sooner had he sat down than he heard a deep voice speak.

"I shall now tell a story," said the voice.

The boy jumped up and looked around. No one was to be seen.

"Who are you?" said the boy.

"I am Great Stone," said the rumbling voice which seemed to come from within the Earth. Then the boy realized it was the big standing rock which spoke. "I shall now tell a story."

"Then tell it," said the boy.

"First you must give me something," said the stone. So the boy took one of the partridges and placed it on the rock.

"Now tell your story, Grandfather," said the boy.

Then the great stone began to speak. It told a wonderful story of how the Earth was created. As the boy listened he did not feel the cold wind and the snow seemed to go away. When the stone had finished the boy stood up.

"Thank you, Grandfather," said the boy. "I shall go now and share this story with my family. I will come back tomorrow."

The boy hurried home to the longhouse. When he got there he told everyone something wonderful had happened. Everyone gathered around the fire and he told them the story he heard from the great stone. The story seemed to drive away the cold and the people were happy as they listened and they slept peacefully that night, dreaming good dreams. The next day, the boy went back again to the stone and gave it another bird which he had shot.

"I shall now tell a story," said the big stone and the boy listened.

It went on this way for a long time. Throughout the winter the boy came each day with a present of game. Then Great Stone told him a story of the old times. The boy heard the stories of talking animals and monsters, tales of what things were like when the Earth was new. They were good stories and they taught important lessons. The boy remembered each tale and retold it to the people who gathered at night around the fire to listen. One day, though, when the winter was ending and the spring about to come, the great stone did not speak when the boy placed his gift of wild game.

"Grandfather," said the boy, "Tell me a story."

Then the great stone spoke for the last time. "I have told you all of my stories," said Great Stone. "Now the stories are yours to keep for the people. You will pass these stories on to your children and other stories will be added to them as years pass. Where there are stories, there will be more stories. I have spoken. Naho."

Thus it was that stories came into this world. To this day, they are told by the people of the longhouse during the winter season to warm the people. Whenever a storyteller finishes a tale, the people always give thanks, just as the boy thanked the storytelling stone long ago.[14]

Human beings are creatures of story. We make sense of our world by telling stories - what our day was like, how we came to understand an experience, what happened to us on vacation. Through stories we imagine our lives into being. As astrologer Caroline Casey says, "A good story conjures the reality." We shape the universe through this storytelling capacity. It is a very right-brain, feminine talent. And yet, it is what stories we choose to tell that make all the difference between hope and despair, fullness of life and scarcity, life and death. There are also cultural stories which can feed a people with visions and dreams of their future, or close off all hope of fulfillment. They can make us insecure and fearful, or inspire us to courageously stand up to oppression and death. When a people lose touch with their cultural stories, they lose touch with their souls and with their place in the cosmos. This has happened with all conquered peoples when their stories are taken away from them. It is what is happening in America and around the world today. We are in danger of losing our individual, cultural and spiritual stories to the corporate story.

Are we thankful, like the young Indian boy, for the stories our culture tells us? Do these stories teach us important lessons? I believe the answer to both questions is no; first, because most of the stories the media creates no longer spring from the imagination, but rather deaden it, and second, because we no longer trust stories to teach us anything. Our culture does not value the bard or the storyteller as a teacher; so many people do not take the lesson of the good story to heart. We have lost touch with our child-like imagination, which can see worlds in a drop of dew or hear music in the fall of a leaf. We do not let the world tell us stories anymore, and we are afraid to listen to what our imaginations whisper in the night.

George MacDonald is the writer that many of our best modern fantasy writers revere as their mentor. He wrote, in the 19th century, stories and plays for the *childlike*. He often wrote about what he called the *fantastic imagination* and he insisted that, while this imagination was attuned to certain natural laws, there was no set and final meaning in stories he wrote. The story contained a meaning only if the listener perceived one. But he always hoped to *awaken* something in his readers, something that was akin to what happens when we hear beautiful music.

> The best thing you can do for your fellow, next to rousing his conscience, is—not to give him things to think about, but to wake things up that are in him; or say, to make him think things for himself. The best Nature does for us is to work in us such moods in which thoughts of high import arise. Does any aspect of Nature wake but one thought? Does she ever suggest only one definite thing? Does she make any two men in the same place at the same moment think the same thing? Is she therefore a failure, because she is not definite? Is it nothing that she rouses the something deeper than the understanding—the power that underlies thoughts? Does she not set feeling, and so thinking at work? Would it be better that she did this after one fashion and not after many fashions? Nature is mood-engendering, thought-provoking...[15]

To rouse the something deeper than the understanding—this is what the imagination and dream-creating function of the soul does for us. This type of consciousness is the myth-making aspect of psyche, either creating mythic themes within individual's dreams and fantasies, or creating cultural mythologies. This is the aspect of psyche that relates to the archetypes, the instinctual patterns of human behavior that Carl G. Jung postulated are the contents of the Collective Unconscious.

The Archetypes of the Collective Unconscious

Archetypes are those pre-existent forms of behavior, apprehension and perception of experience and reaction that make us human.[16] Similar to our instinctual knowledge, they help us shape and meet life in a human way. But we can only perceive archetypes through their archetypal images, for they themselves are unknowable. Archetypes are not inherited images, but inherent psychic structures responsible for the production of these images.[17] These archetypal images in turn give rise to the myths, dreams and stories of individuals and cultures. Jung believed that these transpersonal patterns of images are not located within human beings, but rather human beings are located in and subject to the intentions of the archetypes.

> Our personal psychology is just a thin skin, a ripple on the ocean of collective psychology. The powerful factor, the factor which changes our whole life, which changes the surface of our known world, which makes history, is collective psychology, and collective psychology moves according to laws entirely different from those of our consciousness. The archetypes are the great decisive forces, they bring about the real events, and not our personal reasoning and practical intellect.... The archetypal images decide the fate of man.[18]

It is through the psyche that we have direct contact to the archetypes, the basic patterns of human behavior. Another way to say this is that each person has a spark of divinity within, called soul, which is made in the image and likeness of God/Goddess and which shapes our humanity, for good or ill. This spark of divinity within each person pursues aims and intentions that are beyond our ego control, intent on achieving optimum health and well-being. This sacred Other within us sends us information through dreams, visions and fantasies to help the ego come into balance with the larger forces of the Collective Unconscious.

65

The Lost Language of Symbols: A Language of Meaning

What we have lost with the repression of the imagination is our understanding of symbolic language. Because imagination has been repressed, it is easier to manipulate it and us, because the symbols retain their power, even when we are unconscious of it. A symbol always points beyond itself to something unknown. It is a bridge between the Unconscious and consciousness, for, although the meaning of a symbol can never be exhausted, it is the best way to represent the unknown reality that is trying to be expressed. Symbolic language speaks of such intangibles as feelings, moods, values and ideas that cannot be rationally understood and explained.

It is a language women prefer, even though it has led us to be called incomprehensible. It is a language of deepening, a language that wakes things up within us, and gives us an experience of our own depths. It is the very voice of Lady Wisdom, for it is the way we learn of and relate to the ways of the cosmos.

This is the education that our people have been denied. This is the knowledge that can bring *the healing of the passions of matter*, for the symbols and the stories connect us to the patterns which make us human, the patterns which can take us past the stuck places or the hurdles in our lives and onto the next part of our journey into life. These archetypal images contain and focus our energies and help up tame the passions that would keep us unconscious of the meaning of our lives.

And yet, our western educational system does not teach us how to work with the imagination, or even how to think about and understand our place in the universe. We no longer look to nature—Earth's cycles and laws—for an understanding of our own human nature, for the rational mind has pre-empted that knowledge for itself. We are not taught about the patterns of human behavior or the necessity of suffering for growth in consciousness.

Modern education shunts people into an economic structure. Our children are often not trained in the gifts of creativity and imagination that are their birthright, for these talents are not valued by the corporate entities that run the world. The most amazing gap in our education has to do with the very thing all human beings desire most: we do not teach our people how to be in relationship, either with the Self or another. The very thing we want most is the biggest mystery to us, for though love will always remain a divine mystery, we could learn to become vessels for the power of this mystery.

It is time to give service to our community and to our nation because it is only in this way that we can know what we value. We need guiding images to contain and express the energies of our people. We are divided within ourselves: we say we value honesty and truth, yet our politicians are dishonest, our bankers commit fraud, and we admire power and wealth over simplicity, humility and individuality. The story of the Tower of Babel comes to mind: we are all talking gibberish and can no longer understand each other. We are divided within and without. We have forgotten how to be simple and direct or how to attune ourselves to the spirit of life. Most often, we seem to be enfolded in the arms of the Angel of Death, and we would rather stay with a known dis-ease than struggle with the unknown in life.

The only way to meet Death is to face it. If we are to come through this chaotic time into a new birth, we must reclaim the use of our imaginations, so we can give birth to new images that will describe our new experience of life and the world. This coincides with a return of Feminine Spirit, for the Goddess is the Birther and the Great Transformer. The East calls her Maya of the 10,000 Faces. When we meet and name those 10,000 faces, we will finally understand the voice of Lady Wisdom, who is the spirit in nature, both the world's nature and our human nature. And we can only come to that place with a loving heart, otherwise we will continue to misunderstand and misuse the power of images. The poet Rainer Marie Rilke understood Feminine Spirit, women and symbols.

> For there is a boundary to looking.
> And the world that is looked at so deeply
> wants to flourish in love.
> Work of the eyes is done, now
> go and do heart-work
> on all the images imprisoned within you;
> for you overpowered them:
> but even now you don't know them.
> Learn, inner man, to look on your inner woman,
> the one attained for a thousand
> natures, the merely attained but
> not yet beloved form.[19]

67

Like the famous storyteller, Scheherazade, I hope the images and stories I tell you will keep you wondering about what is coming next. I want to *shower your right-brain with images*, as Matthew Fox once said at a workshop. Perhaps some image will speak so strongly to you that you will follow it to a new place and a new wisdom. The power of the imagination must be respected and understood, so we can make choices that are honorable and life-giving. With the proper use of the imagination, we can create a new reality.

The story of Scheherazade is a wonderful example of the power of stories and images to transform consciousness. Although safe because she was the daughter of the Sultan's Vizier, she made a free choice to try to change her world. Through her bravery and cunning and storytelling ability, she saved the women of her kingdom. And she saved her man. What's better than that!

We live in a society that is mythologically and imaginally illiterate, where mistrust and misunderstanding of the imagination has led to a psychic wasteland. We have lost touch with our collective stories that shape a world of hope and aspiration. Hollywood has polluted our psyches as we have polluted our world. We need to clean out and clean up our collective psyche. We need to re-mythologize our world and come up with creative solutions if we are to birth a new world and evolve to a new level of human consciousness.

The Cosmic Story of Our Times

That is why it is important to look at the *End Time* stories that are influencing our very masculine, western society in these turbulent times. Once we know the story, we can enter into it and understand it from the inside. So far, we have seen how our culture uses force and antagonism, a very masculine way of dealing with differences, to solve problems. What can a more feminine wisdom, which is inclusive and synergistic, bring to the global table?

The most important issue women are pondering today is the question of our spiritual purpose. Women want to know what Divine Spirit wants us to do with our lives. We have to look in our hearts and remember what we love the most and then go do it! The *Woman clothed with the Sun* can help us understand our life's purpose. She helps us incarnate the sacred and she has a part to play in the transformation of our individual and cultural lives. She is Lady Wisdom. And she calls us to service.

To return to a feminine sensibility, we need to be telling stories, sharing images and dreams, seeing what myths can bring about a transformation of consciousness. Images hold power. They are transformers. We can let the media shape our images for greed and misuse of power, or we can let new mythologies be born within each of us. These new mythologies can transform each of us and they can transform the world. It is time for us to re-learn symbolic language. It is our mother tongue. That is why symbols affect us so deeply; they imprint us in the womb with the genetic code of our being human.

Symbols hold power and can cause great evil if they are twisted by a person, a nation or a corporation for personal power. The Nazis used the ancient, world-wide symbol of life, good luck, happiness and blessings, the swastika, to elevate their political agenda. But when we learn the language of symbols, we are taken into a deeper understanding of what it means to be human, for symbols contain the wisdom of our genetic code. And out of this deeper sight, we can imagine and create a future that will serve the best in us.

As you read this book, enjoy the stories and information, and use these examples to learn the language of the psyche. Do not be afraid to step into an image or a story. Wander around, take on each character, go on the adventure, dive into an image and watch the story unfold. What does the story bring up for you? How does it answer your questions about life?

Story Water

A story is like water
that you heat for your bath.

It takes messages between the fire
and your skin. It lets them meet,
and it cleans you!

Very few can sit down
in the middle of the fire itself
like a salamander or Abraham.
We need intermediaries.

A feeling of fullness comes,
but usually it takes some bread
to bring it.

Beauty surrounds us,
but usually we need to be walking
in a garden to know it.

The body itself is a screen
to shield and partially reveal
the light that's blazing
inside your presence.

Water, stories, the body,
all the things we do, are mediums
that hide and show what's hidden.

Study them,
and enjoy this being washed
with a secret we sometimes know,
and then not.[20]
Rumi

What images and stories have influenced you? Make a list of them and see if they are still an important source of inspiration for you. If not, dig deep and find some new stories you can center your life around.

Learn to understand symbolic, imaginal language so you can contribute your vision to these transformative times. The best way to learn this language is through your own dreams. As you work with your dreams, figure out how they speak to what's going on in your life. Keep a dream journal next to your bed, and write down whatever images you remember, even if it's only one thing. Your psyche will know you are paying attention and you'll begin to remember them more easily.

The Maidens of the Wells

In ancient times, Logres was a rich country but it was turned into a Wasteland when the kingdom lost the voices of the wells and the maidens that lived in them. These maidens would offer food and drink to wayfarers. A traveler had only to wish for food and seek out one of the wells and a maiden would appear from out of the well with the food he liked best, a cup of gold in her hand. No one was excluded from this service.

But King Amangons broke this custom. Although it was his duty to guard the maidens, he raped one of them and took away her golden cup for his own service. After that, no maiden was seen issuing from the well and the only service which wayfarers received was done invisibly. The king's vassals followed their king's actions and raped the other maidens, carrying off their golden cups. And so the service of the wells ceased. The land was laid waste: trees lost their leaves, meadows and plants withered and the waters were dried up so that no man might find the Court of the Rich Fisherman, he that once made the land bright with his treasures.

When King Arthur instituted the Knights of the Round Table, they heard this story and were determined make amends. But though they made vows to God, they could never hear a voice from the wells nor could they find any of the maidens. One day, the knights did find a group of ladies and knights in the forest. They captured a knight and he told the following tale. "All of us are the children born of the maidens whom Amangons and his men raped. We are bound to travel together through this land until God wills that the Court of Joy be found, for that will make the land bright again."

So Arthur's knights decided to seek for the Court of the Rich Fisherman, who was a shapeshifter. Although many knights sought it and few found it, none asked the right questions when the Hallows were processed about the hall of the Rich Fisherman. At that table the Grail appeared by itself and served all who sat there, providing food in great variety.

On the day that the Court of the Rich Fisherman was found, and the correct answers received by the seeker, the waters flowed again, fountains which had been dried up ran into the meadows. Fields were green and fruitful and the forests clothed in green leaf on the day that the Court of Joy was found.[1]

Chapter Three
Recovering a Feminine Standpoint: A Teaching Story

Who cannot love herSelf cannot love anybody
who is ashamed of her body is ashamed of all life
who finds dirt or filth in her body is lost
who cannot respect the gifts given even before birth
can never respect anything fully.
—SUSAN COOPER,

Story opens our hearts, nourishes our souls, awakens our minds,
refreshes our Spirit. Story is the vehicle we use to pass on wisdom
that is so intrinsic to our human nature that story is the only way
we can express it. Story is in all times and in all places.
—CLARISSA PINKOLA ESTES,

The Rape of Feminine Spirit

Like the maidens of the wells, the voices of women's wisdom have been raped away by centuries of masculine domination and rationalism. We thought we could live without the feeling and intuitive, imaginative and symbolic voices of Feminine Spirit. But like Logres in this tale, western culture has become a materialistic Wasteland without the healing presence of the waters of the wells of feminine wisdom. In the last 40 years, we have experienced the return of Feminine Spirit in all her many forms. Despite the backlash against the women's movement and the latest *war against women* in the US, women are standing up for financial equality with men and shattering glass ceilings. Women in business and politics are stepping forward with innovated ideas that come out of their feminine experience, their feminine brain and their feminine imagination. And those companies who have women CEOs and women in higher management are reaping the financial rewards of their innovative style. Women's voices are speaking out and being heard, asking the right questions and giving the smart answers.

As women re-discover our unique powers of love, interconnection, vision and healing, purpose and wisdom, we invariably give our gifts to the people, and the world, we love. Like the Maidens of the Wells, women give freely of our gifts to all who ask. This is our special magic-the more we give, the more we have to give.

To understand the heroine's journey in the 21st Century, we have to understand that besides re-learning our mother tongue of the imagination, women need to reclaim our unique feminine standpoint and voice. For long centuries, a woman's sense of herself has been undermined by social and religious authorities. When we look to our sisters in the East, we are justly outraged by their plight in countries like Afghanistan and the brothels of Thailand. And yet, it was only 300 years ago that women in the West were burnt at the stake for being witches and seductresses, healers or merely old, and it has only been in the last century that western societies have given women the right to vote. Women are finally free and yet what woman feels free from all the old prejudices and fears that seem to be programmed into our genetic code after thousands of years of repression?

Our sisters in Afghanistan have had to deal with the Taliban, and women in the West have had to deal with our own *inner Taliban*—all those nasty voices that judge us, criticize us and put down our self-confidence; that create fear, depression and anxiety and that cover up our truest and best selves. We know that the patriarchal demands on women have twisted our feminine natures to conform to masculine standards of behavior and belief. These inner terrorists are hard to point fingers at because they are invisible tormentors. These inner suicide bombers would rather see us dead than free of their old lies and beliefs.

It is by experiencing how we are *not* really free and equal to men, in the political arena, in the business world and in our personal relationships, that women come into our true freedom. No matter how successful a woman is—which is really a measure of how well she has acclimated herself to the masculine hierarchy—she still has to confront these negative voices, both within herself and also in her environment, for often men still do not understand or validate her standpoint. That is why we must reclaim a truly feminine standpoint, and know it for what it is. Perhaps then men will stop expecting us to be, think and act like them and finally take it upon themselves to understand us in our true feminine form.

Understanding Feminine and Masculine Energies

More often than not, the concepts of feminine and masculine lead to general statements, confusion, conflict, and sometimes, argument and anger. These terms describe two complementary forces in the universe that are intangible archetypes. It's been suggested that the best course might be to get rid of gender stereotypes altogether and just agree that all attitudes and behaviors belong to both sexes. C. G. Jung pointed out that each of us has a contra-sexual psychic element operating within us. Psychologically as well as biologically, maleness contains recessive feminine traits and femaleness contains masculine traits.

We could just get rid of our concepts of masculine and feminine and say everyone is the same, an easy way out of a difficult situation. But being equal does not mean that we are the same. Women are equal to men under the law, but we must still demand that the feminine perspective on life is equal to that of the masculine. Our modern rationality so often is willing and eager to dismiss questions that disrupt our view of reality. We have become lazy thinkers! What we are having trouble with are the *stereotypes* of gender, not the reality behind them. That still remains a mystery, and its deepest reality always will remain one. But we can dismantle our stereotypes and allow new images to arise from the depths of life. Stereotypes are merely the outer husks of an archetypal reality, a shell or image that has lost its power to express that reality in life. These husks are what need to be discarded, so we can begin to discover where the life that was once theirs has been reborn. We are living in a time of transition and transformation, and we must be willing to explore the possibilities of a renewed understanding of these two different, yet complementary, ways of being in and experiencing the world.

Why do we want to neglect that most lovely mystery of our differing sexuality—our dual nature as human beings—and its reflection in the inner and outer worlds? Why devalue our bodily differences when we can explore the mysteries of our bodies as symbolic of the mysteries of the basic principles and dynamics present in ourselves and our world? Why not imagine that the chaos in our understanding and of the times we live in is the *prima materia* of a new consciousness, the forerunner of a new evolution in spiritual understanding, the dissolving and transformation and rebirth of the masculine and feminine manifestations of spirit and their eventual re-union?

Many people are already engaged in this work as we work to heal the wounds in our lives and in our society. The alchemists found that the Philosopher's Stone, the divine essence within each person, was born of the chaos of the *prima materia*. This *prima materia* had to be distilled, and burnt to ashes, and separated and worked, until it yielded up two essences, which were symbolic of the King and the Queen, Sol and Luna, the Masculine and the Feminine, Yang and Yin. It was only after the separation and discrimination of the elements that a new union was possible. This was achieved in the *hieros gamos*, or sacred marriage, which produced the Philosopher's Stone, or in Jung's terminology, the Self.[2] The reality behind these images renews itself through new images; the worn-out images and beliefs of past ages can be left behind if they are no longer life-enhancing, for new images will arise that will integrate the new truths that are being born.

Being in a state of transition, the concepts of masculine and feminine can be imagined in many ways. The fact that all cultures make the distinction between maleness and femaleness indicates the given nature of this polarity in the collective psyche. Therefore, the opposition and complementarity of the masculine and feminine archetypes are the underlying symbols of our experience of duality. The ancient Chinese speak of this polarity as the cosmic principles of Yin and Yang, and all other polarities have been connected to this sexual polarity: solar and lunar, light and dark, initiative and receptiveness, heaven and earth. These polarities are not fixed and static, but interweave in various proportions throughout all of creation.

In our western tradition, the masculine principle has come to be associated with left-brain activity, as well as solar symbolism and consciousness. It represents spirit, logos, creativity, the striving for individual consciousness, discrimination, separateness, discipline and order. It is represented by the image of the great solar hero who slays the dragon and triumphs over the darkness.

The feminine principle, represented by right-brain activity, is usually associated with the Moon and lunar consciousness. This principle has been devalued in western culture, and so we know less about it - it is more unconscious for us. It symbolizes actualization and manifestation, the senses and sensuality, body and soul, creative play and imagination, and the realm of dreams and fantasies. Lunar consciousness is much more opened to the realms of the magical, mystical and psychic dimensions of life, to the intangible, intuitive, feeling side of life. It is these elements of our psyches which we are re-discovering and which will eventually birth a new collective consciousness. On the whole, women know more about solar consciousness than men do about lunar consciousness because women have had to adapt to a masculine culture, while men still distrust and diminish feminine ways of knowing.

C. G. Jung defines solar consciousness as the ego-consciousness of modern humanity, while lunar consciousness gives rise to the more feminine workings of the Unconscious. Jung also felt that creativity, new births, new stories, and new possibilities emerge from this feminine realm. A Cartesian mechanistic world-view has been the paradigm of western science since the 17th century and the Age of Enlightenment, and it has trained us in a separatist masculine consciousness, which ignores the emotional, mental and spiritual implications of our materialistic culture. It is the more feminine, holistic world-view of the new physicists which experiences a holographic universe, a universe which is seen as a dynamic web of interrelated events, and which postulates the interconnectivity of all things.[3]

Some feminist writers assert that since most of the masculine qualities once belonged to the Great Goddess of antiquity, they should be considered part of the feminine, or at least not only masculine. The Celtic Goddess of War, the Morrigan, is a dark, war-like aspect of the Great Mother, such as Kali in India. Today, we think of war as something more closely related to masculine occupations, although women fought and died as soldiers in both Iraqi Wars. Yet, the ancient Celts saw war as a feminine preoccupation! There has been a change in consciousness since those days and the newer differentiations have settled into the Collective

Unconscious. To reject all differentiation or to consolidate all qualities under the umbrella of one concept can lead to the continued domination of the dominant viewpoint, i.e. the masculine viewpoint.

It is Feminine Spirit and its consciousness of images, rhythms, play, body, mystery, soul and being which has been devalued by our western civilization. To recover a feminine standpoint, we have to find out what it is—learn about it, experience it, and live it. When these aspects of life are renewed and reverenced, understood and made available for the purposes of life, we will have a conscious feminine standpoint. Then we will live the image of the *Woman clothed with the Sun*: a feminine consciousness which can balance a new masculine consciousness. Our old masculine consciousness needs renewal, because for too long it has repressed and used feminine consciousness for its own purposes, instead of honoring it as an equal. A new relationship of equality between these two primeval forces, working through men and women, can help us all heal the Earth, our relationships and our society.

The Power of Story

Another way to understand these two forces or types of consciousness is through an imaginal approach—the way of learning through images. This way speaks to the heart; it evokes knowledge from within instead of defining and categorizing it. As the writer George Mac Donald once wrote, "It is there not so much to convey a meaning as to wake a meaning."[4] As we have seen, stories embody one form of this imaginal consciousness. Our great spiritual teachers have used stories to impart knowledge of the mysteries that cannot be expressed rationally. A story can touch our intuitive and feeling faculties, instantaneously imparting knowledge *through the heart,* which is the seat of feeling. The Native Americans believed that humans learned and thought with the heart, and they often imparted their wisdom through teaching stories.

All fairy tales are teaching stories. We have relegated them to the nursery, but they really speak of the hidden, psychological processes— the archetypal patterns—that can help us work through our complex problems. Fairy tales are the purest and simplest expression of archetypal processes. Just as the hero has a thousand faces, so too does the heroine. Most stories are variations on a basic motif, and show how different components of an archetype are stressed and transformed under different circumstances. There are over seven hundred variations on the Cinderella theme, each reflecting a slightly different way to deal with not only the human problems of envy, suffering and redemption, but with redeeming the spiritual energies of life from the ashes. Many fairy tales deal with the issue of what happens to a woman when there is no positive mothering, nurturing principle in her life, and then it shows her how to find that nurturing within herself. Other tales deal with the negative dominance of the father, which spurs a woman on to her own individuality, and which is the major psychological task facing women today.

There is a teaching story that tells us something about the Masculine and the Feminine Spirit in transition, and I feel that it speaks to what we are experiencing today in the bewilderment we feel about what it means to be a woman or a man. It is a fairy tale that teaches us how to achieve a conscious feminine standpoint. It speaks to the necessity of working with different types of consciousness; of understanding images and letting their transformations teach us something about the essential qualities of our dual nature as human beings. It says that through women's struggle to find our freedom, a whole new way of life is possible for both men and women. It is a story that can teach women how to incarnate the *Woman clothed with the Sun*. There are many variations of this story throughout the world, for it is a story about walking the path of feminine wisdom.

So, imagine if you will a small cottage in the forest. It is nighttime, the stars are out and the crescent Moon floats in the western sky. Inside the cottage there is a hearth fire, and a few candles glow as everyone settles down around the old woman sitting next to the hearth. She beckons to us: "Gather round as I tell you a tale of a beautiful princess who was intelligent, brave and resourceful, who accepted hardships, pain and silence, and who, in the end, knew herself and drew to herself the king of her desires."

There was once upon a time a King whose Queen was the most beautiful woman on Earth. Besides the grace of her form and face, she had the most beautiful golden hair. Their love was legendary, and even the birth of a daughter paled beside their obsessive love.

No one knows how it happened, but it came to pass that the Queen grew ill, and as she lay dying, she called the King to her one last time. She looked him in the eye and demanded that he make her a promise. As he loved her beyond measure, he agreed to whatever she wanted of him. "When you marry again after my death, you must find someone who is just as beautiful as I am and she must have the same golden hair. You must promise me that you will do this." Now the King protested that he would never marry again, but the Queen insisted, and so when the King finally gave his promise, she closed her eyes and died.

For a long time, the King would not be comforted, and gave no thought to taking another wife. Finally, his councilors insisted that the country needed a new Queen. That's when he remembered his promise and said that he would only marry someone who was as beautiful as the late Queen. But although there were many beautiful women who were fit to be Queen, they did not have the same golden hair.

Now the King's daughter had grown up quite alone, at first ignored because of her parents' obsessive love and then because of her father's grief. This princess was just as beautiful as her dead mother and she had the same golden hair. One day the King finally noticed her and saw that in every respect she was like his late wife, and suddenly felt a violent love for her. Then he determined to marry his own daughter. Although it went against all the laws of Nature, the King would not be dissuaded.

The princess was shocked when she became aware of her father's desire, but hoped to turn him from it. She told him, "Before I fulfill your wish, I must have three dresses, one as golden as the Sun, one as silvery as the Moon, and one as bright as the Stars. Besides this, I wish for a mantle of fur, made using a piece of skin from every animal in your kingdom." For she thought it would be quite impossible for her father to do this. The King, however, had the cleverest maidens in his kingdom weave the three dresses. And he had his huntsmen catch one of every kind of animal in the whole of his kingdom, and take from it a piece of its skin, and out of these was made a mantle of different kinds of fur. When all was ready, the King brought the dresses and the mantle to his daughter and set the wedding for the next day.

When the King's daughter saw there was no hope of changing her father's mind, she resolved to run away. In the night, she gathered three of her treasures - a golden ring, a golden spinning wheel, and a golden reel - and she put the three dresses of the Sun, Moon, and Stars into a nutshell. Then she put on her furry mantle and blackened her face and hands with soot and secretly left the castle. She walked the whole night until she reached a great forest, and because she was tired, she hid in a hollow tree and fell asleep.

The Sun rose and she was still sleeping when it was full day, so she didn't hear the hunt led by a new King who owned the forest. When his dogs came to the tree, they sniffed, and ran barking round it. The King told his huntsmen to see what kind of wild beast had hidden itself there. The huntsmen obeyed his order, and when they came back they told him that a wondrous beast was lying asleep in the hollow tree, one whose hide they had never seen before. So the King told them to catch it alive and then fasten it to the carriage so they could take it with them.

When the huntsmen laid hold of the princess, she awoke full of terror. They were amazed to hear her speak and asked who she was. She told them that she was a poor child, deserted by both father and mother, and asked them to have pity on her and take her with them. And so they called her Fur Skin and told her that she would be useful in the kitchen where she could sweep up the ashes. Then they put her in the carriage and took her home to the royal palace. There they showed her a closet under the stairs, where no daylight entered, and told her she could live and sleep there. She was sent into the kitchen, and there she carried wood and water, swept the hearth, plucked the fowls, picked the vegetables, raked the ashes, and did all the dirty work.

The princess lived there for a long time in great wretchedness. Then one day a feast was held in the palace, and she asked the cook if she could go upstairs for a while and look on. She promised to stand outside the door where no one would see her. And the cook gave his permission, but demanded that she be back in half-an-hour to sweep the hearth. So she took her oil-lamp, went into her den, put off her dress of fur, and washed the soot off her face and hands, so that her full beauty once more came to light. And she opened the nut, and put on her dress which shone like the Sun and went up to the festival. Everyone made way for her, although no one knew her, for she looked like a king's daughter. The King came to meet her and danced with her, and thought in his heart that he had never seen anyone so beautiful. When the dance was over she curtsied, and when the King looked round again she had vanished, and no one could say where she had gone.

She had run into her little den, however, and quickly taken off her dress, made her face and hands black again, and put on the mantle of fur. When she went to the kitchen, the cook told her to leave the cleaning till morning, and make the soup for the King while he went upstairs to take a look. So when the cook went away, the princess made bread soup for the King, and when it was ready she fetched her golden ring from her little den, and put it in the bowl in which the soup was served. When the dancing was over, the King had his soup brought and ate it, and he like it so much that it seemed to him he had never tasted better. But when he came to the bottom of the bowl, he saw a golden ring, and could not conceive how it got there. So he ordered the cook to appear before him. Well, the cook was terrified when he heard the order and told Fur Skin, "You have certainly let a hair fall into the soup, and if you have, you shall be beaten for it." Then he went before the King, who asked who had made the soup. When the cook replied that he had, the King said that it was not true, for it was much better than usual, and cooked differently. When the cook acknowledged that Fur Skin had made it, the King sent for her.

When Fur Skin came, the King asked: "Who are you?" Fur Skin replied, "I am a poor girl who no longer has any father or mother." He asked further: "Of what use are you in my palace?" She answered: "I am good for nothing but to have boots thrown at my head." He continued: "Where did you get the ring which was in the soup?" She answered: "I know nothing about the ring." So the King could learn nothing, and had to send her away again.

After a while, there was another festival, and once again Fur Skin begged the cook for leave to go and look on. He told her she could but she had to come back again in half-an-hour, and make the King the bread soup which he liked so much. Then she ran into her den, washed herself quickly, and took out of the nut the dress which was as silvery as the Moon, and put it on. Then she went up and was like a princess, and the King stepped forward to meet her, and rejoiced to see her once more, and as the dance was just beginning they danced it together. But when it was ended, she again disappeared so quickly that the King could not observe where she went. She, however, sprang into her den, and once more made herself a hairy animal, and went into the kitchen to prepare the bread soup. When the cook went upstairs, she fetched the little golden spinning wheel, and put it in the bowl so that the soup covered it. Then it was taken to the King, who ate it, and liked it as much as before, and had the cook brought, who once again was forced to confess that Fur Skin had prepared the soup. Fur Skin again came before the King, but she answered that she was good for nothing else but to have boots thrown at her head, and that she knew nothing at all about the little golden spinning wheel.

When for the third time the King held a festival, Fur Skin asked to go up to the ball and the cook said: "Fur Skin, you must be a witch, because you always put something in the soup which makes it so good that the King likes it better than the soup I cook." But he let her go up at the appointed time. And so she put on the dress which shone like the Stars and entered the hall. Again the King danced with the beautiful maiden, and thought that she never yet had been so beautiful. He had given orders that the dance should last a very long time and while they were dancing, he slipped a golden ring on her finger without her noticing. When the dance finally ended, he held onto her hands, but she tore herself loose, and sprang away so quickly through the crowd that she vanished from his sight. She ran as fast as she could into her den beneath the stairs, but as she had stayed more than half-an-hour, she could not take off her starry dress, but only threw over it her mantle of fur, and in her haste she did not make herself quite black, but one finger remained white.

Then Fur Skin ran into the kitchen, and cooked the bread soup for the King, and as the cook was away, put her golden reel into it. When the King found the reel at the bottom of it, he summoned Fur Skin, and saw the white finger and the ring which he had put on it during the dance. Then he grasped her by the hand and held her fast, and when she wanted to run away, her mantle of fur opened a little, and the star-dress shone forth. The King clutched the mantle and tore it off. Then her golden hair shone forth, and she stood there in full splendor and could no longer hide herself. And when she had washed the soot and ashes from her face, she was more beautiful than anyone who had ever been seen on earth. And the King asked her to marry him and she agreed, for he was the King of her desires.[5]

Fairy Tales: Stories of the Archetypes of the Collective Unconscious

This fairy tale became one of my teachers, for it made me explore and question what was going on in my own life and in the culture at large. As I struggled to find a sense of my identity as a woman, these marvelous images illuminated my path. This story speaks of a feminine initiation, a process by which a woman can achieve a conscious feminine standpoint. At the same time, it explains how the feminine transformative mysteries deepen and enrich our connection to both the masculine and feminine spirit, and how these forces are renewed in the culture. For the question we are all asking ourselves, collectively and individually, is, "How do we find a new spirit, a new orientation, a new way of being alive?"

It is important to remember that the thing that makes these fairy tales and myths so compelling is their connection to the archetypes, those unknown factors in the psyche that manifest through archetypal images. The archetypes are the patterns of behavior inherent in human beings. As Jung and his colleague, Marie-Louise von Franz, have pointed out:

> Fairy tales are the purest and simplest expression of collective unconscious psychic processes. Therefore their value for the scientific investigation of the unconscious exceeds that of all other material. They represent the archetypes in their simplest, barest and most concise form. In this pure form, the archetypal images afford us the best clues to the understanding of the processes going on in the collective psyche.[6]

The fairy tale is its own best explanation, for its meaning is contained in the totality of its motifs, connected by the thread of the story.[7] However, a symbolic and psychological re-telling of the tale is necessary since our ability to understand the language of images has been diminished by our dependence on left-brain rationality. Just as many of us have difficulty understanding the logic and images of our dreams, so too we have to look at the separate elements in a fairy tale before we can see it as a whole. We have to track and stalk the symbols and images and even the thread that holds the story together. We have to let our imagination play with it. We have to look at it from different perspectives, using our intuition, feeling, thinking and sensation, and we have to bring our psychological understanding and experience to it, for our age is engaged in the discovery of this old and yet new psychic reality.

Fairy tales, like dreams and myths, are expressions of the things left out of collective and individual consciousness. Throughout the ages, different stages of human development have fostered stories that reflect different phases of individual development. *Fur Skin* is one of the many variants of the story of Cinderella. The Cinderella motif is also concerned with the re-discovery of the feminine principle, hidden away among the ashes and dirt of life. On a more spiritual level, it depicts the search for Wisdom. *"Among the ancients, 'Wisdom' implied Love and Knowledge blended in perfect and equal proportions."*[8] Matthew Fox speaks of the dying of Wisdom in our culture and the need to search for it. He describes Wisdom as belonging to Earth and creativity.

...Wisdom is of Mother Earth, for nature contains the oldest wisdom in the universe. Wisdom requires the right brain as well as the left, for it is birthed by both analysis and synthesis. Wisdom requires imagination and nurtures it. Wisdom often comes via the creative spokespersons of a culture, in the handing on of stories, sagas, myths, and images from the past and from the future.[9]

Many of the names of the heroines of these Cinderella tales imply the idea of the Light-Giver, the bright, shining one.[10] In Robin McKinley's wonderful and heart-wrenching modern re-telling of this tale, *DeerSkin*, Princess Lissar is named for the light. Fur Skin's light is symbolized by her three dresses, hidden under the robe of fur, that is, within the earthy instinctual nature. This motif of three dresses is used in many fairy tales about redeeming the Feminine Spirit, and brings to mind the ancient tales of the Heavenly Sumerian Goddess Inanna, who disrobes as she descends into the Underworld, where she suffers a death and a rebirth, and then ascends once more to the heavens, robed in glory.[11]

On Being a Father's Daughter

Fur Skin depicts this process in a manner that speaks to our times, for collectively we are in the situation of demanding the Father's gifts, as women look for equality on the level of masculine achievement. And if this is the only kind of equality we know to look for, women will stay wedded to the Father. Women most especially need to reconnect to our own earthy wisdom, for equality comes from an inner spirit, and not an outer form.

The theme of renewal is personified in this fairy tale by the fact that there is a king and a queen in the beginning of the tale, and a new queen and a new king at the end. The images of the king and the queen symbolize wholeness, a unity of forces or factors that make up a paradigm, a cultural dominant, or a psychic identity. The king and the queen are the kingdom, or our self-identity, in microcosm. It is only when masculine and feminine are united in a common vision that the kingdom can prosper. Hopefully, men and women will come to this realization soon, for we must also heal our relationships if we want to heal our culture.

The king in fairy tales symbolizes the central, dominant content of collective consciousness, the central god-image that dominates a civilization. This king represents our patriarchal culture, which has been influenced by Christianity, and later, the rational, scientific outlook, which led to the domination of nature's resources. Our emphasis on the economy is another collective dominant. These masculine dominants keep pushing for the search for perfection and continuous expansion, and therefore, they have given rise to a very large shadow-the repression of all that is seen as imperfect or impediments to progress. Individually, the king represents this patriarchal attitude in subjective consciousness or our ego attitude. He is the inner king who sets up standards and rules for our behavior and belief.

The queen is the inner partner of this king, and represents the intangible, intuitive, feeling side of this cultural belief system, the aspect that gives life and energy to our collective and individual stories. She is the passion and enthusiasm which drives the collective impulse of our capitalistic economic system or the deep spiritual viability of our religions. If the queen dies, the energy invested in a particular system of belief is siphoned away. When a cultural dominant, a crucial paradigm, a religious orientation, wears out and needs renewal (and this is a natural and necessary occurrence), the first thing to die out is the feeling attachments to it.

When we begin to realize the devastation that our economic system has caused to the environment, it is hard to believe that *progress is our most important product*! When religions cannot give their people a viable connection to Spirit, people stop attending their religious services. The images of that particular dominant no longer capture the feelings and imaginations of the people. Western culture is experiencing this death-we no longer believe what our ancestors once did. On an individual level, when a conscious attitude is no longer life-giving, the feeling tone is lost, and the psychic energy goes back into the Unconscious. Life loses its meaning. Individuals go into a depression and we get a society that is depressed, addicted, obese and unbalanced.

When a cultural dominant dies, we witness the tremendous energy and chaos underlying the need for renewal being expressed in the many fads, cults and excesses that abound in modern times. Human beings seem to need a dominant, some form of psychic wholeness to relate to that helps them channel the tremendous energies of life. The king and the queen represent that psychic wholeness.

In *Fur Skin*, the fact that the queen dies implies that the predominant spirit of the times is in need of renewal. But what form will this renewal take? The tale tells us that women are called upon to find our own feminine standpoint, independent of the expectations of the old masculine culture, if a new wholeness and perspective is to be achieved. Of course, men must engage in this struggle too, but I feel that it is women who must incarnate this renewal in our lives, and stop selling out to masculine values.

The basic rejection and denigration of feminine values as compared to masculine values is the heritage of our historically patriarchal culture. This has resulted in a situation in which the feminine individuation problem has become a pioneering task that perhaps is meant to usher in a new period of culture.[12]

For women today, and for our culture, the dying queen represents the aspects of the feminine that support the patriarchy. For far too long, women have shaped our lives to masculine ideals of womanhood. We often repress our own concern with personal authority and the satisfaction of our own needs for the sake of others. We struggle to transform our mature, womanly bodies into that of young teenage girls to attract men's attention. Our wise, womanly mothering wisdom is discounted in political and academic circles.

The devaluation of the feminine over the past 4000 years led to the second-class status of women, and women began to accept this view of our own sex. We were told that, like our mother Eve, we were the source of humanity's fall from grace, as well as being the source of temptation for men. Women, liberated women, still have a sense of guilt when some strange man follows them home or molests them! They cannot help thinking that somehow, they are at fault. And this theme is carried over into the stories our culture tells itself, such as movies about the obsessive woman in *Fatal Attraction*, or the violence depicted against women in movies like *Sleeping with the Enemy* or *The Silence of Lambs*. The dark side of the feminine, the earthy, often uncanny, aspects, were vilified by men who were afraid of it, and so women lost touch with our sexuality, our feelings, our imagination, our mystery, and our wild freedom.

The queen in this fairy tale carries the projection of the masculine ideal of womanhood. No dark, mysterious woman is she, but rather a heavenly light being. This is symbolized by her golden hair, which is emphasized in the tale. Hair often symbolizes the life-force, and the golden color indicates that it is a sun-like, rational force. This feminine aspect is removed from the Earth, from the darkness that is also a part of Feminine Spirit. This feminine dominant serves the heavenly, and in western culture, masculine ideals. She is like the Greek Goddess Athena, the virginal daughter of the Father, in the Father's service, open and receptive to his spirit alone.[13] Like Athena, this queen carries and reflects and defends the masculine spirit in all things. Why else would she demand that the king only marry someone who is as beautiful as she, with exactly the same golden hair? This demand assures the continuance of this particular masculine dominant, whether or not it is the necessary and beneficial thing to do. Instead of promoting change, which is life, she stops it. She is the epitome of a Father's Daughter, a daughter of patriarchy. Unfortunately, most Father's Daughters have been cut off from the earthy knowledge of the cycle of life.

This queen is removed from her feminine roots, which would connect her to the natural rhythms of life, death and rebirth, which are so basic to the feminine mysteries and Feminine Spirit. In fact, she resists those rhythms by demanding the king make this promise. This is an aspect of the patriarchy which we often overlook; namely, that there is a feminine element that wants to perpetuate the old value system. Part of the reason we overlook it, and therefore why it becomes so troublesome, is because it is unconscious. Psychologically, the fact that the queen dies symbolizes that this feminine component has worn out and has sunk back into the unconscious. It now rules the king unconsciously, through the promise, and so keeps him tied to outer forms, regardless of his own inner feelings and their demands.

The queen herself condemns her daughter to marriage with the Father. This could only happen in a culture or an individual where a true feminine standpoint is lacking. If the feminine viewpoint brings into life feeling values, imagination, natural rhythms and unity, then we find that this dead queen operates behind the scenes to keep this life force from entering into our governmental, economic and religious structures. This is an apt image of what happens when the American government, in the name of democracy, liberty and justice, supports tyrants and their repressive regimes. Or when we are told that our liberties need to be curtailed for our own security. Or that we must make war to bring about peace. The promise that the king makes to the queen reflects the refusal to trust that life renews itself, and that it will bring about the necessary changes if we let it. The promise stops the flow of life into new forms; it would rather see the old husks live on past their time. This is an image of the dragon that would devour the *Woman* and her divine child in the *Book of Revelation*. Psychologically, the collective or individual dominant has become rigid and petrified, dry and lifeless. It becomes a Wasteland.

We are all Father's Daughters, women who have been sold out by mothers who have forgotten their own feminine wisdom. We make our decisions about life based on a belief system that does not value the gifts of Feminine Spirit. How do you feel about it? Are your life decisions based on what your heart knows or what your head thinks?

The Transformation of the Feminine

The fairy tale states that it is this princess, this daughter without a mother, who must solve the problem. The princess represents the new, emerging feminine consciousness, an evolution in the form of the eternal feminine principle, who is Lady Wisdom. Just as humanity is hopefully evolving into greater consciousness, divine awareness enlarges as our own consciousness deepens. In fact, Jung believed that the Divine Spirit needs humanity's capacity to know It in order to know Itself.[14] With the development of this new feminine consciousness will come a deepening and enrichment of the images of the Divine in both its masculine and feminine aspects. The princess brings new energy and passion to life, and a new connection to Feminine Spirit as well.

This princess has no mother, only a father who falls passionately in love with her; not seen for herself, but valued for his expectations of her. Having no mother cuts her off from her feminine roots and feminine nourishment. Many women I know have felt this in their own lives. How many of us have fervently worked to ensure that we are nothing like our mothers! This princess, like us, has to get her nourishment from the Father's spirit, collective masculine ideals, and her personal father. The spirituality of the feminine principle and its mysteries are lost to conscious life.

The princess takes on the life of masculine spirit, so of course her father is enchanted with her! Men seem to want a woman who meets their own anima projections. It keeps them in control. Robin

McKinley's *DeerSkin* makes this part of the tale very concrete, for the father *will* have his daughter, whether she will have him or not. He brutally rapes her. We women know, however, that there are many forms of rape, and this fairy tales speaks to all forms: physical, mental, emotional and spiritual. But all forms of rape injure our spirit, and women have to find healing before we can be free of the father, free from being owned and free to make choices about our bodies and our lives.

But this princess, perhaps because she is a father's daughter, cannot be so easily overpowered by his demand. After all, she's learned so much from him. Although she looks very much like her mother, she is both like and unlike her. She probably has the same strong spirit as her mother, for she stands up to the king without fear. But she is not her mother, and she knows that something is wrong that her father should love her so. She very rationally decides on a course of action that she believes will defeat his purpose.

To turn her father aside from this unholy marriage, she demands three marvelous dresses and a fur mantle. Clothes, dresses, and shirts can hide the true personality, as in the case of certain uniforms: nurse, policeman, doctor, or priest. This is when clothes represent the persona, the mask with which we meet the world. But clothes can also symbolize an attitude which we try to incorporate and then manifest to the world. When we're teenagers, we need to dress just like everyone else so we can feel comfortable with our peers. As we mature, we choose clothes that fit our individual style, so that what we wear says something about who we are at a glance. Psychologically, this often means finding the right mode of expression, or the right type of consciousness with which to meet a situation. In this story, these three dresses have a cosmic significance, and represent different ways of knowing, or different types of consciousness, which the *Woman of Revelation* integrates. The price of her father's passion is the possession of all the knowledge of his kingdom.

Today's women have taken our political freedom and learned all there is to know about the world. We excel in business, science, the arts, sports, and politics. And yet, patriarchy is still alive and well in Russia as well as in the Middle East, in South America as well as in the United States, in Africa as well as in Asia. The old order of the patriarchy makes a show of giving women equality—like the dresses given by the father—but in both subtle and overt ways, women have to emulate the prevalent masculine viewpoint to win acceptance and validation. There is still very little respect for or even understanding of a truly feminine standpoint. The real freedom for women comes when we live in our mantle of furs and reclaim our wildness and our instinctual knowledge of life. That is when women can truly claim these three dresses as our own.

All the Riches of the World: The Four Types of Consciousness

These three dresses and the mantle of furs symbolize different types of consciousness, just as their colors represent the differentiation of light. They represent the four-fold aspect of our nature: our body/physical, our individual ego consciousness/psychological, our unconscious imagination/imaginal and our spiritual consciousness/spiritual. When Fur Skin appears in these dresses, she is manifesting the image of the *Woman clothed with the Sun, standing on the Moon, crowned with Stars.*

The golden dress of the Sun symbolizes the solar, masculine, left-brain consciousness of our culture, which likes to differentiate one thing from another. It is our psychological consciousness. The solar principle is a strong, fiery, life-giving force. It is concerned with *logos*, the Word spoken before the beginning of the world. It is our ability to name a thing, which helps us understand its nature more fully. It represents our rational mode of consciousness, in that it brings the possibility of seeing, with great clarity, causes and effects. It stands for the principle of order, of differentiation, of individuality.[15] It can also be death-dealing, like the Sun in the desert, for cold rationality can objectively look on death and destruction without qualms.

The silvery dress represents the lunar, feminine principle. Lunar, right-brain consciousness supports the claims and needs of the reality of life. It is a consciousness attuned to rhythm, tides, needs and the feeling side of life.[16] It is a receptive consciousness, ready to listen, wait, trust, take in and yield to situations, and to allow things to happen in their own time. It nourishes and embraces all things, for like the moonlight, it blurs distinctions and gathers together disparate elements.[17] In its highest form, it is the imagination developed to its fullest.

These two types of consciousness see the world through different eyes, and as the scientific study of the brain shows, both types of consciousness are available to us. As stated before, most of us have overdeveloped our solar consciousness at the expense of our imaginal, lunar consciousness. Getting these two dresses represents developing the ability to use both types of consciousness, to see with both eyes.

The dress of the brightness of the stars relates to the divine dimension of life and is concerned with mystical vision. This dress represents our third eye. Stars symbolize the spark of divinity within humanity. Paracelsus, the famous medieval alchemist, states that within each of us is an 'astrum' or star, which drives us towards great wisdom.[18] This divine image within each person is comparable to Jung's concept of the Self. Jung says that Paracelsus "beholds the darksome psyche as a star-strewn night sky, whose planets and fixed constellations represent the archetypes in all their luminosity and numinosity."[19] The archetypes within and the patterns of stars without combine to help us find the meaning of our lives and our place in creation. The star dress represents our relationship to the Divine, to the ground of our being. This dress is very much present in our society, for it is made up of all the accumulated spiritual wisdom of all times and ages, and it is available to us in books, through yoga and meditation practices, from spiritual gurus and teachers, and most directly through our own inner work. People seeking this kind of personal connection to Divine Spirit are trying to live in their star dress.

Leaving the Father's House

When the princess gets ready to flee from her father, she puts these three dresses into a nutshell. This symbolizes the fact that she must take the essence of each type of consciousness with her, reduced to its essential state, for the image indicates a dark, enclosed, germinating place. This image of germinating is repeated a second time when Fur Skin falls asleep in the tree, and once more in the tale in the image of the closet beneath the stairs, where no daylight enters. This is where Fur Skin sleeps and lives; this is where her new life is enclosed and germinating. Like Harry Potter, we have to accept that we might go through a time of being marginalized for our attempts to find our own power. Harry is given the room under the stairway because his aunt and uncle will not admit that he is a wizard. But it also becomes his own special sanctuary where he can dream. There is a sense of interiority, of going within, that is needed for this task, for the princess' task is this: to take these dresses and make them her own. They must grow within her so that she can express them in her life. They cannot be 'things' that she knows about or 'puts on'; she must integrate them so that they are expressions of her essential being. These three dresses help her develop the capacity for wisdom.

This occurs in a woman's life when she finally realizes that she is responsible for her own life. It is our values that make us who we are: we have to work to live by them, taking responsibility for how those values shape our life and also accepting how they shape the world we live in. It is the only way to learn how to listen within for the voice of Lady Wisdom. This, of course, is the hard part, and the rest of the fairy tale speaks of how this must be accomplished. The princess must live in the mantle of furs.

When we take responsibility for our lives, we begin to listen to ourselves.

The Mantle of Furs

The mantle of furs is very different from the three dresses. It represents the very thing that the old cultural dominant lacks. When the father king falls in love with his daughter, she is horrified. In Robin McKinley's version of the story, the father rapes his daughter. She is brought abruptly and cruelly into an awareness of her womanly body, and all she experiences is pain and terror. She is lost to herself, for the father has ravished her. Men have ravished women for long centuries, and some of them are still at it today. When women are ravished, we lose our voices and no longer have the capability to share our wisdom.

The patriarchal, dominator mindset has turned sexuality, the most sacred act between people, into a weapon of torture, humiliation and pain for some people, such as the women and children who are still being sold into sexual slavery as you read this! Whether the rape is physical, or if it is *only* mental and emotional, women have to escape into our instinctual nature if we are to heal these wounds to our Feminine Spirit. Sometimes the psychic incest is worse for a woman, because the wounds are invisible and we doubt ourselves and do not understand why or how we were wounded. But the wounds are there in all of us, because they are part of our soul history as well as part of our genetic inheritance.

The problem with this cultural dominant (the father king) is the confusion between instinct and spirit. Our culture has lost our connection to our instinctual nature, for we have come to believe that it is evil and unworthy of the human spirit. But the Native peoples knew that we learn about life through our animal nature. Chief Letakots-Lesa of the Pawnee tribe says that

> In the beginning of all things, wisdom and knowledge were with the animals; for Tirawa, the One Above, did not speak directly to man. He sent certain animals to tell men that he showed himself through the beasts, and that from them, and from the stars, and the sun and the moon, man should learn. Tirawa spoke to man through his works. [20]

We have lost the wisdom of our instincts, and of Earth's laws, and so we distrust them. The king's promise makes him fall in love with his daughter, and this twists the natural instincts. This promise is what keeps a woman split off from her true nature and purpose. In reality, the king has married his daughter now for many centuries.

> Patriarchal societies have forced women into stereotyped roles: the understanding, virtuous, and self-sacrificing woman, or the passionate, seductive, and frightening woman. Both feminine images are controlled through the body's appearance, attitudes, gestures, and movements. These categories tear up a woman and rob her of her strength. She has to be very careful not to be misunderstood. To be respected and taken seriously, she tries to hide her femininity and constrict her body into an emotional corset. Split into saints and witches, women were at once put above and beneath the reality of life; either way, they were robbed of all real participation in the development and the shaping of society. They were supposed to derive happiness and satisfaction from a peripheral existence, supposedly in harmony with their "natural" role, namely self-sacrifice and submission. [21]

On a cultural level, the king wanting to marry his daughter is comparable to companies like DuPont Chemical getting environmental awards for having invented something safer than CFC's, safer meaning that these new chemicals will destroy the ozone layer slower than the old chemicals did. The king trying to marry his daughter occurs when the old order tries to make use of the new feeling life that is arising in the collective. U.S. citizens put the environment at the top of their list of concerns, and so the very companies that have caused the environmental problems in the first place are scrambling to prove how environmentally conscious they are; they do this not by really working out new manufacturing techniques to eliminate the use of pollutants but by manipulating public fears and sentiments into believing they are trying to be the 'good guys'. This old energy was behind President George W. Bush calling the lowering of air standards the *Clear Skies Initiative* or selling off our national forests to lumber companies and calling it the *Healthy Forest Act*. And we are so far from our instinctual common sense that many people believe them. On an individual level, humans have become so cut off from our instincts that most people did not perceive the danger of the receding waters of the Indian Ocean tsunami in 2004 until it was too late. Reports that animals and the Native tribal people sought out higher ground confirm that there is wisdom in the body's instincts! And death when we are cut off from them!

So the princess' task, for herself and for her kingdom, is to make a connection to her own instinctual life, and she does this by wearing the mantle of furs. She clothes herself in the instinctual, natural life that the forest animals represent. Once again, Matthew Fox says that our search for wisdom must start with the Earth. "Wisdom is of the Mother Earth, for nature contains the oldest wisdom in the universe." When we are lost, when we have no mother (either literally or emotionally) to teach us the ways of being a woman, we can always return to our mother, the Earth. When we go out into nature, in our gardens or in the wilderness, the wisdom is still there to be found. We just have to make ourselves available to it. We have to don our mantle of furs and learn.

A young woman came into analysis because of relationship issues. She is smart, energetic, artistic and witty. But she doesn't have a good sense of her feminine gifts. She had lots of men friends but few lovers. She was in love with a man who chose to stay with a woman he didn't love because she was pregnant with his daughter. My client couldn't understand how a man could choose to be miserable with another woman when he was clearly infatuated with her. But being the good father's daughter that she is, she always gave him an out: by being understanding and by supporting his decisions even though it hurt her. As she started to get in touch with her deeper instincts of self-preservation and self-love, she began to have dreams in which animals tried to speak with her.

In the first two dreams, she is confronted by bears, which represent the primal mothering power that will defend us from danger. The bear teaches us how to combine intuition with instinct. In the third dream, she goes back to her father's house and reclaims the feminine powers of love and sexuality and rescues a kitten from drowning.

Dream 1:

I am in the basement of my Mom's house going through boxes looking for something. All of a sudden this great big brown bear is there. Its lips are moving like it is talking but I cannot remember what it was saying. I think it is mad at me and wants to eat me! So I run all over the house trying to get away. But it keeps pursuing me. Every time I think I've gotten away, there it is, back again. I run out of the house and around the back. I manage to slip back into the house and lock her outside. She is banging at the door to get in. I turn to run, but there she is in front of me. Her lips are moving but I cannot make out what she is saying. I get really scared and wake up.

Dream 2:

I find myself outside this house in my old neighborhood. I remember thinking "I always wanted to see the inside of this house". The next thing I know, I'm inside. There are a bunch of women around the kitchen table, looks like many generations of the family: grandmother, mother, daughter. I tell them I'm sorry to intrude, but I always wanted to see the house. The mother says it's okay, I can look around as much as I want to. I look around and stop at this door. I open it, and there is a stairway leading down. As I go down, a man riding a brown bear crosses by the bottom of the stairs. He is riding it like a horse. Then they come back to the stairs. The bear throws the man off and comes up the stairs after me. She is trying to talk to me. But I get scared and run back up the stairs. I have no idea what she was trying to say.

Dream 3:

I am crossing the street near my grandmother's house. I am quite thin and very scantily dressed and blonde. Next thing I know, I am in my dad's house. I think the goal was to get it ready for my sister and her husband. I remember being in the front bedroom. It is painted a golden yellow.

… I go next door to my Mom's house. On the way in, I decided to check the mail. The mailbox is stuffed - there are all these cards. Christmas cards I think, in natural/tan colored envelopes. Some are ones I have sent out and others are ones addressed to me. There is an endless supply of them. The mailbox remains stuffed no matter how many I pull out. It's like they keep replenishing themselves.

Next, I am in a white bathroom (not one I recognize) and the shower is running. I am in a white tank top and undies. I hear this little voice coming from the shower. When I pull the curtain back, there is a small gray cat/kitten in there. The poor thing is soaked. It is asking me to help it out of the shower because it can't seem to get out on its own. I help it out and it thanks me. Then I wake up.

This young woman is in the process of reclaiming her feminine power as she gets back into her body and her sexuality. She must go to both the inner mother and inner father to reclaim them, and it is there that her instincts speak to her. She has learned to stay true to herself and accept her needs and desires, and in standing up for herself, she is finding the self-confidence to ask for the love she so richly deserves. These archetypal energies are available to take us through our personal transformations if we are willing to do the hard work of becoming conscious and working with them.

In wearing the mantle of furs, Fur Skin follows the demands of her role as princess and future queen. We often think that being a princess entails nothing more than the rank and privilege and prestige of being royal. True princesses have to learn their duty to their people. They have the responsibility and duty to live their lives for their people, to heal the land and to solve the pressing problems of the culture. To be royal means that one is the mediator between the people of the tribe or country and God or Great Spirit. The king and queen are the channels of life for the land. If they do not fulfill their function, the land dies. Since we live in a democracy, that prerogative now becomes the responsibility of each person, for on a spiritual level we each have the potential to live out our *royal* nature.

To wear the mantle of furs, then, is the princess' task, and she has to reclaim on an instinctual level the wisdom of the body and what it has to say about being human and knowing our place in the cosmos. Psychologically, it is through what Jung calls our inferior function that we begin to connect with our new potentials. Jung distinguished four different functions: thinking and feeling, sensation and intuition. Usually, people favor and develop one function more than the others. Jung felt that it was possible to develop three of the main functions fairly well. The fourth function, called the inferior function, remains outside the ego's total control, and it is this more undeveloped, child-like quality that allows spirit to become the bridge for new potentials and promises of new life.[22]

The fur mantle is that part of life which has been repressed, rejected, or just undeveloped, but which can bring new life into a situation, a culture, or an individual life. We can say the same about our re-awakening awareness of our bodies. Through yoga techniques, holistic healing, and natural herbal remedies, as well as new attitudes towards health and sexuality, we are beginning to reclaim a knowledge of our bodies that was lost to us for many centuries. As we work hard to reconnect with our own bodies and our instinctual life, it is like living in this fur mantle.

Listening to our body and sorting out its messages can take a while. Instead of worrying about some part of your body that isn't 'feeling' right, go into that part of your body and ask it for an image. This image can help you understand what is really going on. Perhaps you need to get up and move and stretch. The body wants you to listen.

Transformation

When the princess dons the mantle of furs, she blackens her face and her hands with ashes. There is a stage in the alchemical process called the *nigredo*, in which the material being acted upon is reduced to ashes.[23] It represents the blackness of dissolution and death. This certainly parallels the motif in both Cinderella and *Fur Skin* in which the heroines must sweep up and live in the ashes. The image indicates that she is willing to undergo the process of allowing her old life to die. This is the hard work of letting go of our old habits, our old beliefs, our old hiding places.

Understanding symbolic language gives us entry into a whole other dimension of life, one in which the imagination teaches us the meaning of life. Symbolic language connects us to the archetypal laws that govern life here on Earth. We listen to this story and hopefully feel the pain of Fur Skin's betrayal and toil, and perhaps wonder at the beauty of her dresses. Then we look at the deeper story within the images. We fill out these images with associations and meaning and begin to make deeper connections with our own lives. This is the gift that symbolic language gives us—symbols come alive within us and begin to live through us. The more conscious we are of this process, the easier it becomes. This is how we can use the imagination to transform our lives.

So, let us go deeper into the image of the mantle of furs. Mantles symbolize death, and *a covering up to make invisible*, like the mantle of the Greek underworld god, Hades. In covering herself with this mantle of furs, the princess is trying to find a way to express the instinctual life that the animals represent. She has to give up her ego reliance on the father's rules (her blondness), and try to understand what it is that she is cut off from.

This often feels like a death to many women. If my instincts tell me that the man in my life is not really valuing me, but I can't put my finger on it rationally, I might turn away from what my instincts are saying because I cannot verbalize or prove it. And yet, feminine wisdom is rooted in common sense or an instinctual response to the flow of life, and if a woman can value that response, it can bring about a rebirth through this rejected part of herself. This is part of the standpoint that women need to reclaim as a counterbalance to masculine rationality. It implies trusting oneself, and this is a very hard lesson for most women. But we have to learn to trust ourselves and our own perceptions. This is the only way to find our wisdom.

Wearing animal skins reproduces the paradisiacal state of understanding and speech between humans and animals, and gives us access to animal and instinctual wisdom. The Greek goddess Artemis might represent this stage in the journey and tasks of the princess. Artemis is Virgin, Woman Alone, at-one-in-herself, creating a sense of inviolability and separateness. As *Mistress of Wild Places and of the Animals*, she is the huntress, dancer, lover and slayer of animals, protectress of young ones and teacher of women.[24] She is connected with the ancient shamans, who wear animal skins on their journeys to heaven. Shamans search out heavenly wisdom for earthly use. Artemis leads the dance on Olympus, and this skill is connected to the skill that makes her the *midwife*, for rhythm facilitates the passage from one realm to the next, just as shamans make their passage on the rhythm of the drums. Both dance and birth are set to instinctual rhythms, and it is Artemis' instinctual nature that causes her to prefer the wild places of forest and mountain to the mansions of Olympus.

Artemis is the image and energy to turn to when we must become virginal in the old sense of the word, when we turn within to find out who we are in ourselves. She represents the wildness of the feminine principle, the wildness in women, which can be dangerous to men, and feels dangerous to the masculine consciousness of the West. But she can help us survive the contact with our unconscious instinctual life. She can teach us which instincts to trust and when to use them; she also helps us decide which instincts we need to offer up to the gods. It's important to trust love, and it's a good idea to offer up jealousy to the gods if we want to grow in our ability to love.

She teaches us how to listen to the rhythms of the seasons, the waxing and waning flow of the Moon, the tides and our feeling life, which have a wisdom we need to relearn. As anyone knows who has gone through it, this kind of knowledge is not set out once and for all as rational knowledge is, and so we have to learn to trust it and most importantly, ourselves, for we become the final authority of our own life. Trust is the hard part.

When the princess flees to the forest, she falls asleep in a hollow tree. The forest, as the home of the animals, is the wild place, both literally and symbolically. For westerners, it has come to represent the Unconscious. In many stories and legends, it is the place of testing and initiation, where the soul enters into the perils of the unknown world. The image of fleeing to the forest and sleeping in a tree carries on the theme of a death and rebirth.

Here the tree symbolizes the World Tree or Axis, the place where heaven and earth connect. It is here that the princess comes in touch with the shamanic ability to fly up the world axis and bring back the knowledge that can heal her and her people. But the tree also becomes a mother symbol, for it often represents the Great Mother in her nourishing, sheltering, protecting and supporting aspect. Many techniques in creative visualization call for us to ground ourselves in the Earth, to become part of the Earth. We need to ground the imagination to bring about the real change in attitude and in life. The imagination is no longer *just a fantasy* but becomes grounded in life, valued and built upon. Sleeping in the tree is an image of being within the womb of the Great Mother, similar to the dresses being hidden in the nutshell. It connects the princess in a positive relationship to Feminine Spirit and to the Unconscious. It is also an image of spiritual rebirth through the World Axis, the center of the world, the place we want to be reborn as conscious human beings.

> The tree symbolizes human life and development, and the inner process of becoming conscious in the human being... it symbolizes in the psyche that something which grows and develops undisturbed within us, irrespective of what the ego does; it is the urge towards individuation which unfolds and continues without reference to consciousness. The Self is the Tree, that which is greater than the ego in man.[25]

The Self does indeed give birth to us, and an attempt to be opened to its workings brings us into relationship with other elements within ourselves that have been neglected. The princess who had no mother to raise her is now connecting with a positive feminine element in herself. In returning to an instinctual way of experiencing herself, she begins to reconnect to the feminine principle that is emerging in the Unconscious. She has to begin to live out the dark, earthy feminine, which is rooted in the Earth and her body, and grows towards the heavens. Just as on a cultural level, we have to begin to listen to what our earthy nature is telling us about what we are doing to the world around us and within us. Aren't we repulsed when we see polluted waters or landscapes? Aren't we angered when we see sickness and malnutrition? But what do we do about it? How well do we use our anger to bring about change, or do we just let it go and go back to our ordinary lives? If we do nothing, we are still sleeping in the hollow tree. But fortunately for Fur Skin, something happens.

Discovering A New Masculine Energy

A new king appears now. The forest belongs to him. He is a hunter, unlike the princess' father, who had to get someone else to hunt for him. Hunters are very active; they go out into the forest with a purpose. They learn to live with and in the forest, and they know and respect the life and ways of the forest and the habits of the animals. They are in touch with their instincts, for they have to feel what is going on around them, and they have to use all their senses, just as the animals of the forest do.[26] This king represents the *new king*; he is the masculine consciousness that appears with the Goddess' return, the lover and defender of Mother Earth. He is the Green Man of Celtic legend, the energy of the Earth which floods the world with life and growth. When we meet him, it feels like a return to a way of being that is so natural to us, and which was repressed by all of us in childhood. Do you remember going out to the garden to sit and watch the first crocuses blooming on a sunny March day when you were young? The awe and the wonder that awoke in you seeing those tiny bursts of color after the starkness of winter! It felt like falling in love or seeing God. I knew something that I had never known before; I sensed some mystery about myself and the cosmos that school neither spoke to nor acknowledged. I still feel it every Spring.

The old father king represents the outer, collective values that have lost their inner life now that the princess comes in contact with this new king. The old king wants to do what is expedient, what will give him more power in the outer world. This new king is the inner king of our instinctual nature, the masculine aspect of the Self that will give rise to a new order—new behaviors, new beliefs, new possibilities—both within the psyche of an individual as well as within the culture as a whole. The new king does what needs to be done, with kindness and consciousness, acknowledging the sacrifice and blessing the energetic transformation.

The hunter king is the energy that enables us to go within, and stay within, until we can understand the instincts and energies that are unconsciously working within us. He represents the self-knowledge that is the foundation of the spiritual journey towards wholeness.

The Hunter, the Green Man of the forest, represents a new path to wholeness, one that engages in life through the senses as well as the intellect. When we allow our instinctual nature to come back online, we begin to feel the connection to all life. We reconnect with the Earth and each other. Men as well as women are connecting with this Green Man, who will father a new masculine consciousness in us all.

The Green Man has appeared in many of our myths and legends. One image of this new king is Adam in the Garden of Eden, when he names the animals. He knows the essence of the animals and can speak their own names. Another image is that of the old Celtic god, Cernunnos, the Stag God of the forests who is also a symbol of the instinctual life brought to consciousness. In medieval legends, there are certain knights who are the personification of the feminine ideal of a man: the Knights of Abandonment, such as Tristan and Lancelot, who are willing to forgo the masculine ideals of honor for the love of their Lady. There are many stories about Gawain, the Hawk of May, that connect him with the Green Man in stories such as *Sir Gawain and the Green Knight*. Celtic lore is full of images of this Green Man, and it is a hopeful sign that the ancient Celtic stories and Earth religion are enjoying a revival in our times. Of course, there is also the figure of Arthur himself, the king who will return in time of need, the king who was taught by the magician, Merlin, and who became a shape-shifter himself, becoming the animals of the forest, rivers and the air.

Another potent representative of this king is the image of the Native American warrior and man of compassion, who lives in harmony with the land and his own nature. The Native Americans offer us a different type of spirituality and relationship to the land than our own western heritage. Theirs is a spirituality of the Earth and its rhythms, and for Americans, they represent a way of being which we have savagely repressed and pushed into the Unconscious, just as we savagely killed them and their cultures. This new king represents a new transformation of the masculine spirit that will be concerned with life and the spirit in nature.

The princess, who has been sleeping in the tree, is now awakened by the hunters. *To wake up* in a dream or a fairy tale often means that a new level of awareness has been reached. This proves true in the tale, for the princess now gets her own name, given to her by the king's hunters. She is now Fur Skin, no longer an anonymous princess, a king's daughter, but an individual with her own name, a name that describes her state of being—embodying her instincts.

There is an ancient myth about the goddess Persephone, in which she only gets her name when she is ravished away into the underworld by Hades. Before this she is Kore, the Maiden. Being ravished into the underworld bestows upon her the gift of individuality. Likewise, Fur Skin now has a name, a context for herself and she is brought to this king's palace to work on it.

Women know this power of getting named. When we are left on our own to deal with death or an illness, divorce or trouble with work, when it feels like we have lost everything that makes life worth living and yet we have to go on, we suddenly discover that we are empowered. We discover who we really are. We come to know our own name.

Becoming a Conscious Woman

Fur Skin is put to work in the kitchen of the palace, where she "carried wood and water, swept the hearth, plucked the fowls, picked the vegetables, raked the ashes and did all the dirty work." Fur Skin lived there for a long time in great wretchedness. The work of self-knowledge is now taken into the realm of concrete, everyday reality, working on the concrete, everyday tasks of life. It is long and grueling work, something not undertaken lightly. It takes endurance, patience and perseverance. The task of transformation is hard work, for we have to be willing to "undertake a critical examination of the self and to refrain from projecting the dark, unexamined shadows lurking in the self onto others."[27]

The kitchen is a feminine place, a place of warmth and sharing and the hearth fire, a place of transformation and purification. In the ancient world, the hearth was dedicated to the goddess Hestia, the goddess whose only image was the transformative fire itself. She represented the fire of life, in individuals and in the community.[28] Fur Skin's great labor is a transformation of consciousness, a tending of the fires of life. It is wretched work for an individual in our society, for it is neither valued nor understood. It is hard work, because it is the little, everyday changes that bring about transformation. It is stopping oneself in the midst of everyday activities and asking where old habits and attitudes come from, and deciding if these are still appropriate for this new life. It entails listening to and working with fantasies, feelings and intuitions: it includes getting in touch with our bodies and their needs. It is something women are beginning to do as we learn to stand on our own, and it will be our gift to the collective psyche in the years ahead.

Women working on change often feel isolated, lonely and guilty. A woman's whole conditioning is contrary to seriously finding out what she wants.[29] As a woman begins to explore her own feelings about herself and her life, she comes up against all of those societal values that have shaped her life thus far. They are voices which tell her what she is expected to be and how she is expected to act. That inner Taliban again! She has to struggle to validate her feelings and intuitions, because whenever she feels she is right about something, someone will inevitably tell her she is wrong and selfish—usually herself!

Women soon find out that we do not even have concepts and names for what we are experiencing. We have to recreate the way we think about things, making up new categories, and seeing emotions, such as anger, resentment and dependency in new ways. We begin to shine a whole new light on things—the light of a feminine, right-brain consciousness and standpoint. When I was working this out for myself, it was sharing these new insights with other women that helped quicken the transformation. And now we have so many feminist, religious and scientific writers examining different aspects of this kind of consciousness that we no longer have to worry about being crazy or not. We're in good company! So much has been written on psychic abilities in the past decades that women are no longer afraid to listen when they get a hunch or when they *see* something about someone. In the end, though, we must each go through our own process alone, for no one else can do it for us. As women and men integrate this feminine awareness in their lives, the Divine Spirit will open us to still deeper wisdom and creativity.

Dancing Our New Lives Into Being

In the midst of Fur Skin's labors, the king holds a festival. In ancient cultures, festivals were times of ritual, times to come into relationship with the gods and goddesses, totems and holy ones. These rituals were enacted in sacred time and sacred space, and they always entailed dance. The sacred power of dance is a natural way of attuning oneself to the powers of the cosmos and to one's own inner being. All dance aims at achieving an identity with what we are dancing out.[30]

> When we dance, we can rise above the little self into the world of mythology and have the chance to become one with the human longing to understand life. Our pain and suffering thus become part of a long story, the human story; this comforts individuals and gives them heart. The heart can then soften and give space for love and understanding. People learn to forgive and grow from a state of isolation into the world of unity.[31]

Dance brings the imagination into the body and out into the world. The way the body moves through space images what the psyche feels about its freedom to move with imagination. Dancing to different rhythms brings a consciousness of what kind of energy levels we deal with in our lives, and how comfortable or uncomfortable they make us feel. In a movement and imagery workshop I led, there was a woman whose movements took up very little space, and who quite literally backed herself into a corner! When I asked her what she was feeling about her movements, she said that she felt she was being very powerful and perhaps taking up too much space! This woman is so afraid of overpowering people that she tries to make herself invisible, or at least unobtrusive. Something that she could not see happening in her life suddenly became obvious through acknowledging this movement's meaning. Inner and outer become one in the dance. No wonder many religions condemned dancing as sinful if dancing can show us our true nature so clearly.

In ancient times, people prayed with all of their being. The emotions and feelings of prayer were not separate from the body. "The whole body shook with worship, and dance helped them open themselves completely. People used their bodies as tools to reach a new level of spiritual awareness. Their bodies gave them the opportunity to dissolve the self and come closer to the divine."[32] The Islamic mystics, the Sufis, use ancient movements and techniques to reach a state of at-one-ment with the divine. The Arabic word for dance, *raqs*, means "to make the heart quiver and shake."[33]

It is through the dance that Fur Skin makes a connection with the King and with her own inner Feminine Spirit.

> We dance to become one with the rhythm that was here before us and will remain after we are gone. Through dancing a human being can move beyond limits, into a world of great thoughts where the yearning for transformation lingers and where the majesty of the true self is recognized. With dancing, each human being becomes ancient and universal. The natural ecstasy released through dancing takes the dancer beyond his or her isolation and feeling of being separate. It turns the drop into a river. Dancing is indeed the fastest way to unite with the divine.[34]

Incarnating Conscious Feminine Spirit: Owning the Three Dresses

Movement now becomes prominent after a time of stagnation and suffering. The three-fold structure of the fairy tale begins to unfold at this point. There were three images of gestation earlier in the tale, and now the rhythm picks up with the three dresses, the three treasures and the three appearances at the three festivals. The number three stands for movement and progression in time, and a conscious realization in time and space. Where one is a unique occurrence, and two might be coincidence, three definitely sets up a pattern. This is the essential meaning of the tale, for what is really going on in the story is a whole new development of the feminine principle and its manifestation in time and concrete life. The fourth element is necessary for wholeness and completion and groundedness, like the four directions in Native American and Celtic ritual. This fourth element is the mantle of furs - the repressed instinctual life, the neglected feminine element, the bodywork that brings about the renewal of wholeness.

Fur Skin appears at the first ball in her golden dress. She is so beautiful that the king thinks in his heart, "My eyes have never yet seen anyone so beautiful." The beauty she manifests is an inner as well as an outer beauty, and Fur Skin now becomes the image of a new feminine value for the king. The golden dress of the Sun is her connection to her authentic Self as well as an expression of her individual ego. It is appropriate that Fur Skin expresses this sun-like, masculine, directed-consciousness in her initial contact with the king. She expresses her connection to the *Woman clothed with the Sun*, and her connection to the goldenness of her hair. This dress, when integrated, is that wonderful sense of Selfhood which so many women find so hard to attain. She *knows herself!* She knows who she is and what she wants. She is a match for the king, his equal and ultimately his mate.

It is through the dance that they connect. There is a dance that must be danced out, whether it's the erotic one between a man and a woman or the dance of the energies of masculine and feminine. With men and women, there are the subtleties of the courtship dance. With the energies of masculine and feminine, there is the flow and movement that ultimately brings the right balance of energies. The princess begins the courtship by first appearing as the life-giving source of light, and exhibits her capacity for discernment and rationality by meeting the masculine on its own ground. She takes action by asking if she can go to the ball. She knows she is ready for her first test. This is the first step that women take on our journey to equality with men and masculine consciousness: we must demonstrate our ability to think rationally before men give our ideas the time of day, and we must know our minds and abilities so that we are not swayed by their perceptions of us.

Fur Skin brings an added dimension to this rational consciousness, for once she has truly integrated it into her own feminine standpoint, this ability to discriminate enables her to see a thing as it truly is, and so *name* it. In ancient beliefs, if you know someone's true name, or can name a power, you have control over it, like Solomon's ring which gave him power over the Jinn, those elemental powers of nature. It is often very hard for us to judge someone or some action, because our cultural upbringing has already told us what things are, or else our personal feelings get in the way. It is as if an illusion has been set over things, and we must use some kind of truth-seeing in order to glimpse what lies beneath it. This new Feminine Spirit can see what lies beneath the outer shell, shining the sunlight of clarity onto what her instincts tell her.

The princess then goes back to her hairy covering, to her body wisdom and to her senses because there is a rhythm in the manifestations, and it is happening in space and time. This too is part of the dance. It does not happen once and for all, even though we think we would want it to. It takes time for this new wisdom to sink in and get integrated into consciousness. With each new situation, she must work out this new way of seeing, learning to trust her instinctual response at the same time as she depends on her rational consciousness to understand. In doing this work, she nourishes the king directly.

In the tale, she makes bread soup. Both bread and soup are humanity's earliest nourishment. In fact, in many languages, the word for soup is synonymous with the whole notion of meals and food. Bread soup is still made by Eastern Europeans and Germans, and it is a thick, hearty soup. Fur Skin makes the king's soup so she can nourish him with the wisdom she has gained. It is important to note that in both Hebrew (hokmah) and Latin (sapientia) the word for Wisdom means "to taste." She is letting him taste of her new-found wisdom.

Fur Skin hides her golden ring in the soup. The new wisdom she shares has to do with this ring. The ring is a symbol of the Self, but it represents a specific function of the Self. In general, a ring symbolizes connectedness, such as the wedding ring that symbolizes the union of man and woman in marriage. Gold is generally associated with incorruptibility and immortality; it is the transcendent element, the most valued of our precious metals. Here she offers the king an important new understanding of the power and use of this solar consciousness through the ring. She has made a conscious connection with the instincts and now she wants to connect with the new masculine energy of the king. The specific function of the ring is to awaken in the king the awareness of soul and of the feminine dimensions of life, for the realm of the feminine is our interiority, our inner life and connection to Spirit. This ring that the king finds in the soup is that connection to the Self which recognizes the union between inner and outer realities, between instinct and spirit. It is no longer Sauron's Ring of Power and domination, but Lady Wisdom's Ring of Love. Discriminating and naming these realities brings the possibility of true union, just as the first step toward taking responsibility for one's life is to live out one's inner truth-which involves trusting our instincts.

When we wear the golden dress and bestow the golden ring on our inner masculine energy, we consciously decide to act a certain way, to stand up for our true values, to name ourselves rather than let others name us. Have you discovered your true name? Are you willing to be true to yourself rather than be subject to collective opinions?

One of the strangest parts of the fairy tale for me was the questioning of Fur Skin each time she makes the king's soup. Why does she hide herself from the king? He asks her who she is (an orphan) and what she does (good for nothing but to have boots thrown at her head!). Why can't she answer? Women often feel alone on our journey to wholeness (being an orphan), cut off from any external power. But what does having boots thrown at your head mean? I have experienced this when I am talking with people who are caught in their complexes—that is, women and men who need to be right and so make sure that you know that you are wrong or crazy or stupid! Just as the boots are used as projectiles (throwing a standpoint at you), so too, these are usually projections. But is this the entire answer?

I believe this is about an attitude about Feminine Spirit that has been imprinted onto the feminine psyche. Women have been told often enough, and in many devastating ways, that we are worthless. Women have accepted this projection for our safety, and even when it's not really believed, it affects us on many levels. So when we begin to reclaim our powers, we run into this voice. For when something is young and new, when something is in the beginning of development, we cannot always see the end result. We cannot always articulate the new thing we are feeling or doing. And we can see more clearly the old habits of putting ourselves down. We rush to tell people how worthless we are before they have a chance to tell us! When we undergo transformation, we often cannot trust that it is really happening. When we first learn that certain qualities that we once despised might really become our new strengths, we can hardly believe it.

It is also important to remember that when something new is being born, we need to keep silent about it with others. It is a mystery, so it cannot be explained or revealed. To speak too soon about it might spoil and contaminate the new thing with others' opinions, for we are in a state of incubation when we are wearing the mantle of furs. Like the Virgin Mary, who silently ponders on the mystery and meaning of her divine Son, it is often necessary to keep silent about the divine mystery taking place within the soul and psyche. It is kept a mystery until it can manifest concretely in the world.

Wearing the dress of the Moon signifies the integration of a lunar consciousness that flows and changes, sometimes waxing bright, sometimes leaving one in the dark. It is the realm of the imagination and the imaginal. It is the light in the darkness, the light of the Unconscious. It is our ability to live with paradox. It is an intuitive consciousness, attuned to unseen powers and energies. It picks up other people's feelings and leaves us pondering about what to do. It moves in cycles of flux, in cycles of growth, decay and death, then growth again. It has to do with the blood mysteries of a woman's body, with her sexuality and the mystery of inner growth. When a woman integrates this type of consciousness, she is no longer overwhelmed or afraid of following her imagination and intuitions about where her life is going. It takes courage to follow the path of your dreams, never fully knowing if they will lead you to insanity or to sanctity. It takes trust and faith in the Self, that it will truly guide you to the place that you need to be, especially when it leads through suffering and calls for patience.

Fur Skin gives the king her golden spinning wheel after this second appearance at the ball. The spinning wheel is the emblem of all ancient mother goddesses, a symbol of Feminine Spirit that weaves the web of life. Through its motion, the thread of life is created. The mystery of giving birth is associated with the idea of spinning and weaving, bringing together natural elements in a coherent pattern. The Fates spin the thread of life. Lunar consciousness helps us to recognize the thread of our lives, through all the sorrows and happiness, making a whole pattern. It shows us that life has its rhythms, which will support us if we work with them. Lunar consciousness stories us with our own mythic life.

We touch on this lunar knowledge when we use the mythic imagination, when we find archetypal stories that speak to our lives. How is the king nourished by this golden wheel of life? We need to acknowledge that our instinctual life has meaning; it is not just a savage, chaotic aspect of humanity that must be held in check. The archetypes are the images of our instincts, and when the archetypal images are wedded to instinct, we understand the meaning and purpose of what we are going through. When Masculine Spirit incarnates into life, when it treads the stately measures of life instead of bulldozing its way through life, it too is life-giving rather than the death-dealing patriarchal consciousness that typifies western culture. If President Bush had been given this spinning wheel of life, perhaps he would have given the U.N. sanctions against Iraq more time to work. Surely, there would have been less death and destruction and more life than what has resulted. He did not take into consideration the overall tapestry of life that he was dealing with. Perhaps we Americans will never know the full extent of the suffering that this war caused the people of the Middle East. Only time will tell. But lunar consciousness feels the jarring truth that *might never makes right.*

Our Moon dress helps us open up to our imaginations. Music, art, writing and dance itself open us to our feelings and give us the opportunity to work with the energies of our life in a productive and healthy way. So if you're stuck, put on your favorite music and move your body. Your Moon dress will show you what you have to do next.

The third time Fur Skin appears at the ball, she is wearing the dress as bright as the stars. Again, we see her as the image of the *Woman crowned with Stars.* The king is waiting for her, for he desires her and her wisdom now. All this time the king has been nourished by a mystery, and he wants to know who and what this new Feminine Spirit is. At the same time, the princess has undergone her transformation through the energy of this new king. The binding connection between them is once again symbolized by a golden ring, this time one which the king gives back to Fur Skin. The circle is now complete. Reality is wedded to imagination. Anything and everything becomes possible.

When Fur Skin wears the Star dress, we see her personal relationship to Divine Spirit shine forth in her extraordinary beauty. She has integrated the inner spiritual values and realities that the stars represent, and she can manifest a true spiritual wisdom that is rooted in the Self. This wisdom now includes the body and the sensual aspects of life that were once rejected by her and by the collective. It also includes the heavenly aspects of wisdom, and knowledge of the cosmos and its workings. This is Gnosis, belief based upon experience. The integration of the Star dress brings to women a mystic vision, which sees connections, which knows that everything fits into the Great Round of Life for a purpose. This consciousness is the imaginative, unitive experience of the mystic, and it operates through compassion, which is the awareness of the interconnection of all living things. These are gifts that women so readily share. It is time to reclaim them for the world.

The last treasure to go into the soup is a golden reel, and it is also connected to spinning and sewing, for it is the spool around which the thread is wound. It is that eternal core of Being around which the thread of life must be wound if it is not to tangle or break up, just as the mystic vision of our human divinity is the consciousness which must be at the center of a new cosmology upon which we can build a united world. Human nature needs to relate to something greater than itself, something which gives life its meaning. We humans are made in the divine image, and our life can become whole only if we ground our being in that greater life. The princess has come to understand that this divine essence comes from within herself, and in helping the king to understand this, she leads the way towards a new responsibility and a new hope for herself and for her kingdom.

The Star dress, which under the Father symbolizes our religion, now becomes the vehicle of our personal spirituality. Spirituality has a direct connection to Feminine Spirit; it is our ability to go within ourselves and connect to the deepest levels of life. Do you have a spiritual practice that grounds and centers your daily life?

The Rebirth of Feminine Wisdom

With this third appearance, the process of rebirth and transformation is completed. Fur Skin still tries to hide herself, perhaps because the world does not take kindly to the demands of Spirit. The cook accuses her of being a witch, for anything out of the ordinary is looked upon with suspicion. It is the king who must make the final move—he has to allow for the revelation of the mystery. In committing himself to this beautiful woman, the king sees through her disguise. He sees the star dress underneath the mantle of furs, for it is the Feminine Spirit in nature that Fur Skin brings to light. It is Lady Wisdom, God's Sophia who comes down into life to redeem us all. The king has also integrated the wisdom Fur Skin has given him. He willingly recognizes her as his bride and beloved, for to him, she is more beautiful than anyone who had ever been seen on Earth. There is now a new king and a new queen, a new collective ideal that the princess has brought to light, which is powered by the love and compassion of a Feminine Spirit that has suffered much and revealed more.

The new feminine consciousness which women are birthing will give rise to new ways of living and meeting the tasks at hand. At the same time, men are valuing women's standpoint and going within and meeting their own inner Feminine Spirit, which is vibrating to the change we women have initiated. They too will integrate these gifts that the Goddess is birthing, and they will bring the energy of transformation into the world and father it. These men can meet women as equals and support them and their vision for the world.

When we go through this process of leaving the Father's House with Fur Skin, we find our individual freedom. But it is so much more than that! The process gifts us with the ability to co-create with Feminine Spirit.

Fur Skin is a story about our times, a time when Feminine Spirit is transitioning from being the Father's Daughter to being the divine archetype of feminine wisdom, the *Woman clothed with the Sun*. Although we might not realize it, most of the feeling life of the culture, and many women in our culture, are working to support men and masculine consciousness. That is the job of the Father's Daughter—in all things she is for the masculine. This is the incest that the story depicts, and this incest has been perpetuated on all women, whether physically or psychically.

It is time to run away from the *right* thing to do, the collectively acceptable thing to do, and learn to listen to our instincts. They will not lead us astray if we are noble and true to ourselves. We can begin to trust ourselves, and to make our own decisions about what is important in life. We await the return of the king-if not a literal king, at least our own inner king. It is up to women to find this king, for like Arthur, he is sleeping in Avalon, the isle of women, awaiting our call. He is the king who is waiting within men for the 'most beautiful' woman to connect him to his soul's desire. And he is the king within woman who will make her strong enough to create a new world.

Fur Skin is a story that teaches us how to connect with Lady Wisdom. I have also used this fairy tale as a teaching story so that you might begin to understand how to work with symbolic language. As much as people have a great desire to find a new relationship to Feminine Spirit, there is a great lack of understanding when it comes to this type of consciousness. Instead of definitions, there are images. You have to get inside them and live with them to cull their wisdom. Sometimes you have to turn to books to get an idea of what the big archetypal images have revealed to earlier times. Find stories that speak to your heart, and then listen to what it has to tell you. Go watch the movie *Dirty Dancing* if you want to see a modern re-telling of this fairy tale! In the process, you will learn to understand and to use symbolic language. It involves knowing and naming, intuiting and sensing. But it is also playful and energizing as well.

Women and men both contain elements of masculine and feminine energy; we both have the use of our left and right brains. But we do have different life experiences, which shape our knowledge. I believe that women have to undergo this initiation and transformation if humanity is to develop a more just and nurturing consciousness. Women are here to incarnate and manifest the gifts of Lady Wisdom. This is our gift to the world. This tale tells us how this transformation is accomplished and it assures us that once we have undergone this initiation, we will have the wisdom to meet the problems of our world with hope and creativity. I hope that this tale about the process of leaving the Father's House, detailing the journey with its trials and joys, will encourage people to discover the *Woman clothed with the Sun* within themselves and let Lady Wisdom live and love and work through us to transform our world.

What is your reaction to Fur Skin's story? Go through the fairy tale along with her and discover if you can wear your own golden dress of the Sun, your silvery dress of the Moon and your shimmering Star dress. Perhaps you'll find that you're more comfortable with one dress more than another. If so, begin to learn more about your other two dresses. Learn to know which dress to wear on what occasion – if you are trying to understand what you want to do about an issue in your life, wear your Moon dress to get an image or story. Then use your Sun dress to understand why that image or story spoke to you. Then don your Star dress to decide what to do, based on your values and beliefs

The Marriage of Sir
Gawain and Dame Ragnell

One day, King Arthur was out hunting in the forest with a small group of companions. But when he was alone, dressing his kill, someone stood watching; when Arthur sensed it, he looked up to see a mighty, well-armed knight. The knight joyfully called out a greeting, because he had wanted to catch the king alone for many years.

"Well met, King Arthur!" said the big man. "Many years you have done me great harm, and now you will meet your death." Threatened with immediate death, the king quickly reproached the knight, for what honor could there be in killing an unarmed man. The king's argument touched on knightly honor, and so the knight was forced to relent a little. He required that the king swear to return to the same spot on the same day the following year, unarmed, to answer this riddle:

"What do woman desire most in the world?"

The king gave his pledge. But when he caught up with his companions, his nephew, Sir Gawain noticed his dejection and drew him aside to ask what had happened. The king explained in secrecy and after the two talked it over, they decided to ride off in different directions, and whatever lands they came to, they would ask men and women how they would answer this riddle. And so they prepared for their journeys and departed.

They received many answers, which they put down in two books. Some people said that women desired beautiful clothes; some said that women loved to be adored; some said they loved a sensual, passionate man and some said jewels would do the trick. Some said one thing, some said another. But upon returning home, Arthur was still uneasy with these answers.

Only one month remained to solve the riddle. Needing to meditate, the king rode into the forest, and was surprised to meet the most ugly hag mankind had ever seen: face red, a snotty nose, a wide mouth with huge, yellow tusks that hung down over her lower lip, a long thick neck, and hanging shriveled breasts. After his first horrified glance, he noticed that she had a lute slung over her shoulders, and she was riding a richly saddled mare. It didn't seem right that such an ugly hag would have the gift of music.

She rode directly to the king and greeted him. And then she quickly told him that none of the answers he and Gawain had found would do him a bit of good. "If I do not help you, you are dead," she said. "Grant me, Sir King, only one thing, and I will save your life; or else you will lose your head." "What do you mean, Lady?" asked the king. "Tell me why my life is in your hands and I promise you anything you ask." The hideous old creature replied, "You must let me marry Sir Gawain. I promise that if your life is not saved by my answer, you do not have to keep your promise; but if my answer saves you, you will let me wed Gawain. Choose now, and quickly, for it must be so, or you are dead!" The king was horrified at this choice and told the hag that it was not for him to decide, but Gawain. And the lady replied, "Well, go home now and speak fair words to Sir Gawain. Though I am foul, yet am I gay!"

The king returned to the castle, and when he told Gawain of the lady's demand, Gawain answered courteously that he would rather marry her than see Arthur dead. Which answer proved that Gawain was indeed the flower of knightly virtues.

Dame Ragnell was the name of the hag. When King Arthur returned to her and gave her his promise and that of his nephew, she replied, "Sir, now you will know what women desire most of high and low. This is the prime desire in all our fantasy, and that now you will know:

We desire of men, above all manner of thing, to have the sovereignty."

Of course, this was the only answer that would save the king, and when he told it to the big knight, he had to give up his quarrel and spare the king's life.

Now King Arthur had to give Dame Ragnell as wife to Sir Gawain. As they rode into the courtyard together, Arthur was greatly ashamed of her. But as all there wondered where so foul a creature had come from, Sir Gawain stepped forth without any sign of reluctance and pledged his troth. Dame Ragnell said, "God have mercy. For your sake, I wish I were a fair woman, for you have such good will."

All the ladies of the court and the knights felt great sorrow for Sir Gawain, for his bride was so very ugly. And she insisted that the wedding take place at once. Nor was she to be put off with a quiet little wedding, but insisted upon a high mass and a banquet in the open hall with everybody there. At the banquet, she gobbled up all the meat and drank all the mead!

That night, in bed, Gawain could not at first bring himself to turn and face her unappetizing snout. After a time, she said to him: "Ah, Sir Gawain, since I have wed you, show me your courtesy in bed. It may not rightfully be denied. If I were fair, you would not behave this way; you are not valuing our marriage. For Arthur's sake, kiss me at least; I pray you, do this at my request. Come, let's see how quick you can be!"

Gawain collected every bit of his courage and kindness. "I will do more," he said in all gentleness, "I will do more than simply kiss you!" But when he turned to her, he saw that she was the fairest creature he had ever seen.

She said: "What is your will?"

"Sweet Jesus!" he said, "who are you?"

"Sir, I am your wife; why are you so unkind?"

"AH, lady, I am to blame; I did not know. You are beautiful in my sight - whereas today you were the foulest sight my eyes had ever seen! To have you thus, my lady, pleases me well." And he embraced her and began kissing her, and they had great joy of each other.

Later she said, "Gawain, my beauty will not hold. You may have me thus, but only for half the day. And so the question is, would you have me fair at night and foul by day before all men's eyes, or beautiful by day and foul at night."

"Alas," replied Gawain, "the choice is hard. To have you fair at night and no more, that would grieve my heart; but if I should decide to have you fair by day, then at night I would have a hard time bedding you. I want to choose the best course, but I don't know what to say. However, since this involves you more than anyone else, my dear wife, let it be as you would desire it; I rest the choice in your hand. For I love you more than my own life.

"AH, sweet mercy, courteous knight!" said the lady. "May you be blessed above all the knights in the world, for now I am released from the enchantment and you shall have me fair and bright both day and night."

And then she recounted to her delighted husband how her stepmother had enchanted her; and she was condemned to remain under that loathsome shape until the best knight in the land should wed her and yield to her the sovereignty of her own choice. "Thus was I deformed," she said. "And you, courteous Gawain, have given me the sovereignty for certain. Kiss me, my dear, even here and now; be glad and of good cheer." And there they made joy out of mind.[1]

Chapter Four
Enlightened Earth: The Mother of Us All

*Will you teach your children what we have taught our children? That
the earth is our mother? What befalls the earth befalls all the sons
of the earth. This we know: the earth does not belong to man, man
belongs to the earth. All things are connected like the blood that unites
us all. Man did not weave the web of life, he is merely a strand in
it. Whatever he does to the web, he does to himself.*[2]
—ATTRIBUTED TO CHIEF SEATTLE

*Earth and nature teach us how to be embodied in this world. We have to
awaken to our senses, feel what our body is saying to us and get back in
touch with our natural instincts. Wearing the mantle of furs means coming
to our senses.*

The Sovereignty of the Earth

When women step away from the Father's House and don our mantle
of furs, we often feel like Dame Ragnell. As we undergo this most
crucial transformation of consciousness, people ask us, "What's happened
to you? I don't understand you anymore?" We feel the same way. But
we know that something 'most beautiful' lies beneath our furry skin.
We know it, but it is also important that someone else recognizes our

beauty, hidden behind the enchantment of a patriarchal curse. For many thousands of years, women have been denied this sovereignty and until all women everywhere have the right and capability to make their own choices in life, women will never be truly free. When feminine wisdom is not honored, we lose the precious counter-balance that alone enlivens masculine knowledge and power. And so we all lose our freedom.

Feminine sovereignty is grounded in the perception that women and the Earth have a lot in common. In ancient times when people honored the Earth for sustaining their lives, they also honored women, who were the source of new life. This is why the problem of sovereignty is an issue for women as well as the Earth. And this is why both issues need to be addressed. Fur Skin is not just reclaiming her connection to her own body by wearing the mantle of furs. She is trying to solve the collective problem that her parents left her to solve: what will be the new relationship her kingdom has with the Earth?

All cultures develop a relationship to the Earth, their home. Our modern relationship has been to take what we need regardless of the consequences. But we are seeing that we have to change, and we don't yet have a clear vision of where we are headed beyond the fact that we have to be better stewards of the Earth. The ancient Celts honored the Earth as their Mother, and they understood the archetypal figure of Lady Sovereignty, who embodies the power of the Earth. Dame Ragnell's story from the Middle Ages indicates how important this problem of their relationship to the Earth was for them. For the Celts, Mother Earth was a shape-shifter. She could appear as the most ugly hag or as the most beautiful maiden. Both these aspects were hers to be understood and loved.

In the Irish story of the *Sons of King Daire*[3], the Sovereignty of Ireland says to Niall, her chosen king, *'As thou hast seen me loathsome, bestial, horrible at first and beautiful at last, so is the Sovereignty; for seldom it is gained without battles and conflicts; but at last to everyone it is beautiful and goodly.'* Sovereignty is worth fighting for – both for the Earth and for women. But women can't just stop at demanding our lawful equal rights. Sovereignty demands equal rights for women's wisdom and vision. This means that each woman is responsible for reclaiming her personal freedom, for sovereignty demands the search for our unique identity and purpose. And for that, we have to rediscover women's ancient wisdom—the wisdom of the Earth.

The Wisdom of the Earth

The Earth has been communicating with us all along about the problems our consumer lifestyle causes her. But we haven't been listening. Or else, we listened and chose to ignore her call. But we are finally acknowledging the scientific evidence of climate change, as well as experiencing its devastating effects in the change and intensity of world-wide weather patterns. This change is forcing us to reconsider our relationship to the Earth.

Connecting to the Earth entails more than keeping our carbon emissions low and recycling, although these are ways we try to clean up the pollution generated by our modern life-style. Connecting to the Earth isn't just going for a hike in the mountains or swimming in the ocean, although these are times when we can commune with nature. Connecting to the Earth demands that we become conscious of our bodies, our own private bit of Earth. Connecting to the Earth begins when we can feel reverence for our land, our air, our waters, when we can love our neighbors and the Earth as ourselves. Connecting to the Earth makes us one with her.

Connecting to the Earth begins when we re-examine our beliefs about our place in Earth's ecosystem. Can we use the Earth's resources however we want without consequences? Or are humans just as much a part of Earth's ecology as wind and fire and water? We need to discover what our relationship to the Earth is. Are we the stewards of the Earth or perhaps Earth's consciousness itself? Unless we discover our place in the Earth's living biosphere, we won't know how to honor the Earth.

Before humanity looked to the heavens for their gods, we looked to Mother Earth as the supreme Goddess of life. We were Earth's children, just as the animals, land, plants and waters were hers. As we face the results of our own misuse and abuse of the Earth, we have to admit we haven't treated our mother very well. Who among us would rape, degrade and pillage a beloved mother and nurturer in this way? And yet we do, because our forefathers told us that the Earth was dead matter and we were special, meant to rule the Earth, not care for it. And so we kill off species without a thought. Unfortunately, as we kill the animals and plants and pollute the air and water, we are killing ourselves.

Women's Bodies: Women's Wisdom

Now that we find ourselves at a crossroads of consciousness, we need to turn to our mother the Earth again to re-discover her wisdom so we can find the answers to our problems. Women can do this by donning our mantle of furs and living in our bodies, and by understanding the proper ways to reverence and live on the Earth. To really live in our body means being mindful about what our body is feeling, and listening to its instinctual responses to what we do to it.

As Father's Daughters, women are cut off from our instincts because we have been told to restrain our feelings, intuitions, passions, fantasies, romantic ideals and sexuality for a morality and logic which overtly discriminates against women's ways of knowing and being. How can a woman be happy living like this? When a woman's instincts kick in, if she is a Father's Daughter, she will go into her head and find all the reasons she shouldn't follow her instincts. The rules and morality of the Father's House often cause her to turn away from something that she longs for. While a good Father's Daughter will be proud of herself for standing up for her values, she probably missed an opportunity for growth and relationship by ignoring those instincts instead of exploring them. If we used our intelligence to understand which instincts to trust and which ones we need to ignore, we would be happier and healthier.

So often, we ignore our body until it gets sick, or we abuse it with food, drink and drugs because we don't know how to deal with its pain. As we work in our fur mantle, we learn to listen to and understand what our bodies ask of us and perhaps we remember that our bodies are the temples of our souls. Working with the imagination can help us speak with our bodies through images that arise spontaneously from the Unconscious, the interface between body and soul.

Instead of ignoring or drugging your body, take the time to get to know what your body is trying to tell you. Meditate on where the pain is and ask it for an image to work with.

This is the way to begin to reclaim our feminine standpoint, which is grounded in the body and on the Earth. We each have to balance the four-fold aspects of consciousness within ourselves: the physical (earth), the psychological (air), the imaginal (water) and the spiritual (fire). When all four layers are open and aware, we become wise in our choices and in our creativity.

We need to distinguish between instincts, intelligence and intuition.[4] Instinct goes straight to the heart of life, through an instantaneous sure feeling. This is the gift of the mantle of furs. We act on instinct. But when we want to choose our actions, we also need to develop our self-awareness, which means working with our thinking and feeling. Intelligence is the faculty that creates ideas, words and theories that can be used in our collective culture—the structures we operate in. When Fur Skin wears her dress of the Sun, she has learned to name instinct with her intellect. A *Woman clothed with the Sun* understands what her instincts are telling her to do.

She does this by taking her stand on the Moon, deepening her experience of life through her imagination and feelings. When we wear the dress of moonlight, we discover the meaning of our experiences through the symbolic language of images, memories, dreams and feelings. These tools of our lunar consciousness make our instincts conscious so we can understand them with our intellect.

Then we have our intuition: instinct which has become objective, self-reflective and transformative. This is the sphere of the archetypes, the Creative Imagination, the place where everything originates, which opens us to the magic of the moment. When we understand the basic pattern within the experience, we can change it. When we become aware of the archetypal laws of life, we consciously shape our life toward the spiritual purpose of our existence. That is when we wear the dress of starlight.

Being a Father's Daughter has taken us out of our bodies and into our heads, away from the feelings and intuitions that ground us in feminine wisdom. So when we leave the Father's House and find our freedom, we will encounter our Sacred Initiator, Aphrodite, the Goddess of the Body, Love, Sexuality and Wholeness. It is Aphrodite who initiates women and the soul through the power of Love. But first we have to find our lost Mother.

The Search for Our Lost Mother

Whether we acknowledge it or not, we are held and sustained within the arms of Mother Earth. Just as surely, the life of planet Earth is now in our hands. Earth is the only home we have. How could we have gotten so separated from our home that we would come close to destroying it with our poisons and our waste, our wars and our unsustainable economy and population? We are faced with the stark truth of climate change, which is disrupting our weather, melting the glaciers at alarming rates and cooling down the Gulf Stream, which could bring on another Ice Age. By allowing our governments to ignore the signs of environmental unbalance, we are taking away our children's future. If women can remember our relationship with our mother the Earth, we can become spokeswomen for her sovereignty. We have a choice, and we are responsible to our children's children for seven generations. Through each woman, the *Woman clothed with the Sun* can become the consciousness and the conscience of the Earth. When we incarnate Lady Wisdom, we give the Earth back her essential power and mystery, based in the fullness of life and the testing of death.

Most ancient cultures that lived close to the Earth—the Celts, the Aborigines, the Native Americans, and western culture itself until the sixteenth century—revered Earth as the Mother. They knew they were made from the dust of this Earth, that they shared this Earth with the other animals, the trees, the rivers and seas. They knew that they were part of the Great Round of Nature, one with all the other works of the Mother. They knew that just as the animals gave up their lives to feed and nourish human beings, so too, human beings gave back their lives to the Great Mother when death took us. They understood the wisdom and necessity of the cyclic processes of her mysteries, and they lived within that cycle of gestation, birth, death and regeneration as in the protective circle of a mother's arms. For them, the Earth was animate and divine; she set the rhythms of life for all her children. She was the divine nourisher and sustainer, giving humans beautiful children and plentiful harvests; she was also the divine destroyer, taking back her own. She was, and is, the bedrock and foundation of all that draw their life from her. The Greeks saw her this way:

> *The Mother of us all, the oldest of all*
> *Hard, splendid as rock*
> *Whatever there is that is of the land*
> *It is she who nourishes it,*
> *It is the Earth that I sing.*[5]

We have come a long way from our origins, and today, our consumer-driven culture is such that we have forgotten this generous and dangerous Mother. While our western religions have strengthened our individual sense of morals and values, for the most part they separated us from a positive relationship with the Earth. Christianity saw the ancient Goddess as evil, and later condemned all things of the Earth as illusionary and sinful. Since the Industrial Revolution, our scientific rational world view taught us that Earth was only inanimate matter. Rejecting her divinity, and even her aliveness, we felt safe defiling, raping and poisoning the Earth. Leaving science to investigate the complexities of life, people no longer honored Earth's mysteries of life, and so we forget that we are also a part of the Great Round of Life.

As we learned to control and use the Earth, we found that we could also control our instinctual nature, and the mind and the ideal of pure spirit (the Queen's golden hair) became more important than the body and its experience of soul. We removed ourselves from living contact with our Mother Earth: by covering the land over with our cities and roads; by explaining her mysteries as nothing more than scientific facts; by living in our heads rather than in our bodies. We substituted a one-dimensional observing of life for the wisdom of the experience of life.

The Native Americans treasured the wisdom of the Earth. Luther Standing Bear, a Lakota (Sioux) medicine man, wrote:

> The Lakota was a true Naturist—a Lover of Nature. He loved the Earth and all things of the Earth, the attachment growing with age. The old people came literally to love the soil and they sat or reclined on the ground with a feeling of being close to a mothering power. It was good for the skin to touch the Earth and the old people liked to remove their moccasins and walk with bare feet on the sacred Earth. Their tipis were built upon the Earth and their altars were made of Earth. The birds that flew in the air came to rest upon the Earth and it was the final abiding place of all things that lived and grew. The soil was soothing, strengthening, cleansing and healing.
>
> That is why the old Indian still sits upon the Earth instead of propping himself up and away from its life-giving forces. For him, to sit or lie upon the ground is to be able to think

more deeply and to feel more keenly; he can see more clearly into the mysteries of life and come closer in kinship to other lives about him... .

Kinship with all creatures of the Earth, sky and water was a real and active principle. For the animal and bird world there existed a brotherly feeling that kept the Lakota safe among them and so close did some of the Lakotas come to their feathered and furred friends that in true brotherhood they spoke a common tongue.

The old Lakota was wise. He knew that man's heart away from nature becomes hard; he knew that lack of respect for growing, living things soon led to lack of respect for humans too. So he kept his youth close to its softening influence. [6]

We have indeed become hard-hearted to each other, to the Earth and to ourselves, and I believe it is because of this separation from the Earth, from the feminine realms and from our own souls. This created a split in our psyches, plaguing us with all the neuroses of modern society. We no longer understand the beauty of the laws of nature or of our nature, and so we live constantly with the fear of the unknown, just as the early settlers must have feared the vast and wild lands of the American continent.

When these settlers came to this new land, they brought with them the memories and shapes of their old land, the land their ancestors were formed by. Cultures and personalities are shaped by the land: mountain dwellers are different from sea peoples. Just look at the United States, with our hard-driving, intellectual East coast, our salt-of-the-earth plains people and our laid-back West coasters. We know about the hardships that accompanied the settlement of America, but it must have been a great psychological hardship as well, for the land was re-forming the people who came to settle it. Perhaps it was that great psychological wrenching which caused the terror and fear and which contributed to the American determination to dominate and control the vastness, strangeness and wildness of this new continent. And so the *enlightened* Christian belief that it is man's place to dominate nature won out over the Native American reverence for and care-taking of the land.

And the Native Americans, who were formed by this land, also became the victims of this fear of the white peoples. Luther Standing Bear ventured into the white man's world, and came to understand this about his conquerors.

> The white man does not understand the Indian for the reason that he does not understand America. He is too far removed from its formative processes. The roots of the tree of his life have not yet grasped the rock and soil. The white man is still troubled with primitive fears; he still has in his consciousness the perils of this frontier continent, some of its vastnesses not yet having yielded to his questing footsteps and inquiring eyes. He shudders still with the memory of the loss of his forefathers upon its scorching deserts and forbidding mountain-tops. The man from Europe is still a foreigner and an alien. And he still hates the man who questioned his path across the continent. But in the Indian the Feminine Spirit of the land is still vested; it will be until other men are able to divine and meet its rhythm. Men must be born and reborn to belong. Their bodies must be formed of the dust of their forefathers' bones. [7]

Today, many of us feel that connection to the land and are beginning to understand and meet her rhythms. We understand the need for parks in our cities and open spaces saved from developers. The ecology movement and groups fighting to protect the oceans and waters, the wilderness, animals, ancient forests and rainforests are signs of this connection. People working to develop safe and renewable energy and to reduce waste are another sign of this return. We go on vacations back to the land for refreshment for we recognize the irreplaceable importance of this connection to the land for our psychic well-being. We fight to save our wilderness areas, knowing that if we lose the last of our wild places, our psychic equilibrium will be destroyed. Our children, through Earth Day activities and school courses, are learning to honor and respect the Earth as our *home*. These are steps away from fear and into integration. We are beginning to listen to Earth's song once again.

The Earth and Feminine Spirituality

Another way we acknowledge the importance of the land comes through the Women's Spirituality Movement. As women leave the Father's House, we often return to an ancient way of relating to the Earth by celebrating the old seasonal holidays. These are times when the energies of the cosmos rejuvenate the Earth's energy grid, and when people participate in these rituals, they too share in the renewed energies. By honoring these seasonal gateways, we can consciously integrate these energies, learning to age gracefully as we are renewed and supported by the Earth and the cosmos. Women find great comfort in connecting to the Earth's seasons as well as the Moon's cycle, so connected as it is to our menstrual cycles.

It is important that culturally we re-connect to the natural laws here on Earth for many reasons. Sadly, our young women are being seduced by the pharmaceutical companies into using contraceptives that disrupt the natural internal rhythms of their menstrual cycles so their feminine biology won't get in the way of their very hectic, work life. But what price does the body pay, especially when later on, these young women find they are not fertile enough to have children without expensive medical procedures?

The Wheel of the Year

The Wheel of the Year is the cycle of seasonal gateways which celebrate the changing relationship between the light and the dark, markers of the year. On December 20-22, Winter Solstice is the celebration of the Rebirth of the Light in the time of greatest darkness. We know that the Sun is at its extreme southern declination, so in the northern hemisphere we experience the shortest time of daylight and the longest night. We feel the weight of the darkness and long for the return of longer, lighter days. (Of course, in the southern hemisphere, their wheel is reversed; it is Summer Solstice there.)

So we create religious holidays to welcome the Divine Child of Light once again into the world. The planetary energies work to unite with the physical and emotional energies of humanity, awakening the feminine energies of love and birthing. It is a time to go within ourselves, so we can give birth to the light within our inner darkness.

We seek to awaken passion and curiosity and Feminine Spirit's gift of new life and love. This is the time to set the stage for the New Year to come. Feminine Spirit births the light, and the light that grows now is the *yang* or masculine part of the cycle. This part of the cycle initiates the cycle of manifestation.

Six weeks later, we celebrate the Celtic festival of Imbolc, also called Candlemas or St. Brigid's Day by the Catholic Church. It is the Festival of Quickening, the time when seeds split open, the light grows stronger and creativity stirs in our depths. Celebrated on February 2nd, Ground Hog's Day, we look to predict the return of Spring through the strength of the returning sunlight. And we look within for signs of new life and new creativity for the coming year. We might be called to learn a language, take up a musical instrument, start to write, learn to cook or crochet, learn a new sport. Something within us tells us that yes! life is still with us. All is not dead, even if the snow and cold have frozen everything around us.

The next gateway is Spring Equinox (March 20-22), when life bursts out from the seemingly barren Earth, and the chains of darkness and winter are broken for another year. There is a balance of light and darkness, and we breathe in the knowledge that the light is growing and the days are getting longer and warmer. The Sun has reached the equator and will begin its journey north. It is at Spring Equinox that we celebrate the resurrection of Jesus Christ as well as the Jewish holiday of Passover. The symbolism of death and resurrection is played out at this balance of light and dark, life and death. Now we begin to express the masculine energy of life as we assert our creativity more dynamically and bring our creative talents to bear on new projects. The masculine force of *will* is released in the Spring. This force wants to have greater external expression in our lives to balance the internal feminine energies of Winter.

At this time, the fertility of the Easter bunny, named for the great fertility goddess of northern Europe, Oester, captures our imaginations. There is a story about Oester that exemplifies this balance of feminine being and masculine doing. *A bird came to her one day, and told her that she had fallen in love with a land animal, a rabbit, and wanted to be changed into a rabbit to be with her beloved. So Oester blessed her and changed the bird into a rabbit, and in gratitude the rabbit laid eggs for the goddess for the rest of her life.* The ancients knew that the great Goddess of Life grants our wishes for life and love and happiness in Spring. And that the correct response is to offer our respect back to her through our actions. We feel the truth of this story that something divine is behind the gift of life. And that respect is due this mystery. At Spring Equinox, we move out of our winter hibernation into action.

On May 1st, we celebrate the Feast of Beltane, when *sweet desire weds wild delight* as the colors return to nature and flowery perfumes intoxicate our senses. This is when we experience, each time as if for the first time, how awesome Earth's beauty is, seeing and feeling the gift of life that we have been blessed with; a time to know joy and hope and desire and passion, for these are the gifts of life that we remember as the Round of the Year circles on. Beltane marks a time when we celebrate the gift of life's possibilities. We have come from birth into youth and flowering. On Beltane, we dance around the May Pole, weaving the masculine and feminine energies to create the passion that sparks new inventions, new creativity and new life in partnership with each other.

Now the Wheel of the Year turns to its second half and the cycle of maturity and fulfillment open up, followed by the slow decay and death of Autumn and Winter. This begins the *yin* or feminine part of the cycle. First comes the Summer Solstice (June 20-22), the time of the longest day and the shortest night, the marriage feast of Heaven and Earth when we feel the fullest potentials of life. At the time, life's spiritual, mental, emotional and imaginal awareness is aligned with our physicality to promote greater spiritual awareness and growth. This is a time of union, when we can blend the feminine and masculine energies within as well as without. Nature is open to us, assisting in this new integration. This is the time when we know what our purpose is and are fully engaged in it. The Sun is at its most northern declination and the northern hemisphere is bathed in light and life. It's *summertime and the living is easy!* (Of course, in the southern hemisphere, they are celebrating the Winter Solstice.) This is the moment when we celebrate the power of light. This spiritual light brings with it a new consciousness, new illuminations, new beauty and vision as we consummate our life. But in the very moment of this longest day of light we know that now the cycle is turning and imperceptibly the darkness begins to grow and the light lessens.

On August 1st comes the Festival of Lammas, or Lughnasadh, which marks the beginning of the end of Summer and the coming of Autumn. Now we begin to notice that the days are shorter, giving way to cooler days and longer nights. This festival highlights the fading power of the Sun as well as celebrates the first fruits of the year's harvest. It is the time of year when the abundance of the harvest is apparent and we begin to see the first fulfillment of our creativity and hard work. It is a time to give thanks for our lives and the good things in it. This is the time to dedicate the first fruits of the harvest to Mother Earth, an offering that reminds us that all things come from this divine source. Our masculine, *doing* energy begins to take the back seat as we prepare ourselves for the Autumn when the feminine *being* energy takes over once again.

Next comes the Autumn Equinox (September 20-22), when once again we hang in the balance between the energies of the light and the darkness, but a very different balance than we experience in Spring, for we are moving out of the light and into the darkness. As we accept the decline of the light, we also accept the gifts of the harvest. These gifts often entail healing, balance and greater strength of body, soul and spirit. This harvest is not only of the foods that sustain our bodies, but the harvest of another creative year of our lives. Hopefully, we have grown and matured through the year and have something new in our lives to show for it. This time of harvest is a time of celebration, but also of purification and preparation. We have to look at our values and determine which ones center us in our lives. We have to consider how our harvest went and what new goals we might want to pursue in the coming year. We are preparing for the death of the year, for without death there can be no new life. This time of year teaches us how to let go of what no longer serves our life. Life demands that we recognize that we are growing older and that we must learn to accept the inevitable death of our youth, of our middle age and ultimately of our lives.

This death is celebrated on Samhain, our Halloween night, on October 31-November 1. It is not a time of evil forces, but rather the night when the veils between the worlds are thin, and the spirits of the dead may once more walk among the living, so that we remember and honor what has gone before us. This night celebrates the opening of the gate between life and death; when in accepting the fact of death, we allow ourselves to open to the birth that will come once again on

Winter Solstice. This is the time to let go of our fears, our failures and our unfulfilled goals so that they can go back and be composted for rebirth at Winter Solstice. As we experience the withdrawal of life force into the depths of the Earth for renewal, we learn that we too can let go of those parts of ourselves which no longer serve us, because as Earth's children, we are assured of new life to come.

So the Wheel of Life continues its round. In celebrating these sacred times, women and men are once again acknowledging that ancient wisdom which the Earth offers to her children: first, that human beings live in cyclical time as well as linear time; second, that our human lives are regulated by the cycles of birth, growth, decay and death that the Earth herself is subject to, and third, that we have an opportunity at these times to direct and influence how we use and store this energy of life to use for our spiritual growth.

Because of our one-sided emphasis on directed, masculine consciousness and the rejection and repression of the feminine in all its manifestations, the problem of really internalizing the Earth as Divine Mother needs to be met on many levels. At the same time as we reconnect with the outer Earth, we must also make contact with the inner Earth, or foundation, of our being. Since our psychic life is based on primordial images, we have to listen to those images just as we have to listen to our bodies and to the Earth to find the wisdom to make the right choices about our lives. Just as the Earth was a divinity to ancient peoples, she must become a psychic reality for us, for both our bodies and our souls need her nourishment. We need to be grounded in the reality of the Earth's laws to balance out the superficial reality of our modern culture. If our society is ever to connect to the Earth in a new way, it will be through the gift of feminine consciousness.

Mother Earth's Wisdom and Modern Women

Let us look at some of the ancient stories of the Earth.

The ancient Earth Goddess was a fertility goddess who sheltered, protected and nourished her children. While the fertility of the land and women were her literal province, symbolically this includes our inner fertility and creativity. Nature's abundance is also available to us if we look to the Earth as our teacher. One of the first lessons she teaches us is to allow all things to grow—weeds, flowers and grasses all grow in the same field. There is no right or wrong, no moral judgments connected with her creativity. All things grow: some grow strong and re-create in time, while others grow and die and go back into the soil to nourish new growth. This truth allows us to experience all aspects our lives without judgment, without trying to control what we experience. This also speaks to our creativity; we have to understand that for creativity to blossom, we have to allow our ideas to spill out and excite us until we find the one thing that calls to us to nurture it and develop it to its fullest capacity.

This is the truth which demands that we ask what our experiences mean, rather than feel victimized by those experiences. It is a masculine, left-brain trait to always try to control what life brings to us. It also indicates a psychological addiction to perfection. It is often through our mistakes (the weeds?) that we learn about the truths of life. Our culture desperately needs to learn this lesson, for we are so afraid of failure that we often by-pass the very lessons that would make us grow strong. And it forces us to live in fear of that failure.

I believe that we are learning from a mistake that came out of the Feminist Movement, which at first placed a higher value on having a career then on the more traditional roles of raising children and caretaking a marriage. As women were educated and developed their intellectual capacities to the fullest, they gave these talents to an essentially masculine model of society. The pendulum swung to the other extreme, making marriage and child-rearing less important and desirable in many women's eyes. Unfortunately, women who stay home to raise their children feel that they are not as valued as women who have a professional career. Not only do they feel less competent, but the unique knowledge they've gained from motherhood is also disregarded. When Caroline Kennedy dropped out of contention for Hillary Clinton's New York Senate seat, a male reporter said that she'd basically only been a mother and so did not have the experience necessary for the job. As if mothers know nothing about life after responsibly raising our children. This attitude has made the masculine experience of making money and having worldly power more important than the feminine experience of loving interconnectivity and nurturing. We are coming to realize that both motherhood and partnership are as important as career and worldly success, and that this feminine wisdom must be valued in both our private and collective lives.

Earth says that women are fertile and that we are here for life. When women value their jobs more than their motherhood, we have a problem. The Father King has raped his daughter and instead of running away, she has allowed herself to be married to the Father. And we do have a problem, because our children are being raised by strangers and by television and the Internet, and so are losing out on the love and grounding that unstressed mothers can provide. This is not to say that mothers should stay home and never realize our full potentials! I am not advocating a return to the idea of 'a woman's place is in the home'. I do know, however, that we have to once again value the feminine tasks of life and find ways to live our lives that allow enough time and place for them.

The pendulum is swinging back, though, and now that women have to work for a living, they are realizing how much they would really rather be home raising their children. As do our men. If there were only one choice for the most important job in the world, it would be raising our children to become responsible human beings. Otherwise, why have children at all? This is a problem that all of us have to solve, for we need to fight for our children's welfare, which means fighting for a future that includes a healthy environment, a secure lifestyle and which values our unique creative potentials. Women want to balance their work with childrearing, loving partnership and community building. And women are the ones who usually teach our children how to use and value their emotional intelligence and intuitive vision as well as their intelligence and career goals.

Would we have valued this new/old wisdom if we had not rushed into the workplace to test ourselves against the men? Hopefully, we will value our roles as mothers and fathers more because of it. Allowing for weeds helps us learn!

We often encounter the Earth's fertility as inner creativity, and allowing many choices is an important first step, not only for the things we may hope to create in this world but also for finding out who and what we are. This allowing, though, is not *doing what we please*, as we have come to associate with the idea of *finding ourselves*; allowing has to do with inner patterns of growth which make demands on us, which have internal laws and inherent disciplines which direct the life flow of psychic energy, and which give strength to the new growth in personality. Allowing means that we do not dictate what a person should or should not do with her life. Allowing means being open to our instincts and learning how to follow through on them to see where they bring us.

I did this in my own life. At the time, I was feeling pressure to perform, to make more money and to achieve more success. But this was the time when I was busy being a single mom raising four children and, psychologically, wearing my mantle of furs and learning to listen to my instincts. I had this dream.

> I am in a store, looking at a picture and a calendar. I cannot find a salesperson to pay, and after a long time, I finally decide to just take them. As I leave the store, I go through an apartment where a woman is painting someone's portrait. As I walk out the door, the woman painter says (about me), "She's a 12th House person." I come back into the room and ask her how she knew this, because it is true - I have many personal planets in the 12th House in my astrology chart.
>
> This woman starts to ask me why I have taken the picture and calendar. At first, I won't acknowledge that I have them. She tells me that she painted the picture and that I have changed the waning moon to a waxing moon. I still refuse to give them back. Then she calls many children to come into the room and they dance around me, imploring me to give back the things that I have taken for their sake. And I do give them back.

This dream showed me that I could not rush the process that my soul was engaged in, which was leaving the Father's House. While the dream is connected to the Moon dress (through the calendar) which we will discuss in the next chapter, it also had ramifications about the birthing process of my Self. My ego wanted to believe that the time was right *now,* for changing the waning Moon to a waxing one means that I was rushing to begin something new when I had to complete something already in progress. I felt I had the right to take charge of the timing (the calendar). I was tired of giving myself away to others and wanted to feel as if I was in charge of my own life. Raising four children takes money as well as nurturing.

The woman artist, who radiated power and compassion, is an image of the Self. She needed to stop me from moving out of my process just to make more money. She did this by calling to the children, both my inner and outer children as well as the other people who needed me. In this way, my psyche sent me a message about what kind of growth was being demanded of me. I needed to mother these inner/outer children, which I wouldn't have done as well if I was concentrating on power and making money. She also implied that learning to live in harmony with the natural cycles and rhythms of my life, waiting to see what new things were growing in me, was more important than forcing the issue. That was hard to hear for a Father's Daughter!

I have always felt that the main task of psychology is to help people find out who they are; to discover what stories make up their lives. To help them name themselves rather than apply generic collective labels to their talents, or to pressure them into a life they don't want or need to live. Jung calls this process *individuation*, meaning the process of learning to live out the demands of the Self. To do this, each of us must find a positive mothering ground within ourselves. Like many Father's Daughters in my generation, I was brought up with the idea that making a mark in the world was more important than being a mother and being a conscious person. But my individuation demanded that I learn the lessons of motherhood rather than the lessons of worldly power. Perhaps those lessons will come in future lifetimes, because what I have learned is that nobody can do everything in one lifetime. And that since the Earth's natural laws teach us that we will return again, I can do the task at hand knowing that those other lessons might already have been learned or will be learned at some future time.

Researchers and psychologists stress the importance of the initial bonding between mother and child, where we gain a sense of ourselves through this primary relationship. It seems the severance of the bond between human beings and nature has created a corresponding severance of the bond between mothers and children. Our mothers were disenfranchised from their feminine roots, so how could they provide us with a firm grounding in our own feminine nature? Instead of being grounded in a sense of our feminine gifts, we have been nurtured on the collective values of the patriarchy, and our grounding is in the shallow soil of outer values and ego-consciousness. We have been brought up in the Father's House. This has led many women to look for and recover our bond to the positive, deep mothering ground of our being.

Gaia: The Ancient Earth Mother

An ancient story about the Greek Earth Mother, Gaia, provides us with a deeper understanding of how to do this. Hesiod's Theogony states that

> … first there was Chaos, and then appeared broad-bosomed Earth, who bore, first of all and as her equal, the starry Sky, Ouranos. Then she bore the great mountains, valleys, plains and the Sea, and after that she mated with Ouranos and bore many children, among whom were the Titans and Titanesses, the ancestors of the Olympian divinities, who represented the 'titanic' forces of the earth. Yet, although Ouranos came every night to mate with his wife, Gaia, from the very beginning he hated the children whom Gaia bore him. As soon as they were born, he hid them and would not let them come out into the light. He hid them in the inward hollows of the Earth, and it is said that he took pleasure in this wicked deed.
>
> The goddess Gaia groaned under this affliction, and felt herself oppressed by her inner burden. Therefore she devised a stratagem. She brought forth gray iron and made a mighty sickle with sharp teeth. Then she took counsel with her sons and daughters, asking who would avenge her for this wicked deed. Only Kronos (Saturn) took courage and agreed to act on her behalf. So Gaia rejoiced, and hid Kronos in the place appointed for the ambush, giving him the sickle and telling him her plan. And when Ouranos came at nightfall, inflamed with love and covering all the Earth, his son thrust out his left hand and seized his father. With his right hand he took the huge sickle, quickly cutting off his father's manhood, and cast it behind his back into the sea.
>
> Gaia received in her womb the blood shed by her spouse, and gave birth to the Erinyes—the strong ones—and to other creatures. The father's genitals fell into the sea, and it mixed with the foam and gave birth to Aphrodite. Since that time, the sky has no longer approached the earth for nightly mating.[8]

139

As with any story, this one must work on your heart and your imagination. What it has to say about life and creativity is significant, for the Earth gives birth to the whole world, just as our experience of the Earth, and our personal relationship with nature, gives birth to our own world-view. This myth says that first there is *chaos, or nothingness,* and then there is Earth, or form. If we look at this story as we would a dream image, that is, more as a picture than as a narrative, we would see that chaos and form appear at one and the same time. This way of looking at chaos and form would imply that within chaos there are inherent forms. Each moment of chaos has shapes within it, or "each chaos mothers itself into form."⁹

Admittedly, it is very hard for most of us to imagine living within the chaos, for we are troubled by any confusion in our lives. But this image also warns us that there is a need to allow some chaos, for there is always the danger that we will try to get rid of the confusion too quickly, thereby losing whatever new forms are about to emerge from it. The very nature of creativity entails chaos and times of daydreaming, as any artist will tell you. Joseph Campbell said that "Until you are willing to be confused about what you already know, what you know will never grow bigger, better, or more useful."

There are fallow periods in our lives and in our days when nothing much seems to happen. (Oh, how hard that is on our masculine consciousness!) What do we do with the fact that the very nature of our being is chaotic? The truth is, we consistently create ourselves and our realities each moment and those moments do contain the chaos of creation.

Ouranos symbolizes the Divine Plan before manifestation, the cosmic laws that order the universe, the urge for perfection, the ideal vision of life. It is very hard for the ideal to manifest in all its perfection. Therefore, like Ouranos, the first masculine consciousness who takes pleasure in the feminine but rejects the fruits of their union, we may too quickly impose some form or agenda on our chaos; the *shoulds* and *oughts* of our lives are imposed too readily onto our inner and outer chaos and children. Perhaps this myth explains why our modern masculine consciousness has such a hard time giving over power to feminine consciousness: the masculine likes order and control and loses itself too readily in the chaotic processes of creation.

There is always a tension and antagonism between the creative idea and its manifestation. Overwhelmed by the power of our ideal vision, our own creativity (which is of the Earth) rebels and might retaliate—because of time constraints, day to day pressures or just plain giving up under the pressure (Saturn/Kronos as worldly authority and time and constriction)—by cutting off the source of inspiration, the Creative Imagination.

Potentials of new life are often rejected and kept hidden away within us because it frequently comes into consciousness as a hated or ugly thing, like Dame Ragnell; that is, something that we have been taught to regard as wrong. It is often our unconscious instincts that know what we need to do, but our ego consciousness cannot accept the alternative offered. Often these are aspects of our psyches which have never been allowed to live in the light of day. Being kept in the dark, like seeds, they gather energy for new life, as we saw in the tale of *Fur Skin*.

But before this new life can become viable, we must face the stunted thing, the old fantasy that is stuck—the very thing that we have rejected for so long. Jung spoke of these stuck potentials as the Shadow, areas of our psyches which carry buried within it the very thing which is lacking in consciousness, the thing that has been missing from our lives which is required for further growth and development. We saw this rejected aspect in the mantle of furs, which symbolizes the earthy, instinctual aspects of life. It was only when the princess accepted her rejected instinctual nature that she came into her own Selfhood. We saw it in the collective question of 'what do women want?' that Sir Gawain had to acknowledge and accept by marrying Dame Ragnell.

Besides these stunted potentials that need breath and light, there is also the new life that grows spontaneously from within our inner chaos. This is the mystery of continuous creation we need to open ourselves to. This is the mystery of Spring, of new life that comes out of seeming death. Our directed, goal-oriented, reasonable ego consciousness hates mystery, and is afraid of the creativity of feminine consciousness because it is wild and passionate, unpredictable and chaotic, and often demands the death of old, worn-out ego ideals before it can create something new. Perhaps this is why Ouranos feared to let his children out, for then he would have had to change and adapt, and not live in absolutes. We all need to face our fears; which means facing our creativity and our

141

desires. Can we let the forms as the images that are inherent within us come into the light of day? Can we allow them a place in our lives so we can be co-creators of our lives? There is so much potential within each one of us if we can only allow it to gestate in the chaos.

To begin to do this, we have to learn what it means to mother ourselves, which is essentially to give birth to ourselves. If we can accept the image of mother as our grounding and nurturing as well as our sense of lack, the dark abyss, Chaos, we might discover a more fulfilling way to live life.

Here is a dream of the Goddess as Mother, a dream that asks the dreamer to accept deep love and mothering from her inner dark Goddess. When she accepts this nurturing, she is restored. She is a beautiful woman and the whole universe is hers!

> I am an infant, lying alone in the grass. A great Being picks me up. She is huge and black skinned. She has a beautiful face and large soft breasts. She has the kindest smile I have ever seen. She holds me and sits down on the great stone steps of an alabaster temple. She nurses me with the milk of human kindness. I grow into a woman. We are dressed in the most beautiful garments. I have on a rose madder color robe and she has on an ultramarine robe with small silver stars on it. It is the entire universe.

Why Patriarchal Consciousness Fears Death

With the advent of the Cartesian scientific world view, a distortion occurred in our Judeo-Christian belief that we are stewards of the Earth. Christianity, fearing the growing influence of scientific thought over people's beliefs, unfortunately refused to incorporate this new scientific understanding into its cosmology. The result is a twisting of both beliefs that has caused a great amount of damage to the Earth and our psyches. As scientific thought moved further and further away from any belief in a Divine Spirit at work in matter, religion rejected the spirit-in-matter. The result is that we were disenfranchised from our earthly heritage.

Our western cultural dominants, both science and religion, have cut us off from our instinctual knowledge of life. These dominants represent the Father King who is so removed from life that he would marry his own daughter. This is not to say that either science or western religions are evil; just that they have created an imbalance that adversely affects us all. Because they devalued the Earth and the life of the body, when we experience something new or upsetting, we don't know how to let our bodies tell us what to do. The Body Knows! But our minds challenge that knowledge and we get stuck in the pros and cons of indecision.

More importantly, as we separated ourselves from the Earth, we lost touch with the wisdom of the natural cycle of birth—death—rebirth, and so death became a mystery and the fear of the unknown attached itself to this inevitable part of life. And as we rejected the feminine body and instinctual wisdom of the Earth, we lost track of the cycles that allowed for the fallow times. Our masculine consciousness wanted it all-always alive, always moving forward, always being in control.

In the end, this fallow time of unconsciousness and chaos (nothingness or formlessness) and its silence became equated with death, and so death became a fearful thing for us, suddenly split off from life instead of being a natural part of life. When the scientific community began to view the Earth as dead matter, the western psyche further split off from its grounding in the body, which the Church had already damned as a major source of sin. A new god-image arose, one in which the Earth, the body, as well as women, who were seen as the source of earthly life and pleasures, were condemned as *the devil's playground* and we began to believe that life was an opening for sin, and sinners could not even hope for peace after death, for death brought them their just punishment. As our beliefs about the intrinsic goodness of the physical world changed, it created a split between our body and spirit, between our consciousness and our unconscious. Rejecting the life of the Earth cut us off from the wisdom of her cycles. We hungered for more life, and fought against death itself, because we had lost our understanding of the necessary connection between life and death. The images of our deep-seated fear of death entail either an image of pain and suffering or nothingness and chaos, rather than the ancient image of death as a doorway to new life (which Christ's resurrection also showed us).

Death is still an inconvenience and a terror to us, and so we continue to misunderstand it. We do not say, as many Native Americans warriors did, "It is a good day to die!" for we have very little understanding of what death means to us. It is a psychological and symbolic truth that our rejection of death constellates the very death we fear. Perhaps this is the reason we live in a society that is destroying our environment and our health, and creates death all around us.

In Ursula Le Guin's wonderful *Earthsea Trilogy*, she images this fear of death as a shadow, a shadow that drains all the joy and color out of life. In *The Farthest Shore*, the archmage, Sparrowhawk and the young king, Arren, go on a journey to try to restore the balance of life and death, which has been disrupted by a sorcerer who is so afraid of death that he has opened the gates between life and death and now cannot close them. The young king wonders why men are destroying the trees and the Earth, and the mage explains that they have no guidance, no king to show them how to live in the Balance.

In his youthful innocence, Arren wonders how this one fearful man could so easily destroy the balance of the world as his fear spreads.

And he asks the mage, "Where are the servants of this (man) Anti-King?"

"In our minds, lad. In our minds. The traitor, the self, the self that cries I WANT TO LIVE, LET THE WORLD ROT SO LONG AS I CAN LIVE! The little traitor soul in us, in the dark, like the spider in the box. He talks to all of us. But only some understand him. The wizards, the singers, the makers. And the heroes, the ones who seek to be themselves. To be oneself is a rare thing, and a great one. To be oneself forever, is that not better still?

Arren looked straight at Sparrowhawk . 'You mean that it is not greater. But tell me why.... . I have learned to believe in death. But I have not learned to rejoice over it, to welcome my death, or yours. If I love life, shall I not hate the end of it?

... 'Life without end,' the mage said. 'Life without death. Immortality. Every soul desires it, and its health is the strength of its desire. But be careful, Arren. You are one who might achieve your desire.'

'And then?'

'And then - this. This blight upon the lands. The arts of man forgotten. The singer tongue less. The eye blind. And then? A false king ruling. Ruling forever. And over the same subjects forever. No births; no new lives. No children. Only what is mortal bears life, Arren. Only in death is there rebirth. The Balance is not a stillness. It is a movement - an eternal becoming.'[10]

Are we one of those who would deny death, thereby denying the soul and the possibility of rebirth? Or can we passionately love our lives and give them over to an eternal becoming?

Reuniting Life and Death

We still unconsciously associate life with Mother, because we associate death with a withdrawal of love and warmth and comfort; death is abandonment and annihilation. This is the psychological underpinning of the negative mother complex. It is a devouring, a torment, a reduction to nothingness. The negative mother complex is strong within our psyches because these feelings are associated with our fear of death rather than with the knowledge of inevitable change. How can we grow if we don't also leave the Mother's House of childhood and grow into our individuality? The negative mother within us is the energy that forces us to face the dark and the dead in our lives. When we learn to face her and accept that at some points in life we will feel abandoned and loveless and tormented, we will indeed become wise.

In the East, the positive and negative mother is still united and therefore death does not hold such fear for people. One of the most glorious forms of the devouring side of the Mother is seen in India's goddess *Kali*, "dark, all-devouring time, the bone-wreathed Lady of the place of the skulls."[11] This image is scary when we cut off life from death, when we split up the attributes of the Earth Mother. But in India, *Kali*, which means *Terror-Joy*, is worshiped as both Creator and Destroyer, both good and terrible Mother, just as the primal forces of nature are both life-giving and death-dealing. It makes death easier to accept when we believe that life, comfort and joy lie on the other side of the experience. And it makes our life experience deeper and richer to know that it won't last forever. That death has a claim on us as well.

The Earth Mother's mysteries are the transformative mysteries of birth, love, death and regeneration. What she tells us is that life flows into death, which flows into life once again. A woman had a dream:

> I am standing with another woman watching all sorts of demonic creatures emerging from a gray mist and floating quickly, one after another, before our eyes. They do not bother us or seem to be aware of our presence. I think to myself, "My God! This is the Chaos of Hell." Then the woman recognizes one of the creatures and says, sadly, "Oh, Famine, not you - not again…" I realize I am viewing the afflictions of humanity.
>
> The scene shifts. I find myself caught up into an enormous orgasmic experience. The atmosphere is electrically charged with creative energy of tremendous proportions.

This woman, in her mid-forties, felt that the dream makes it clear that the forces of creation are linked forever with the forces of destruction; that both forces are necessary for the weaving of the fabric of life. The *orgasmic experience* of recognizing this fact unites her to the universe. The creative potential of this realization is enormous, because once we no longer fear death, especially the ego-death that the second half of life demands of us, the possibilities of creation open before us.

This is what happens when we turn to face destruction as a necessity of life. Doesn't our attitude change the nature of our ability to deal with chaos and death? If we can begin to accept that death is a blessing, will we not be willing to work toward changing the things in our lives and in our culture that are outworn and no longer appropriate to the health of the world? Can it be as simple as cutting dead wood? When we no longer fight against death, will we not have energy to meet it in new and creative ways?

The Earth can help us understand this mystery of life and death. Isn't Winter the season that gives us this experience of death? It is cold and dark and the life of the Earth goes dormant, frozen and covered over with snow. Although we can escape into our heated homes and cars and work places, we still end up going within in some form or another. The coldness and darkness torment many people and the inwardness of the winter months are like a mini-death to some. And yet, the Earth holds up a mystery to us: the mystery and meaning of death is our constant companion in the winter months, but out of that death comes new life every Spring. Why do we doubt that we also participate in these mysteries when we are children of Earth?

Death is always an unknown, a mystery; it does not, however, have to be met with terror. We say *'I feel like I'm dying'* when we feel lost. But being lost is not the same as death. We experience death many times in our lives, and so we have many chances to grow accustomed to death. Besides the concrete deaths of a loved one or of a relationship, there are also those psychological deaths, the death of old habits, complexes and beliefs, the point when we can simply let go of our hold on life and let life itself carry us along. We hang on to old complexes and ways of experiencing life, even when they hurt us, because we have no conception of what will come after we let them go.

There is also a spiritual death we must undergo –the dark night of the soul—when we have to face our aloneness and emptiness. I had a dream at a time in my life when I had to make the decision to believe in myself and in what I knew to be true. I had to re-evaluate my belief system, my old way of seeing the world. Was it still viable, could it still guide me in my life decisions? I finally recognized that it was really keeping me from new life. In the dream, facing this knowledge was portrayed as facing my potential death.

> I am in a house and very frightening things begin to happen around me. The wind outside the house is blowing fiercely. The Ark of the Covenant [I had just seen Raiders of the Lost Ark] is in this house, and I realize that the power of God is manifesting in dangerous ways. The other people with me do nothing, so I walk around, making sure that everyone and everything is alright.
>
> Two men appear out of the Ark. One is very tall, with dark hair and heavy features, reminding me of Frankenstein's monster. The other is a little man in a black suit with a black high hat and a black beard. They both come at me with terrible power. I am terrified and try to get away, but they have me cornered. I invoke God's name and keep trying to get away. I make the sign of the Cross as the tall man comes toward me and he laughs at my attempts at calling on God's help. He tells me that it will do me no good.
>
> Then I realize that the only thing left for me to do is to stop running and face them. I tell myself that they can only kill me. I am still afraid, for they are powerful, but I am no longer

terrified. I turn to face them, and somehow that is the only attitude to take that can defeat them, for they can no longer harm me. I also realize that I will have to face them again at other times in my life, but now I know what I must do, as well as what I can do.

This dream taught me about facing and accepting death; it taught me about my own bravery and strength and gave me the courage to act. In terms of my spiritual growth, the God whom I had been taught to believe was my heavenly Father was trying to destroy me. My old beliefs would not hold or save me. The dream opened me to the idea that my deeply held belief in the goodness of the Father God, the patriarchy and the authority of masculine consciousness was dangerous for me. That it was no longer serving my life to act in the old ways, and to believe in the old gods. They had turned into monsters for me. Like Fur Skin, I had to finally face what the Father's Spirit was doing to me, and like her, I succeeded in finding my own standpoint in relation to Feminine Spirit.

One part of facing your own death is to face your life. By this I mean taking responsibility for what you want and what you do; by taking your life into your own hands, you no longer have anyone or anything to blame for your condition. Life is, and your death becomes a part of that life. Don Juan Matus, the Yaqui Indian, taught Carlos Castaneda about facing his death.

> "Death is our eternal companion," don Juan said with a most serious air. "It is always to our left, at an arm's length. It was watching you when you were watching the white falcon; it whispered in your ear and you felt its chill, as you felt it today. It has always been watching you. It always will until the day it taps you."
>
> …"The thing to do when you're impatient," he proceeded, "is to turn to your left and ask advice from your death. An immense amount of pettiness is dropped if your death makes a gesture to you, or if you catch a glimpse of it, or if you just have the feeling that your companion is there watching you."
>
> He leaned over again and whispered in my ear that if I turned to my left suddenly, upon seeing his signal, I could again see my death on the boulder.

His eyes gave me an almost imperceptible signal, but I did not dare to look.

I told him that I believed him and that he did not have to press the issue any further, because I was terrified. He had one of his roaring belly laughs.

He replied that the issue of our death was never pressed far enough. And I argued that it would be meaningless for me to dwell upon my death, since such a thought would only bring discomfort and fear.

"You're full of crap!" he exclaimed. "Death is the only wise adviser that we have. Whenever you feel, as you always do, that everything is going wrong and you're about to be annihilated, turn to your death and ask if that is so. Your death will tell you that you're wrong; that nothing really matters outside its touch. Your death will tell you, 'I haven't touched you yet'.... One of us here has to ask death's advice and drop the cursed pettiness that belongs to men that live their lives as if death will never tap them." [12]

How often do any of us take death as our advisor? Try it for a day, and you will find that the pettiness of your life will give way to a strength and standpoint that only a real acceptance of death can give to life. I know now that as I get older, I have dropped the pettiness and worries of my youth. This acceptance of death is not foolhardy; it is not so much that the fear of the unknown disappears, but rather, it can no longer cause me to abandon what I feel and know I need to do. The truly brave face their fears and grow from the experience.

The World Mother as the Vessel of Our Feminine Spiritual Evolution

When we accept death as a natural, though unknowable, part of life, and re-unite within our own consciousness the cycle of life and death, we begin to glimpse another aspect of the Earth Mother. Earth becomes the World Mother and we see her archetypal power as a vessel of life. The womb and its symbols of cup, vessel or container have always been symbolic of the feminine divinities. The womb is a woman's center of gravity and as such, needs to be valued and its spiritual power released. The mystery of having a space within, a space from which new life issues, is a metaphor of the process of transformation. Feminine wisdom is imparted to us through this image of a vessel. For example, look at the idea of power. Women's wombs are metaphors for the fact that we are all really vessels for power to flow through. Once we stop trying to *be powerful* and *hold onto power* as our old masculine, ego consciousness desires, and start becoming vessels in which power can manifest, perhaps *powerful* will really come to mean *full of power,* creative powers.

When we live in our mantle of furs, we take on the life and powers of our animal nature. We reconnect with our instincts, with our wild natures and with our body, which have been raped, demonized and tamed in the name of the patriarchy.

Ask yourself who are your animal guides? What do they have to teach you? When you dream of an animal, you are being asked to incorporate that instinct. Or you might pick an animal card from one of the many decks available to help you work out a problem. Our animal brothers and sisters have always been teachers. We've forgotten to ask them to teach us about life.

We make the choice to live in the vessel of Earth's instinctual life and evolve our consciousness. For Father's Daughters, living in our mantle of furs isn't easy. We like to think and plan. We don't readily sit in silence and listen to or understand what our instincts are trying to tell us. We have to learn to combine our instinct with our intellect, our senses with our intuitions. We have to learn to accept our instincts, not repress them. So the hard work of naming these instincts and these feelings teaches us what they have to say about our lives so we can make life-giving choices based on our inner wisdom and outer logic.

As Clarissa Pinkola Estes details in her powerful stories in *Women Who Run With the Wolves,* women have lost our conscious connection to our wild, wolfish selves, the Wild Woman who is our deepest instinctive self.

Wildlife and the Wild Woman are both endangered species.

Over time, we have seen the feminine instinctive nature looted, driven back, and overbuilt. For long periods it has been mismanaged like the wildlife and the wildlands. For several thousand years, as soon and as often as we turn our backs, it is relegated to the poorest land in the psyche. The Feminine

Spiritual lands of Wild Woman have, throughout history, been plundered or burnt, dens bulldozed, and natural cycles forced into unnatural rhythms to please others.

...Healthy wolves and healthy women share certain psychic characteristics: keen sensing, playful Feminine Spirit, and a heightened capacity for devotion. Wolves and women are relational by nature, inquiring, intensely concerned with their young, their mate and their pack. They are experienced in adapting to constantly changing circumstances; they are fiercely stalwart and very brave. Yet both are hounded, harassed, and falsely imputed to be devouring and devious, overly aggressive, of less value than those who are their detractors. They have been the targets of those who would clean up the wilds as well as the wildish environs of the psyche, extincting the instinctual, and leaving no trace of it behind. [13]

This wild woman archetype is at the root of Fur Skin's insistence on wearing the mantle of furs and laboring in it. She knows the psychological truth that it is our wild instinctual nature which has been injured by the father's desire to marry her, and which has been injured by her mother's demand of the king's promise. The only way to regain our feminine wisdom and standpoint is to allow the wild energies within us to have their say. These energies move us to dance, to adorn ourselves with beauty, to take joy in our bodies, to come out and play, activities which until recently were forbidden to women by western cultural mores and which are still forbidden to women in Islamic countries. Women are re-defining ourselves outside the patriarchal conditions that have dominated our self-awareness for millennia. A rare and talented storyteller, Estes opens up our understanding of the Wild Woman archetype. Her book is required reading for any wild woman in this stage of transformation.

The Rhythms of Life

Rhythm and movement are ways to open ourselves to the power and energy of our instinctual life. Rhythm at its most primal is expressed in drumming, and the ancient Celtic, Arabian and Afro-Cuban rhythms can teach us the patterns of soulful living. Just as birth occurs through the rhythmic contractions of labor, our dancing bodies also learn the rhythms of life and open us to our creative source. The Goddess Artemis, leader of the dance and Mistress of Animals, invites a woman to become virginal once again, to belong to herself, to know her own being and instincts through reconnecting to her body and its needs. Once a woman knows herself, she can never lose herself again, even when loving a man. Dance centers us in our unique Feminine Spirit.

Through dancing, a woman can oppose the splitting between the social and the natural, as well as the taming of her wilder self, which can start early in a male-dominated history. A woman thus learns to name and express the being that lives deep inside her, waiting and longing to be discovered. This is her other, hidden self, the one who does not match norms or expectations, the one who widens her nostrils like a horse to suck in the wind, who roars like a lioness and shamelessly tears her clothes from her body. This one lives mostly in the background, in the dark cave, deep inside the belly, and only seldom surfaces. She is usually spotted when a person says or does something she wouldn't normally allow herself, when something just tumbles out. It happens without one knowing really how it could come to that. Dancing helps you start to heal this inner split. Dancing offers the conscious and the unconscious, the rational and the intuitive, a space in which they may gradually flow into each other. [14]

Dancing, we experience a sense of freedom and sexuality, as well as learning the right use of our sexuality. For sexual promiscuity is not sexual freedom, but sexual confusion. Dancing encompasses the realm of the sacred, the artistic, and the joyful, sensual play of self-discovery. Without these knowing rhythms in our lives, we might mistake abusing our bodies for freedom.

When you have writer's block, or are stuck in any aspect of your life, move! Dance! The movement opens up blockages and allows energy to flow. Dance is a bridge between our inner and outer worlds, opening us to imagination.

Body knowledge starts by removing attention from the mind and focusing entirely on movement. Independent thinking, thinking with one's own mind, is learned through thinking in feelings and sensations, and thinking in pictures, free from the rigidity of words. With these two different approaches, a whole world of possibilities opens up.[15]

There is an ancient form of dancing that specifically expresses women's power: belly dancing. Any woman can do it. It has nothing to do with how skinny you are or if you have taken dance lessons all your life. Besides being great exercise, you get to play with scarves, expose your belly and feel sensual. It makes you feel like a woman. Belly dancing is a way to express and understand our deepest, sensuous feminine nature.

The movements of belly dancing enable a woman to understand and experience a natural rhythm. In this dance form, she swings her limbs around the center of her body, around the navel of the world, through waves and swinging, rhythmical movements of the pelvis, through movements older than any single woman, indeed older than human civilization. We dance to become one with a rhythm that was here before us and will remain after we are gone.... .

Belly dancing is a dance of isolation, in which the various parts and centers of the body are moved individually, independently from each other, yet end up forming a unity. The polycentric movements of belly dancing develop the body's intelligence and capacity to react, finally resulting in a multi-dimensional body awareness. Just as individual drops unite in the harmonious flow of a river that time and again draws strength from its source, so belly dancing, as suggested by its popular name, finds its source in the belly. Its rhythm originates from inside, from the elemental sound of the heartbeat that we first heard in the cavern of our mother's belly. If a woman wishes to bring new life into the world, she must have this life force, of which belly dancing is the age-old expression.

Strength for her movements is picked up by the dancer from her belly, the lower part of her body where her balance is centered. She links her lower belly's center of gravity to the earth on which she dances and embeds it in a greater circle of energy. Even her finger movements draw their energy from her belly. And every single movement, however tiny, longs to return to this center. The whole body swings around this center, the navel of the world.[16]

The World as Sacred Space

This center, this navel of the world, is also the Earth. Now let the Earth, our planet and the Mother, become *world*, the psychic component that shapes our experience of life. Let the world become the symbolic womb or vessel where we grow into life and where our death becomes a birth into another place. When we come to understand the world and the path of our life through it as a dimension of our psychic reality, we learn that everything that comes to us and everything that we do can be an aid to our growth in life and into death, or that larger life that is a mystery to us now. This is when we can take death as our advisor! The great vessels of transformation—the womb, the breast, the alchemical retort, the cup of the Holy Grail which feeds everyone with the food of their choice—describe the fact of sacred space, the space where the divine and human meet. If we desire it, the World Mother becomes such a sacred space.

We have the ability to look at our lives psychologically, and see that all the incidents and elements that make up our individual lives, both the good and the bad, are necessary conditions for the birthing of our Selves. Jung's idea of synchronicity, the acausal but meaningful relationship between the nonphysical and the physical, is an example of the outer world and our inner world meeting in such a way as to bring us some insights into our psychological state. The Chinese book of divination, the *I Ching*, as well as such divination tools as the Runes or Tarot cards, operate with this idea of ultimate correspondence of inner and outer reality. The Hermetic saying, *as above, so below* is another example of this truth. Therefore, the task is to find out what the world is demanding of us in the way of growth and creativity and life, which might sometimes demand a death. When we do not deal with our inner life adequately, our problems invariably meet us in the outer world.

When Gaia becomes the psychological World Mother, nurturing us into our next evolution of consciousness, she offers us deep feminine wisdom. Remember the myth? Two important transformations and births take place from the castration of Ouranos. One is the birth of Aphrodite, the Goddess of Love. Aphrodite is a goddess who is clothed with the Sun. Aphrodite is the Goddess of the Body, and as such, has been abused more than any other goddess by the patriarchy. Aphrodite, the Goddess of Love, all the many facets of love, is the divine gift of cosmic law that has been given to us here on Earth. I believe that Aphrodite, or Venus as the Romans called her, symbolizes the goddess energy that women must reclaim as we each become a *Woman clothed with the Sun.*

The other event is the birth of the Erinyes, the *strong ones.* The Erinyes were originally called the Furies, whose name means *a spirit of anger and revenge.* The Furies hound all those who have flouted blood-kinship and the deference due it, especially when a mother is insulted or murdered. With the repression of the feminine aspects of life and our disregard for the Earth, I expect that many of us have been hounded by one thing or another in our lives. This hounding comes from the Furies, snapping at our heels, never letting us rest. But these Furies went through a transformation in the Greek play *Orestes* by Aeschylus. This is the story of what happened when Orestes, who murdered his mother, Clytemnestra, to avenge the death of his father, Agamemnon, is brought to trial before the gods. Pallas Athena, the original Father's Daughter, argues his case so persuasively that the Furies agree to become part of the divine order and so become known as the Benevolent Ones.[17]

This transformation of the Furies into the Benevolent Ones is symbolic of the psychological transformation that takes place when we can see the many facets of our lives, especially those aspects which hound us because of a slight or a neglect of a proper attitude to the life source or to our own creativity, as the very source of our continued growth and development. The Furies become benevolent whenever we meet life's hardness and rockiness (also of the Earth), not with anger and a thirst for revenge, but with the transformative question, "What is this here to teach me?" We also need to ask, "What does this situation say about me and my attitudes?" Asking the questions does not imply that the situation or the other person is right any more than that she/he/it may be wrong. It just means that, like the Grail hero who, when confronted with the appearance of the Grail, must ask, "What does this mean?" life poses us questions and we can seek and find the answers that we need. The asking of the question in the Grail story brings about the cure of the Fisher King and the renewal of the Waste Land. Asking the question implies and acknowledges that the experience itself has a meaning. The question acknowledges the Feminine Spirit at work in the world, and the essential soul-full quality of life. The Erinyes are the *strong ones* because in meeting them face to face, they give us the opportunity to develop our own strength.

Just as the world gives birth to each of us as individuals, it presents collective tasks that we have to face as well. And it is women who set the stage for the working out of these tasks. Women quite literally shape the world when we give birth.

> With each generation the entire race passes through the body of its womanhood as through a mold, reappearing with the indelible marks of that mold upon it. The os cervix of woman, through which the head of the human infant passes at birth, forms a ring, determining forever the size at birth of the human head, a size which could only increase if in the course of ages the os cervix of woman should itself slowly expand; and… so exactly the intellectual capacity, the physical vigor, the emotional depth of woman, forms also an untranscendable circle, circumscribing with each successive generation the limits of the expansion of the human race. [18]

When a woman is self-possessed, emotionally mature, stable and secure in her own strength—when she has walked away from being a Father's Daughter and has become her own woman—she will give birth to a whole new human being-perhaps the divine child of *Revelation*. We have it in our biological DNA to grow and evolve, and if mothers evolve, how can they not give birth to children who have evolved as well?

I have only detailed a few of the many images of Mother Earth and there are many books that can help you learn more. There are many mysteries associated with the Divine Feminine Spirit: her fertility, which is experienced within the myths of Demeter and Persephone; her creative gifts and talents, as bestowed by the Celtic goddesses of the Cauldron, Brigid and Cerridwen; the magic of Isis and Morgan le Fey; the dark moon mysteries of Cybele and Hecate; and the beauty and wisdom of Changing Woman, White Shell Woman and Spider

Woman. And yet, all of her aspects speak of the flow of life from one form into another, of life into death and death into life, from seed to flower to fruit to seed again. She speaks to us in the beauty of the life we experience in nature-Spring, Summer, Autumn and Winter. The Great Round of Life defines our path through this world as well as our evolution and growth.

The Earth is Our Seat of Power

There is one more symbol of Earth's powers: the symbol of Lady Wisdom as the *Throne*. All mother goddesses share this aspect of being the throne, or the seat of power. We see numerous statues of the Mother and Child: Isis and Horus, the Virgin Mary and the Christ Child. In Celtic mythology, the Goddess of the Land is the Throne of the King; that is, the king assumed his power by a symbolic marriage to the Land, from which he gets his power to rule. What can we say about this aspect of the mothering power of the Earth, this throne-like quality? What does it mean to be seated in the lap of the Goddess?

The seat of power. What does it mean? I feel that there is both a literal and an imaginative meaning to this symbol. There are literal spots on the Earth where each of us feels most at home, most centered, most powerful. For some of us, it is the mountains; for others, it is the ocean; still others, fields of growing grain. Or perhaps it is forests, rivers, gentle rolling plains, valleys or deserts. These places strike a responsive chord in our hearts. The combination of height, depth, breadth, light and temperature, as well as the peculiar beauty of each landscape, makes us feel something special about the world and ourselves. These places are our power spots, for they refresh and nourish our spirits. They seem to draw out our innermost selves; they make us feel most alive!

The feeling that you get when you are connected with the Earth in this manner can become a seat of power within you. You know the feeling whenever and wherever you encounter it again - in another place where the land is similar, in a dream landscape, or even in a relationship. In recognizing this feeling as an essential part of your being, you can nourish it and be nourished by it. The image and the feeling that you get from the land will lead you deeper into your life. The Native Americans knew this about the land: the land shapes you to itself.

Connected to the symbol of the throne is the Celtic idea of Lady Sovereignty. The king and the people whom he represented gave sovereignty to the Goddess of the Land. This meant that they gave her pre-eminence in recognition of her power and efficacy. This can mean, for us, giving sovereignty to the Earth and her mysteries; it can mean giving sovereignty to the promptings of the soul, which is the spark of divinity and creativity within each of us; and it can mean giving sovereignty, or authority, to our feminine, imaginal consciousness that forms our primary relationship to the world.

As the story of *The Marriage of Sir Gawain and Dame Ragnell* suggests, we have to learn to live with the fact that the Earth as well as women are shape-shifters. Besides taking on animal shapes, Dame Ragnell or Lady Sovereignty could appear to be the ugliest old hag or the most beautiful woman, depending on the question she poses to us. The same goes for the unique individuality of our souls. Our feelings, thoughts and beliefs shift and change because that is their nature—that is the soul's nature. When our ego consciousness is cut off from our soul, we experience life as the Hag, chaotic and brutal. When we wed our soul to spirit, life does become the *most beautiful*. We obviously need new strategies for living once we face our unconscious feminine side and listen to its perspective. The question of feminine sovereignty is still being posed to the masculine world. It will never be understood until our collective consciousness embraces the wisdom of the Earth.

The story promises that once we do accept this wisdom and this wedding, we will make joy out of mind. What a wonderful thing to really *know* that divine spirit lives within our bodies. What a blessed reality when we experience how Feminine Spirit helps our body, mind and spirit develop to their fullest potential. That same Feminine Spirit manifests as the natural laws of the Earth. Once we remember that our souls incarnate onto this Earth to evolve through learning the spiritual lessons of the material world, especially about the nature of love and union, we will honor the Earth and our bodies as temples of Spirit. This is the healing of the passion of matter. This is something that Lady Wisdom can teach us if we give over our ego's standpoint for its larger purpose, which always serves life.

Over the past two thousands year, humanity developed a type of ego consciousness that has given rise to the greatest light as well as descended into utter darkness. But in the past few hundred years, that ego consciousness has been split off from the feminine unconscious and therefore from the Self. When women turn within to listen to our unique feminine voice, and pay attention to the Unconscious, working to re-learn its language, we transform and enlarge our consciousness to encompass our loved ones, our community's needs, and the Earth.

We can no longer ignore the fact that the environment is being ravished by our corporate economy to the point of no return. Climate change is our new reality. At some point in the future, our fresh water supply will dwindle—the corporate takeover of water supplies is already underway. Americans consistently say that we value the environment and yet many of us are unwilling to take on the inconvenience of changing our lifestyle to stop the waste and destruction it generates. People need stories to help them see why a change of perspective is necessary. We have to search for those new stories for ourselves and our world.

Maybe we need to consider giving women, feminine consciousness, and the Earth, our Mother, sovereignty once again. It would mean honoring images and stories. The Earth Mother poses the question, "What is your true nature?" She gives birth to all of us, just as the Self gives birth to us as individuals. If we gave sovereignty to imagination and soul, to Earth as the vessel of transformation, and to women, we might find our way to a different vision with which to see the world, and to a new way of integrating the different facets of our lives. If we dare to express our own creativity, that creativity can form new patterns of life. When we turn to the things in life that really matter to us, to the matter—mater/mother—of our lives, we can allow life's imaginal dimensions to enrich the context of our lives in this world; concrete lives made rich and meaningful by this sacred context.

Earth's Wisdom: The Serpent of Wisdom

While all animals live in harmony with the Earth and her ecosystem, there is one animal that has represented Earth's Wisdom since ancient times. The Snake or Serpent is a symbol of the wisdom of the energies of life and death within our bodies. We have come to associate snakes with evil and the Devil in Christianity, and so women's bodies and sexuality have been vilified by association. It all began in the Garden of Eden.

This one story has been used to subjugate women throughout western history. The snake tempted Eve, and by her sin, we are all fallen from grace. But what exactly was the temptation? The serpent tempted Eve to eat of the Tree of Knowledge of Good and Evil. Now that we know that there were matriarchies before the patriarchy gained power, the knowledge of good and evil already existed. Women had this knowledge. Women have always had this knowledge. It's bred in our bones. To grow, to evolve, to become a conscious human being, each of us must have this knowledge of good and evil. We have to learn to make choices and exercise our free will. And we do this by listening to our bodies and our feelings and then using our minds to make choices. This ancient knowledge is part of our feminine heritage.

And it is Snake who offers us this wisdom. Pictures of ancient priestesses with snakes twinned around their arms symbolize their ability to act on their instinctive knowledge. Snakes were found in goddess temples, especially those like Delphi where prophetic insight was sought. All cultures venerated the serpent, and all cultures acknowledge the wisdom, subtly and healing powers of the snake. In ancient Egypt, the Pharaoh's crown was comprised of the *uraeus*, the cobra which represented divine wisdom and power. And if we look at most world mythologies, there is always a serpent coiled around the Tree of Life.

Serpents symbolize complex energies, both male and female. Serpents represent the transformative energies of death and rebirth, and they shed their skins as examples. They travel underground, and so bring back hidden knowledge. Their coils echo the cycles of manifestation, the ebb and flow of life. The Ouroboros, the serpent which eats its own tail, opens us to possibilities of return and renewal, the infinite powers of creation and destruction. When it coils around the Tree of Life, the serpent brings the dynamism of growth. As a symbol of self-creative manifestation, it is both light and dark, good and evil, healing and poisonous, preserver and destroyer. Only in the West has the serpent come to be associated with only the dark aspects of this energy. And so we have heroes fighting the serpent: Zeus and Typhon, Apollo and Python, Osiris and Set, Marduk and Tiamat. These are psychological stories of the hero ego trying to overcome the Unconscious. Our western religions could never contain the contradiction of opposites. When things are in opposition, they are meant to complement each other, not cut each other off. Because of its inability to unite the opposites,

Christianity's version of the serpent and its wisdom of life is the Devil, the negative, malevolent, destructive, deceitful and cunning adversary of God. The Tempter. But that's only half the story.

Hermes' caduceus has two snakes twinning around a central staff. These double serpents represent the opposites which ultimately have to be united – the union of opposites which finds a third, transcendent function that mediates between the two. In medical symbolism, these two snakes represent healing and poison, illness and health-the twin forces of life and death. Earth's wisdom is that all these opposites are really united. Like the kundalini energy in the body, this serpent power is the energy of life. Once the kundalini rises up the spine through the body and the charkas, it brings us to higher states of consciousness.

The wave-like undulations of Snake as it travels corresponds to the energy and light waves we know of from science. Snake reminds us that all is energy. We can travel to the future on these waves in dreams, or we can raise this energy up our spine for greater awareness. When snake sheds its skin, it reminds us that we live in the midst of constant change, the transmutation of life—death—rebirth. On the physical plane, this energy creates passion, sexuality, desire and vitality. On the emotional plane, it engenders our creativity and dreams. In the mind it creates our personal power and intellect. When this energy reaches into the spiritual planes, it brings us wisdom, wholeness and a connection with Divinity. Powerful indeed!

Snakes and serpents appear in dreams all the time. When there are many snakes crawling around, like Indiana Jones we get *freaked out* by them. All that energy with no place to go! A woman dreamed that she was holding a party for her family, but there were many snakes in the room, which symbolizes undifferentiated and uncontrolled life-force. She and her family have lots of energy and power, but sometimes they don't use it well. Especially when the family gets together, the energies run wild. They have no container for it, and so it becomes dangerous.

Another woman dreamed of snakes, but these snakes gave her power. She dreamed:

> My husband and I are headed into a forest sanctuary. I yell at him to watch out, for a golden snake comes down out of a tree, mouth open, fangs out and bites him in the neck. I go to help him and I grab a cake knife. One golden cobra flings

itself into the air at me. It is so golden it looks like it's covered in jewels. This cobra flings itself down to bite me on the head and as I wake up, my arms and legs are energized.

The dream story describes a very real shift in energy between this woman and man. The husband is now working with his feminine energy and the wife has taken back her power and freedom. The husband is listening with respect to her ideas and learning to understand his own feelings and intuitions. Their relationship is renewed.

As I mentioned earlier, one of my first dreams in Jungian analysis had to do with the birth of a golden dragon. Symbolically, serpents and dragons are often interchangeable in myths. The dragon, especially in the East, represents the highest spiritual and supernatural powers, as well as wisdom, strength and the cycles and laws of life. Dragons are the guardians of treasure and secret knowledge. The winged serpent, a combination of bird and serpent, is an attribute of Quetzalcoatl, the Feathered Serpent, the great culture hero of the Aztecs. The golden color of my dream dragon implies that it is a spiritual energy, like the golden auras around the heads of saints. This dream was both a task and a promise to me: my job was to become conscious of the treasures of the Unconscious, especially the Collective Unconscious.

Earth's wisdom is available to each and every one of us. We receive this wisdom through our dreams, through visions, through feelings, through instincts. Then we need our intellect to understand what to do with our insights. This is the gift that our mother, the Earth, wants us to use. Isn't it time we did?

How Sun, Moon, and Wind Went Out to Dinner

One day Sun, Moon and Wind went out to dine with their uncle and aunts Thunder and Lightning. Their mother (one of the most distant Stars you see far up in the sky) waited alone for her children's return.

Now both Sun and Wind were greedy and selfish. They enjoyed the great feast that had been prepared for them, without a thought of saving any of it to take home to their mother–but the gentle Moon did not forget her. Of every dainty dish that was brought round, she placed a small portion under one of her beautiful long finger-nails, that Star might also have a share in the treat.

On their return, their mother, who had kept watch for them all night long with her little bright eye, said, "Well, children, what have you brought home for me?" Then Sun (who was eldest) said, "I have brought nothing home for you. I went out to enjoy myself with my friends–not to fetch a dinner for my mother!" And Wind said, "Neither have I brought anything home for you, mother. You could hardly expect me to bring a collection of good things for you, when I merely went out for my own pleasure." But Moon said, "Mother, fetch a plate, see what I have brought you." And shaking her hands she showered down such a choice dinner as never was seen before.

Then Star turned to Sun and spoke thus, "Because you went out to amuse yourself with your friends, and feasted and enjoyed yourself, without any thought of your mother at home–you shall be cursed. Henceforth, your rays shall ever be hot and scorching, and shall burn all that they touch. And men shall hate you, and cover their heads when you appear."

(And that is why the Sun is so hot to this day.)

Then she turned to Wind and said, "You also who forgot your mother in the midst of your selfish pleasures–hear your doom. You shall always blow in the hot dry weather, and shall parch and shrivel all living things. And men shall detest and avoid you from this very time."

(And that is why the Wind in the hot weather is still so disagreeable.)

But to Moon she said, "Daughter, because you remembered your mother, and kept for her a share in your own enjoyment, from henceforth you shall be ever cool, and calm, and bright. No noxious glare shall accompany your pure rays, and men shall always call you 'blessed.'"

(And that is why the moon's light is so soft, and cool, and beautiful even to this day.)[1]

Chapter Five
Standing On The Moon:
Another View Of Our World

"Mommy, did you know that we live inside the moon?"
—My son Gregory, age 4

"Why don't you come in, Curdie?" said the voice.
"Did you never see moonlight before?"

"Never without a moon," answered Curdie, in a
trembling tone, but gathering courage.

"Certainly not," returned the voice, which was thin and
quivering: "I never saw moonlight without a moon."

"But there's no moon outside," said Curdie.

"Ah! but you're inside now," said the voice.

—The Princess and Curdie George MacDonald

The Moon symbolizes the doorway to the Creative Imagination where thought-forms, archetypes and stories take shape. Always shifty, always mysterious, light and dark, delusions and imagination are at play. Life itself revealed in images! What possibilities will you chose to live? What story, what symbol will you follow? When we stand on the Moon, we stand at the doorway of creation, the bubbling cauldron of creativity. What will we make of our lives? What will satisfy us? The Moon holds sway here. Change is the only constant. She is process and growth, transparent and veiled. She is our light through the darkness of creation.

We Live Inside the Moon

Like the Moon in this fairy tale, women tend to think of others even when we're enjoying ourselves. Like the Moon, women are nurturers. Throughout the ages though, when comparing women to the Moon, men have most often berated us for our changeability. But changing our minds about something, or being caught up in different emotions throughout a day, doesn't take away the fact of our essential reliability and caring concern. In the midst of our changes, women stay centered in what's important to us: love, family, work, creativity. That's why it is women who will put our minds and hearts into creating change in the world. After all, we do know something about it!

Fur Skin's dress that shines like the Moon symbolizes this gift of change-ability, as well as the psychic component that engenders this type of flexibility: the power of the Unconscious, which picks up clues from our environment and tells us what we need to know to survive, to prosper and to regenerate. Psychic abilities, intuitive flashes, visions, dreams, feelings all find their source in the Unconscious. When Fur Skin wears her dress of moonlight, she uses her imagination to understand her world. And when she listens, she channels that wisdom into her life.

The Woman clothed with the Sun STANDS on the Moon. What does it mean to take this Moon consciousness as our standpoint? To take our stand on the Moon might appear to be risky, since constant change can be pretty shaky ground. A masculine perspective of this image of the *woman* has interpreted it as having domination over that changeability. They were afraid of the Unconscious. But don't forget that the *Woman* also has the Earth as her center, and it gives her the balance to go with the flow and ebb of life.

When my son Gregory told me we live inside the Moon, he spoke with a child's imagination, and he spoke the truth. Jesus said, "Unless you become like little children, you will not enter the kingdom of heaven." I believe it is this childlike imagination that he spoke of. We have to play more with our imagination if we want to become wise.

This imagination is how we understand our part in Earth's ecology. When we are in touch with the natural rhythms of life, we more easily find the balance between work, pleasure, family and creativity. The rhythms of life still beat strongly within us and when we disregard them, we find ourselves ill or at odds with ourselves. My dream of stealing the calendar and being called to stay by the children called me back to the rhythms of life. To understand what these rhythms are, we have to understand the impact the Moon has on us, as it helps to set the rhythms of life on Earth.

The Moon Mother

When we lost touch with the feminine mysteries of the ancient Goddess, we were banished from our home inside the Moon. Small children know and remember their true home, but as we grow up, we forget for the most part, how to live in the natural rhythms of life which the Moon Goddess—perpetual renewal, the measure of time, the weaver of fate—represented to her ancient worshipers. Most of us have no idea what power and effect the Moon has over us or the world around us. However, what was lost can be found, for the Moon still travels across the night sky and still sheds her silvery light upon our darkness.

The first thing we observe about the Moon is that it changes shape, unlike the Sun, which appears the same every day and never fails to rise and set, full and round all through the day. The Moon grows larger, then smaller, waxing and waning as it travels across the sky. It rises at different times during the night and at different spots on the horizon. And it even completely disappears for three nights. But it comes back, and begins the process over again. Small wonder that early humanity projected its imagination onto the Moon, since they experienced it as a monthly cycle that regulated time, its rhythms governing the tides, women's menstrual cycles, plant life and weather.

Ancient peoples observed that the Moon made the fertilizing moisture that makes living things grow and thrive: plants and animals as well as human beings. The Moon Mother, imagined as a vessel of water, fertility and fecundity, was the source of *being* and *becoming*. It was an aspect of the Great Mother who "established a unifying pattern for all living things, living and breathing in harmony, existing in an intricate and ineffable web."[2] And because they could live with contradictions, these ancient peoples also believed the Moon was the land of the dead, the place souls went to between incarnations. Just as the Moon dies and is reborn, so souls go to the Moon to await rebirth. The creative life cycle of birth—death—rebirth is prefigured in the changing Moon.

As I mentioned, women naturally understand this rhythm of change, because our bodies respond to these changing rhythms. Men have a harder time adjusting to this cycle. They don't know how to relate to their own changing moods, and so ignore them as inconsequential. Women's greatest gift, our ability to adapt to change, has been used against us to demonstrate that we are not as *rational*, and therefore not as reliable or responsible as men. Many of us, adapting to the role of good Father's Daughter, have tried to become more consistent. But at what cost?

Once again, men used themselves as the measure of all things, and their own lack of adaptability became the standard. But not anymore! Now the world needs people who can change, who can let go of what is outdated and open to new ideas and new possibilities. It is a perfect time for women to step forward and use our strengths and set new standards for what makes a full and rich life. Life is about change and if women want to live up to our potentials, we have to consciously take our standpoint on the Moon. When the ancient Goddess religions were suppressed under Christianity, her manifestations were split up. On one hand, some of her light qualities were attributed to the Church and to the Virgin Mary. Her darker, mysterious qualities, however, were soon associated with the Devil and with witchcraft, for Christianity accepted the heavenly attributes of the feminine while rejecting the earthy spirit of the Goddess. The Earth and women, who were seen as creatures of the Earth and of the body, were relegated to the darkness of sin. Consequently, our culture developed a split between the heavenly feminine and the earthy feminine. This is the problem the fairy tale *Fur Skin* is trying to solve. How do women reunite our earthy wisdom with the heavenly wisdom we've inherited?

The Uncanny Moon

As a culture, we often focus on the uncanny dark side of the Moon. Our collective beliefs about the Moon and its light are often negative, projecting insanity, lunacy, wild and foolish behavior, moonshine, whimsy, irrationality, *mooning over someone* as the effects of the full Moon. We are fascinated and horrified by the strange bestial transformations we imagine occur under the light of the Moon: people turning into werewolves, witchcraft and black magic practiced in the dark. As we have seen in countless horror films, the *night of the living dead* can burst into our lives at any moment. The shadows of the night still hold terror for us, and it is not the moonlight that dispels these shadows for us, but our electric lights.

There are old English folk tales which show us not only how far we have moved away from understanding the gifts of the Moon, but also how wrong it is that the Moon has been taken over by our darkest fears.

Long ago, in a land of bogs and deep, dark waters, when the Moon shone down at night, she lit up the bog-pools so that people could walk there almost as safely as in the day. But when she didn't shine, out came the horrible things that dwelt in the darkness and went about seeking to do evil and harm.

When the Moon heard of this, she was very troubled because she was kind and good. "I'll see for myself," she said, "maybe it's not as bad as people say."

So at the dark time, she stepped down to Earth wrapped up in a black cloak with a black hood over her silvery shining hair. She went to the bog and looked about her. All was dark and watery.

The Moon drew her cloak tight and trembled, but she wouldn't go back without seeing all there was to see. On she went, stepping as light as the wind from tuft to tuft between the greedy gurgling water-holes. Just she came near a big black pool her foot slipped and she almost tumbled in. She grabbed with both hands at a nearby branch to steady herself, but as she touched it, it twined itself round her wrists and gripped her so tightly that she couldn't move. She pulled and twisted and fought, but it was no good. She was held fast.

As she stood trembling in the dark, wondering if help would come, she heard someone calling in the distance, calling, calling, and then dying away with a sob, filling the marshes with a pitiful crying sound. Then she heard steps floundering along, squishing in the mud and slipping on the tufts, and through the darkness she saw a white face with great fearful eyes. It was a man lost in the bogs, lost far from the path with dead things grabbing at him.

When the poor Moon saw that he was coming closer and closer to a deep pool, she was so upset that she struggled and fought and pulled harder than ever. And though she couldn't get loose, she twisted and turned till her black hood fell back off her shining silvery hair, and a beautiful light came from it and drove away the darkness. Oh, but the man cried with joy to see the light again. And at once all evil things fled back into the dark corners, for they cannot abide the light. So the man could see where he was, and where the path was, and how he could get out of the marsh. And he was in such haste to get away that he scarcely looked at the brave light that came from her beautiful shining hair, streaming out over the black cloak and falling to the water at his feet. And the Moon herself was so taken up with saving him, and with rejoicing that he was back on the right path, that she forgot that she needed help herself.

So the man ran off without helping the Moon. Then she pulled and fought as if she were mad, till she fell on her knees, spent with tugging, at the foot of the dead tree. As she lay there, gasping for breath, the black hood fell forward over her head and so the blessed light went out and back came the darkness. Horrors came crowding round her, mocking and snatching and beating; shrieking with rage and spite, swearing and snarling, for they knew her for their old enemy, that drove them back into the corners, and kept them from working their wicked wills.

These wicked horrors fought and squabbled all night about how to kill her, and soon the poor Moon wished that she was dead and done with, till a pale gray light began to come in the sky. Dawn was near. And when the wicked things saw this, they feared they wouldn't have time to work their will, so they caught hold of her with horrid bony fingers and laid her deep in the water at the foot of the tree. And they fetched a strange big stone and rolled it on top of her, to keep her from rising. And there lay the poor Moon, dead and buried in the bog, till someone would set her loose. But nobody knew where to look for her.

Well, as the days passed, and the time for the new Moon came and went, the nights were so dark that the evil things were worse than ever, for they came closer and closer to the villages. Soon everyone was afraid to step out at night, and then they were afraid to turn out the lights and go to sleep, lest the evil things invade their homes!

The people at last sought out the Wise Woman and asked if she could find out where the Moon had gone. Well, she looked in the mirror, in the cauldron and in the Book of Shadows, but she could not divine what had happened to the Moon. She sent them away, telling them to come back to her if they heard anything about the Moon.

Well, the people went their ways, and as the days went by, and the Moon never appeared, they talked and talked of nothing else at home, at the inn, and at work. And one day, as some of them talked in the inn, a man from the far end of the bog sat up and slapped his knee. "I'd clean forgotten, but I think I know where the Moon is!" And he told them how he was lost in the bogs and how, when he was almost dead with fright, a light shone out and he found the path and got home safe.

So they went off to the Wise Woman and told her about it, and she looked again in the cauldron and in the Book, and then nodded her head. She instructed them to search until they found a coffin. That was where the Moon would be. So they all set out the next night, feeling more terrified than each thought possible. They stumbled along the paths into the midst of the bogs, seeing nothing in the darkness, while all around them they heard sighs and flutters, and felt cold wet fingers touch them. Then all at once, they came upon the dark pool beside the great dead tree where the Moon lay buried. They found a huge stone that looked like a coffin, and so they all knelt down in the mud and silently prayed.

Then they came closer, and took hold of the big stone, and shoved it up. Afterwards they said that for a moment they saw a strange and beautiful face looking up at them out of the black water, but the light came so quick and so white and shining, that they stumbled back dazed by it. The very next minute, when they could see again, there was the full Moon in the sky, bright and beautiful and kind as ever, shining and smiling down at them, and making the bogs and the paths as clear as day. The Moon's light stole into the very corners, as though she could drive the darkness clean away if she could. [4]

This beautiful folk tale speaks to the loss we suffer when we ignore the gifts and blessings of the Moon. Darkness and evil do abound when we lose the capacity for reflection and imagination that the Moon symbolizes. Because this darkness has been projected onto women, the Moon and feminine consciousness, our culture had lost this capacity for self-reflection and so we are left with our own fears undiminished. We forget that the wise woman looks in her mirror, her caldron and her book to discover what is needed to fix the problem. A wise person searches for answers in all different ways.

Moon Magic

Where we see nightmare terrors, people once saw strangeness and otherworldliness, imagining the moonlit night as the realm of the Faerie Folk. The Hollow Hills, lit by the silvery light of the Moon, were inhabited by the beautiful, magical fays or the People of the Sidhe, very like the magical elves of Tolkien's Middle-Earth. Although the faeries have been connected with the spirits of the dead, they are rarely depicted as truly malevolent. At most they are tricksters who make fun of clumsy humans. Like the land of the dead, their land exists out of time; there is no death, no age, no sickness, no ugliness. It is a moonlit land where its inhabitants feast, dance and make music, and while there is no death there, there are many accounts of births.[5]

While there is a psychological danger of getting lost in such a fantasy world, the real peril for a mortal going to the Faerie realm is that you lose your sense of time. The tales say that humans who go there for a night of feasting and rejoicing soon find out upon returning to this world that many years have passed away. We fear getting lost in such a world, but we also fear losing the world as we know it, which is the price of living with this new vision. Faerie is the land of our hopes and dreams. Inevitably, it is the gifts we bring back to our own world from that realm that make the lost time fruitful.

But this realm of feminine, lunar consciousness does not lead to lunacy if we approach it with consciousness. We have to wear the golden dress of the Sun before we can dance in the silvery dress of the Moon. The Moon symbolizes the light in the Unconscious, the ability to bring conscious awareness to those parts of ourselves that are still in the dark, a necessary task if we want to nurture our souls. We do this when we pay respectful attention to our dreams and intuitions, our feelings and instincts; listening to their wisdom gives us greater insights into our life choices and those of others.

If we can look at our nocturnal nature, with its strangeness (which really isn't so strange) and its otherworldliness (worlds which are open for exploration), if we can look at it without fear and terror, we might find its true magic and learn to integrate it in consciousness. Anyone who has worked with her own dreams will understand this. Our unconscious visions and dreams can fertilize our daily lives, and give us direction and wisdom. As a source of our dreams, and therefore of our creativity, the Moon was revered as the Muse of the Arts. And as the cyclic pattern governing all life and renewal, the Moon shows us that times of rest, meditation, vision and gestation (the fallow times) are as important a part of life as times of growth and production. The time spent in Faerie is well spent if we return with creative vision and birth it in this world.

Possibly the reason the moonlight is potentially so frightening to us is that it covers over our daylight reality with enchantment, giving everything a new look, an unfamiliar shaping, an unrealistic blending. The night is alive with shapes and sounds that we do not see or hear in the daylight world, or shut up within our houses. As a culture, we have chosen the daylight and rationality, so we devalue a light and a consciousness which is unfocused and ever-changing.

In the moonlight, the boundaries of things are blurred; new relationships are imaginable. Things flow in and out of each other as the light moves. Dark and light interact in one sphere to create wholeness, unlike the Sun which creates an opposition of light and darkness. Solar consciousness is the driving force behind our culture, and it is associated with the masculine principle. It is a consciousness that separates and discriminates, makes boundaries and creates shadows. Lunar consciousness, associated with the feminine principle, dissolves those boundaries and unites things. It sees discrimination and transforms it into discernment, turns boundaries into transitions and shadows into doorways. Just as the world needs both lights in the sky, we need both types of consciousness. To honor both types of light equally, we have to learn how to feel our way in the dark until it is just as comfortable as moving through the light.

The Dance of the Sun and the Moon

The Moon's light is a function of its relationship to the Sun. The amount of light we see reflected by the Moon changes day by day, waxing to the full Moon, waning to the new Moon once again. This soli-lunar cycle[6] creates an increase and then a decrease in light as the Moon separates from and then reunites with the Sun. Since ancient times, the Moon cycle set the agricultural tempo and farmers and gardeners still plant by the phases of the Moon. This natural cycle can also symbolize the psychological process of growing our consciousness.

The cycle begins at the new Moon, when the Moon travels between Earth and the Sun and is hidden in the Sun's light. The new Moon phase is a time of beginnings, when the Moon disappears from the night sky. This monthly sowing phase, while the Moon travels the daytime sky, is activated by the Sun's position in the heavens and the energies that position focuses. A winter Aquarius Sun is a very different energy and light from a Leo Sun's light and energy. That energy is absorbed by the Moon's conjunction with the Sun, and gets released throughout the cycle's duration. Internally, it activates our unconscious response to life. A new Moon fertilizes ego consciousness by opening the Unconscious like a womb and planting a seed to be nurtured. During this time, we engage in the world subjectively. Each month at the new Moon we have the opportunity to respond instinctively to the present moment without old patterns interfering. We might act spontaneously and impulsively, freed from the conscious mind, child-like and open to new adventures. This is the phase when we listen to our body's response whole-heartedly and trust its wisdom.

A few days later, a thin crescent Moon appears in the western sky at sunset, sitting like a vision and a promise of new life. It is the phase of the Moon when we can see the outline of the whole Moon that will be—-a promise of the full moonlight that will once again shine on us. This phase symbolizes a time when we struggle against inertia, like a new plant struggles to push up through the Earth. Psychologically, we can speak of it as a testing time, when we either fall back into our old patterns and fears or we learn to focus our energies on the new life we sense awaits us. Each time we confront obstacles and overcome our inertia, we gain strength as well as a sense of our own capability and talents. During the crescent phase, we get to move forward into our new growth.

Next comes the first quarter Moon phase, when the Moon stands overhead at sunset. It is 90 degrees away from the Sun and their energies are squared-off of each other. It is time to take some action that will further manifest our goals. In a plant, this is the time when it puts down roots and sends out stems and leaves. Likewise, this is the time for us to test ourselves in the world, taking on challenges that will lead us to our goals. It is a time of decision-making, when circumstances force us to make a choice and then take action on it. We develop our will, courage and confidence when we move forward in our lives and meet the crisis, conflict and challenge of making our own way in the world. We must learn to take control of our own lives, otherwise we are caught up in tensions, frustrations and anger over lost opportunities and inadequate support. Like the hero's journey, this is the time to push through obstacles, both within ourselves and in the outer world. When we do, we commit ourselves to finding workable ways to fulfill the promise of the new Moon.

The gibbous Moon phase occurs when the Moon is growing towards fullness but is not yet completely there. Like a plant that needs more light, more water and more time before it can blossom, during this phase we try to analyze and perfect the goals we've been working toward. Sometimes we experience so much outer resistance or run into unexpected details that we feel dissatisfied and discouraged. On an inner level, this is a time for self-improvement and analysis, a time to disregard the non-essentials and question what we are doing. Through this search for perfection we hone our skills and perfect our techniques.

The first, instinctive part of the cycle finds its completion with the full Moon, when it stands opposite the Sun in the sky, receiving and reflecting back the full light of the Sun. The flower has finally blossomed! This phase is a time of fulfillment if we have worked hard at the previous parts of the cycle, a time when the seed potential begun at the new Moon matures. Since the full Moon begins the second part of the lunar cycle, this is the time when we develop objective awareness. Now we begin to become conscious of our purpose, of the meaning of what we have created. Psychologically, this phase offers us the possibility of consciously pursuing our life's purpose by fully integrating the polarity of the Sun and Moon, of inner and outer, of self and other. It is the internal balancing of these opposites that brings us the clarity and objectivity and self-awareness of this part of the cycle. When we learn to bear the tension of opposites, we discover that a third way, which Jung called the transcendent function, opens up. It is a result of each side understanding the importance of the other. The Sun's spiritual purpose is accepted by the Moon's soulful reflections, just as the Sun accepts that the vehicle for expressing and achieving its purpose is the Moon-shaped personality. It is the alchemical marriage of the Sun/consciousness and the Moon/the Unconscious which engenders a time of revelation and illumination, of creative fullness and conscious awareness. It is always a time to engage ourselves out in the world, to experience the fullness of life, especially through our relationships. We have entered the phase where we must think before we act, so that our actions are considerate, caring and meaningful.

After the full Moon, the Moon starts on its journey back to reunite with the Sun. The light begins to decrease, and the plant to bear fruit. During the disseminating phase of the Moon, we can communicate what we learned during the first part of the cycle, the meaning of our experiences and what we value because of them. This is the phase when we learn to walk our talk. Our lives are changed and we now can teach others how to do the same. This phase opens us to working with like-minded people, sharing information and experiences and creating new forms of group action.

When we reach the dark and mysterious last-quarter Moon that rises around midnight, we find ourselves contemplating what we have learned and deciding if we still believe in it. This phase provokes a crisis in consciousness, a time to confront our belief system and question our assumptions. In the plant cycle, it is the time after the harvest when whatever remains is left to decompose and go to seed. Psychologically, it represents a time when we let go of old ways of thinking about the world that no longer serve us. The energy forces us to confront our old belief systems and discover if they are still viable. If not, we need to let go of them; if they are, we save them like seeds for an unknown future. We have to let go of the past and begin to orient ourselves towards a new cycle. It is time to invest in the future.

The very last phase of the soli-lunar cycle is called the balsamic phase, the old crescent moon that rises just before sunrise and later disappears completely. This final phase of the Moon become a bridge between the old and the new cycle. This is a time to distill what we have learned in the cycle, and to transform it into a vision that can seed the next new Moon. Psychologically, this is a time when we can release and transform old energies. This phase is a wisdom phase, when we have to use both our instincts and our intellect to finish up old business and clear the decks for a new cycle. Living a new vision in the midst of an old collective or personal reality is the lesson here. This is Lady Wisdom manifesting fully. Otherwise, we refuse the lesson and get so stuck in old wounds that the world bears the blame for our refusal to let go and die. You could say that collectively we find ourselves in this situation today-our old way of life no longer works, and instead of distilling its wisdom and envisioning a different future, the *powers-that*-be hang on for dear life and create death all around instead.

It is important to pay attention to these lunar cycles and understand how they affect your body, soul and spirit. Pay attention for a few months to your dreams, especially around new and full Moon. See what comes into your life during the waxing stage and then understand what meaning it has for you during the waning phase. What new wisdom have you discovered? After a few months, look at your astrology chart and see what houses are affected by the monthly cycle. This will tell you what aspect of your life is being worked on. Compare it with your experiences and see if using your chart helps you understand yourself better. Making this cyclic rhythm a part of your life is one way to take your standpoint on the Moon, like the Woman clothed with the Sun.

During this soli-lunar cycle, as the Sun and Moon's relationship to each other changes, the light itself is changed. Fierce golden sunlight is received by the Moon and transformed into a cool, silvery light, a *reflective light*. The Moon implies the art of reflective thought and is certainly a metaphor of the consciousness that sends us our dreams every night, reflecting back to us our daytime reality in the form of objective dream images. Our dreams give us the images that compensate or complement our ego reality. Through the light of lunar consciousness, we begin to see different aspects of ourselves and how they interrelate. Dreams give us a perspective on our lives that is greater than our ego perspective; they give us a symbolic vantage point from which to view our own individual story. The Moon symbolizes a reflective mirror with which to view ourselves and our attitudes, our problems and our joys. This soft light promotes inner growth and evolution, just as it induces plant growth.

How the Moon Nurtures Us

The power of the Moon is implied by the many words connected with its linguistic roots. These words take their meaning of the ancient understanding from the Moon's attributes. Some of the words are: MENSIS, month; MENSES, blood flow; MENOS, Feminine Spirit, heart, soul, courage, ardency; MENOINAN, to consider, meditate, wish; MEMONA, to have in mind, to intend; MANIA, madness, possession; MANTEIA, prophecy; MENUO, to reveal; MANTHANO, to learn; MEMINI, to remember; METIS, wisdom; MATRA-M, measure; METIESTHAI, to dream. All these words stem from the one original Sanskrit root HATI-H, which means thought, intention, measure and knowing.[7]

The Moon, and the consciousness and knowing its light bestows, is therefore necessary for measuring, considering, revealing, learning, remembering and dreaming. It is the bringer of wisdom, as well as of madness and lunacy; it gives the ability to walk in the spirit world, or to be possessed by it or the contents of the Collective Unconscious. It also gives courage, heart and soul to the undertaking of becoming human. The light of the Moon is the consciousness by which we incarnate, the light that brings change and growth to life. At a time when our educational system is breaking down, when our children are having trouble learning because of their time in front of the television and the computer, we need to reclaim the powers of lunar consciousness so we can teach our young people to consider, to learn, to think, to have intention, to remember and to dream. We are slowly beginning to bring programs into our schools which teach our children about emotional intelligence. It is already changing the way they learn and behave.

By the light of the Moon, and through a consciousness of images, we can step over the boundaries of our everyday world into other worlds, just as we can see the stars beyond the Moon in the night sky. The Moon stands on the border of our known universe—men have literally stood there, gazing out at the universe, looking back at the Earth. They shared this experience with us: we have seen Earthrise from the Moon, and it has sparked our imaginations, prompting us to explore who we are through feminine, lunar consciousness. Since that time, women have worked to rediscover our true natures through journaling, sharing personal stories, and looking back to feminine goddesses and mysteries.

If the Earth Mother symbolizes the vessel in which our soul is transformed and brought to birth, the feminine principles of the Moon symbolize the process of that transformation. For we are constantly changing and becoming; sometimes in the fullness of life, sometimes in the darkness of depression and death. The Moon's changing appearance is a sign of that state of ebb and flow in all of life's energies. I find it a more comforting light than the Sun's, because it does not demand a constant high level of performance and a splitting of the light from the darkness. It helps me to accept my comings and goings, my being accessible and being remote, for it allows that life is also like the *inconstant Moon*. Yet we fear this inconsistency, and try to push away painful emotions like men do. Of course, repressing our emotions causes depression, and then we anesthetize ourselves to avoid going down into the Unconscious to discover the reason for the depression. We don't realize it is a call to rediscover the ancient mysteries of feminine consciousness.

The Moon Eye of the Unconscious

Just as the Moon's light grows and diminishes, so too does this type of feminine consciousness. It comes to us in waves and sometimes we don't understand it. It's hard on our ego consciousness to be forced to stay in the dark until something gels. But just because it is not consistent does not mean it is untrustworthy. The knowledge obtained from it can be hard for the ego to accept, for it sees what is immediately there, stripped of pretense, ideals and even relatedness, and then it also sees with a vision clothed in beauty. Like the objectivity of nature, life and death, beauty and ugliness are equally present, like the ancient goddesses of Sovereignty.

The eye of the dark Goddess, or what we sometimes speak of as the Terrible Mother, sees *what is* before judgment of good or evil is passed. This eye gives us the ability to see in the dark, to look into the chaos and discern the forms inherent in it. It is a wisdom which looks beneath the outer forms and structures that we know and accept, the structure that forms our world view. At one time, this vision and this knowing was called the *evil eye*. How interesting that it was mainly old women who had this evil eye and mostly men who were uncomfortable at being looked at with it! This might be due to the fact that this intense feminine vision was most plain to women who had endured a life of hardship under men and patriarchy.[8] Of course, this knowledgeable *seeing* makes it dangerous to the collective consciousness and its values as well. It strips away old perceptions and gets back to the essence of reality.

Like Fur Skin, our task is to get in touch with the rhythms of our instinctual life and learn to trust its messages. Then we can dance in our moonlit dress and give validity to our feelings, our intuitions, and our fantasies. We make those rhythms conscious by becoming conscious of the Moon cycle and how it affects us; by paying attention to our dreams; by listening to our bodies and to our feelings; by letting our imagination take part in our decision-making; and by honoring the Moon as an image of the feminine power of change.

The Power of Three Will Set You Free

One of the powers of the Moon was expressed by the number three, an energy which is so prominent in the tale of *Fur Skin* as well as many other tales. Three is considered a sacred number: we have many old sayings about the power of three bringing good or bad luck. When something happens once, we might ignore it as unimportant. When it happens again, we might say it's a coincidence. But if it happens for a third time, a pattern has been established. Now we know that something important is happening: it carries certainty and power, the energy of forward motion, the power of expression and synthesis.

Three symbolizes the stages of human life: childhood, adulthood and old age. It stands for birth, life and death as well as beginning, middle and end. It makes up the trinity of body, soul and spirit. In numerology, three is the number of creativity, talent and knowledge. And in many religions, there is a trinity of gods or goddesses. Christianity picked up on the power of three and declared their God was Father, Son and Holy Spirit. The Trinity symbolizes unity in diversity.

The ancient Moon Goddess manifested as a triple-figured Being, the Creator, the Preserver and the Destroyer. As crescent Moon she was Virgin and Maiden, as full Moon she was Mother and Partner, and as waning Moon she was Crone and Wise Woman. This triple Goddess represented the three stages of a woman's life, as well as Fate. In many mythologies, Fate is depicted as a triple Goddess, the weavers of destiny. In Greek mythology, they were: Clotho, the Spinner of the thread of life; Lachesis, the Measurer, giving the element of chance; and Atropos, the Cutter, who finally cuts off the thread of life. Like the golden spinning wheel that Fur Skin puts into the king's soup after she wears the dress of the Moon, this lunar consciousness gives us a chance to consciously meet our fate.

The Moon measured time for most cultures, whereas we depend on a solar calendar and so are out of sync with the Moon's time. The dynamic energy of the Moon was worshiped as the Bull of the Mother, whose horns symbolized the crescents of the waxing and waning Moon. The zodiacal sign of Taurus represents this dynamic feminine energy. The receptive, opened, meditative, dreaming energy was worshiped as the new and full Moon and was represented by the sign of Cancer. The Moon set the rhythms of life and so was intimately connected to women's lives. Like my dream of the calendar and having to wait, what did we lose when we were banished from our home in the Moon? Perhaps our sense of timing, but certainly our sense of *the right time*.

The Triple Moon Goddess: Maiden, Mother and Crone

The first face of the Moon goddess, the crescent Moon, is her Maiden aspect, representing youth, expectancy, innocence, newness. She is the dawn, enchantment, seduction and fruitfulness. Through her eyes, we see the freshness and beauty of life and hold reverence and wonder in our hearts. She is open to all experiences for she is unafraid of the unknown.

The Maiden is also called the Virgin. Many of the ancient goddesses were virgin goddesses. A virgin was a woman who *belonged to no man*, a young woman who was unmarried. Possibly this is the meaning of Mary being a virgin when she conceived Jesus. Esther Harding's work on women's mysteries suggests that to be a virgin means to be *one-in-herself,* a woman who accepts her own sovereignty. It did not mean a young woman who is sexually inexperienced. To be virginal means being true to nature and to your instincts rather than giving over to another's needs or demands. Virginity is a creative submission to the demands of instinct, rather than a rejection or denial of those instincts.[9] Virgin forests are not barren places, but rather ones that are especially fruitful, for they are unexploited and still totally natural. How many of us, whether woman or man, know how to be virginal in this sense?

The virgin acts according to her own nature. She gives herself to lovers but is never possessed by them; she is never just the counterpart of a male, either god or man. In ancient Greece, this aspect of the Moon was honored as Artemis, goddess of wild things, and leader of the Dance. This Virgin Goddess watched over childbirth and was the womb opener[10] because childbirth demands that we surrender to instinctual rhythms. In surrendering to her instinctual nature, a woman becomes creative.

Each month, a woman can become virginal again with each new shedding of menstrual blood which prepares the womb for new life. At this time, a woman stands grounded in her instincts, ready with her creative potential to meet the demands of her life. This stage represents young women through their 20's, as they go out into the world to work and to prove themselves in the world. This is a time of adventure and exploration, when we learn how to listen to our own natures and learn to be free.

The crescent Moon is an image this new beginning. It stands as a sign of psychic energy emerging out of the darkness of the Unconscious, continually evolving, continuing to bring us new life experiences. Each month the new crescent Moon stands in the western sky at sunset, shining with fragile beauty, evoking a feeling of hope and new life to come. It is during this part of the Moon cycle that we experience a sense of expectancy, for who knows what experiences are waiting for us. It evokes our youthful sense of independence and individuality that sometimes gets lost in the midst of our hectic lives. Our bodies, our emotions and our thoughts can open to new possibilities, where we think outside the box, start new projects, and permit ourselves new feelings.

As the Moon comes to its fullness, it fully turns to meet the light of the Sun. This second aspect of the Moon is the Mother, a stage that represents the creation and ripening of life, the state of adulthood and parenthood. It is the time to take responsibility for yourself and others, to learn the lessons of patience and self-discipline. As the nurturing mother, this stage knows and teaches the mysteries of life, just as a mother teaches her children how to grow up to be good human beings. This is the stage where we learn the power of Love as an exchange, the energy that connects us to others. We first learn to love ourselves in the Maiden stage so we can learn to love others in the Mother stage. One without the other doesn't work, because if we can't love ourselves, we won't know how to love someone else. Jesus said, "There are only two commandments: Love the Lord your God with your whole heart, mind and strength. And love your neighbor as yourself." We must be grounded in self-love to do everything else right. And this self-love comes to us through honoring our instinctive knowing.

A mother's love is unconditional and compassionate, and yet not without discipline. We nurture our children to teach them the mysteries of life, and sometimes that means not giving them what they think they need, but letting them learn how to get it for themselves. Mother has the wisdom of life at her core, and she teaches this wisdom by example as well as through any creative endeavor she takes up. The care and nurturing she gives her children, both outer and inner, is reflected in the strength and truth of those creations. Full Moon consciousness nurtures the newly born baby, a new behavior, a new creative project or a relationship in the same way—with love and devotion.

In ancient Greece, Hera was worshiped as the Moon cycle, but most especially as the full Moon, as the Lover or Partner. Although the patriarchy gave Hera the thankless role of the jealous wife, she originally embodied the power of the union of opposites, the power that comes from the sacred marriage of masculine and feminine energies. As the full Moon, She was known as *the Perfect One*, and Zeus, her consort, was called *the Perfector*. Her virginal aspect was not lost but brought to its perfection by union with the Other. From the myths, we know that the patriarchal mind could not allow women to own their sovereignty, and so this mighty goddess became a stereotype for patriarchal marriage. We can see why in Greek mythology Hera gets so terribly angry with Zeus' sexual escapades, for he does not allow her to be true to her nature as the *Perfect One.* He refused to complete her. When we are in relationship, we can neither lose ourselves in it nor hold back from it. True relationship is about incorporating two different yet complementary energies, completing each other.

This full Moon experience is the rounding out of an idea, a desire or a feeling by coming into relationship with others or bringing it into the world in some creative fashion. This full Moon consciousness can look at an ego decision, which thinks there is only one truth, and show it another, equally viable, way to see things. It can hold both ideas until the third, transcendent path opens. A young woman dreamed:

> I am looking at the sky at night together with my mother. I see two huge full moons and I tell my mom how amazing that is and that it is not possible. My mother tells me that she has no glasses and she can't see it. Somehow I have her old glasses with me and I give them to her and she can see everything clearly.

This woman can suddenly see both side of the issue. It's her inner mother who isn't sure she can see both sides. Our mothers can only give us what they know. And so sometimes we have to show them the way. Like Persephone, this dreamer knows something that she has to share with her mom. *Something awesome, something new. A larger, more feminine consciousness.* Perhaps her mother can't get beyond her patriarchal mindset without her daughter's help.

Women in their 30's and 40's are in this stage of life. This is the time of motherhood and marriage, where we learn to partner and to parent. We become involved in our schools and our communities as we help our children grow into adulthood. This is when we learn to work with a partner toward a common goal. It is a time when we can be perfected in our sense of ourselves. To really meet the Other entails an openness, a willingness to be totally present in yourself for the Other; it entails an ability to allow new perceptions or awareness so we can meet the world without retreating back to the stability of old habits or values.

In the story, Fur Skin experiences this full Moon openness when she appears at the balls. She goes to the festival openly, dressed in splendor, ready to meet the king on her own terms. This is the hardest part—to be in relationship without losing our sense of self. This is the point when we need the Moon's virtues of spirit, heart and courage, for it takes a firm belief in ourselves and a deep connection to our soul to meet the demands of life in this way. If women can learn to keep this sense of self in the midst of being in relationship, we can heal the wounds that break our marriages apart. For relationships are in the hands of women and it is one of the ways we can bring about the change that is needed in the world and between men and women.

The third aspect, the waning Moon, represents the Crone or Wise Woman. This was the most feared, least understood aspect of the Moon goddess. This is the aspect that was called the Hag, the Terrible Mother, the Witch, the Wise One. This aspect of the cycle deals with death, the end of cycles, and the mysteries surrounding re-birth. The more we fear old age, death, and the unknown, the more we fear this aspect of the cycle. But if we can accept this part of the cycle, we will find the treasure of wisdom that we've been seeking: the wisdom that sustains life, the wisdom to evolve our consciousness.

The Crone, whose name means crown, symbolizes the achievement of wisdom culled from the experience of loving and nurturing that we learned at the full Moon as well as the wisdom of the Virgin who knows herself. Just as we find a peace and harmony within as we grow older-as the fire and impatience of youth is felt but is no longer overwhelming to us-so too the waning Moon is a time of introversion and withdrawal. It teaches us to be alone with ourselves. It is a time to realize what we understand and the wisdom that comes from that knowledge. No one would ever mistake the waning moon for the waxing moon, for there is a wholly different feel to each of them. I am always struck by the beauty of the waxing crescent, which fills me with hope and excitement, whereas the waning crescent rising after midnight always leaves me with a feeling of mystery, of being far away and alone. You can tell the light is sinking toward death.

This is the aspect that was worshiped and later feared as Hecate. In ancient Greece, the power of the Moon also belonged to the goddess Hecate. She was called, like the Moon itself, the *most lovely* and had three aspects: Hecate Selene, the Moon in heaven, Artemis the Huntress on Earth and Persephone the Destroyer in the underworld. Hecate originated in Egypt, where she was the midwife or wise woman, who commanded *the mother's Words of Power*. The Greeks finally came to worship her as the Crone who guarded the triple crossroads, the central axis where the different worlds meet. She held the powers of prophecy and magic, as well as the ability to commune with the dead. We no longer fear, as later Christians did, Hecate as the Goddess of Witches and Magic, for we know that magic is the power to see the energies of life and direct them with our will and not necessarily the work of evil powers. It can be used for evil, but that depends on the person. We create magic when we use the power of intention and ritual to enhance our lives. This is Crone energy, and it represents the power and wisdom of Moon consciousness. Women in their 50's and older begin to feel comfortable with this energy, and as healers and wise women they bring healing to their families, their communities and to the world.

It is the wisdom that facing death can bestow, the energy which sinks into the darkness of the new Moon, the psychic energy that sinks back into the Unconscious to be renewed. The old life must pass away so that new life can come. The wisdom is not lost in that darkness but rather transformed, so that it becomes part of the new virginal energy which re-appears at the crescent Moon once again. With each new cycle, we add to our understanding and go deeper within the mysteries of life.

The Moon Goddess also has a fourth aspect, the dark and hidden side of her nature. This is the mystery, her death aspect, the time of her descent into the underworld, the time of the dark of the Moon. In ancient Greece, this dark side of the Moon was ruled by Persephone, the Queen of the Dead, the guardian of the treasures of the underworld. It is why she is also the Spring Maiden, for she comes back to the outer world with the gifts she has wrestled from the darkness of the unknown. The fact that this goddess was worshiped as life-giving and death-dealing shows that these aspects cannot be separated. But since we have separated them, the terror of death is ever with us. The ancients worshiped this power through the initiation of the Eleusinian Mysteries, which gave them the immediate experience of a death and rebirth which helped them to accept the terror of death and separation from their old life. It is this initiation that we have to undergo if we want to experience the power of feminine wholeness.

The Moon's Initiation:
The Descent to the Underworld

Sylvia Brinton Perera describes this descent in her marvelous book, *Descent to the Goddess.*[11] Exploring the Sumerian myth of the Goddess Inanna's descent to the underworld realm of her dark sister Ereshkigal, her death and rebirth and eventual return to the heavens, Perera describes our need to descend into the underworld of the Unconscious and stand before the dark, repressed feminine that rules there within our psyches. If we can allow ourselves to make that dark journey, leaving behind our everyday attitudes as Inanna left behind her power in her clothes and jewels at the seven gates of the underworld, we will confront a feminine side of ourselves that has been relegated to the darkness by our collective consciousness of the light. We can regain the lost knowledge of the feminine from this dark sister, the wild woman in our psyches, Fur Skin wearing her mantle of furs, if we have the courage to look on her and honor her, which means honoring our deep wounds, our fears, our despair as well as our intuitive knowing and vision. Then we can begin to bring some of her power back up into the light of everyday reality. I believe that this is the renewal we are all searching for, for from this death and rebirth a new Feminine Spirit is available to us, and we will be able to see, with our dark sister's *eye of death*, what it is that we really want and what is demanded of us by our destiny.

Once we have made this initial descent to the dark Goddess and we connect to our repressed feelings, each menstrual period and each cycle of the Moon gives us another chance to go within and listen for wisdom. At the dark of the Moon, or during our bleeding, the new birth occurs. This is a stage of border crossings, when we have the potential to break into other realities, when our ego consciousness sinks into the depths, and we are bereft of light. Outwardly, it is often a time when we feel distant and cold, unrelated and hidden. Life feels barren, like a dead thing. We experience this as a time of depression, grouchiness, being out of touch, yet touchy. This happens when psychic energy goes into the Unconscious, into the experience of being hidden. Our energy is scattered, for there is nothing outside of ourselves that it cares to hold onto. We feel dry and lifeless, for the moist, feeling life has gone through an inner boundary into the darkness of the depths. Usually, we just suffer through it, for we do not realize what is happening to us. But if we can name these times for what they are—a descent to the dark Goddess—we might be able to go into the depths consciously. The way, par excellence, for women to experience this descent, as well as the rebirth of the new cycle, is through our menstrual cycle.

Woman's menstrual cycle is an ebb and flow of energy, a cyclic rhythm we experience in our bodies. If today's ads are any indication, modern women experience it as a disruption in their lives, having no idea of the inner meaning of its rhythms. We only know that the blood flow is a bother, and the only time we look forward to our periods is when we fear we might be pregnant. How far we have come from honoring the gifts of a female body! How will this affect our instincts when women can take drugs and only have their periods four times a year? The menstrual cycle has an inner dimension whose meaning we have lost, for long ago it was called *Woman's Friend* and women knew its hidden mystery.[12] In losing touch with our bodies and the wisdom of our bodies, women lost the means by which we can consciously partake in the creativity and wisdom of Feminine Spirit. For our bleeding wombs are the symbol and the source of life renewed.

The Grail Mysteries

The mysteries of the dark side of the Goddess, which in ancient cultures was seen as the Moon's menstruation, were described again in the medieval myths of the Holy Grail. The Holy Grail is the cup that contained the sacred blood of Christ, used by him at the Last Supper. In the Middle Ages, a body of stories grew up around this legend, and were incorporated into the Arthurian literature. There was a period in the Middle Ages when the feminine principle tried to emerge into collective consciousness. Emma Jung and Marie-Louise von Franz, in their book *The Grail Legends,*[13] see these stories, as well as the emergence of alchemy, as an attempt to re-integrate the Feminine Spirit back into the collective Christian consciousness of the times, the very issue we are faced with again today. Although the attempt seems to have failed on a large scale, there was a resurgence of interest in the more magical consciousness of the feminine imagination.

The Grail stories, which also incorporate some ancient Celtic lore about the goddess Cerridwen's cauldron of plenty, tell of the great quest of the knights of Arthur's court. The Grail appears in a vision to them, and all the knights set out on a quest to find the Grail. They go off alone, making sure not to take the usual tracks into the forest. Only a virtuous knight can even hope to find the Grail, and not many of them succeed. When the Grail hero, whether Gawain, Perceval, or Galahad, finally comes to the Grail castle, he must ask the question, "What is the meaning of this?" or "Whom does this Grail serve?" When the question is finally asked, the wounded Fisher King is restored to health, and the land, which had become a wasteland because of the wound, blooms again. The Grail serves Life, and these knights learn that their purpose is to serve life as well. It is the Grail hero's attitude to the mystery of life, the very fact that he asks the question, which works the magic. Psychologically, this signifies an ego attitude that isn't afraid to look to feminine consciousness for meaning. It is a willingness to ask what meaning our dreams and fantasies have in order to live a balanced and more soul-full life.

Like the story of *The Maidens of the Wells*, when Feminine Spirit is ravished and robbed of its nurturing capacity, the land is laid waste. The medieval stories of the Grail speak of the Cup as the renewal of life, and though associated with the Christian mysteries, it was also about the quest for the hidden mystery of the feminine principle, which is concretely available to women in our own bleeding.

Women's Dreaming Power

In Carlos Castaneda's book, *The Second Ring of Power,* we meet don Juan's women pupils. Carlos learns things from them that not even don Juan can give to him-for he works out don Juan's teachings through his relationship with them, and grows into his power by coming up against them. La Gorda, that most marvelous of women warriors, tells him a secret about *dreaming*, which is the ability to go consciously into the Nagual, or in Jungian terms, the Collective Unconscious.

> "The Nagual [don Juan] told me and the little sisters that during our menstrual periods DREAMING becomes power. I get a little crazy for one thing. I become more daring. And like the Nagual showed us, a crack opens in front of us during those days. You're not a woman so it can't make any sense to you, but two days before her period a woman can open that crack and step through it into another world."

"During that time a woman, if she wants to, can let go of the images of the world," la Gorda went on. "That's the crack between the worlds, and as the Nagual said, it is right in front of all of us women."

"The reason the Nagual believes women are better sorcerers than men is because they always have the crack in front of them, while a man has to make it."[14]

This dark Moon power is this ability to let go of our everyday world and step through it into other realms. We can go within to see visions, feel feelings, grasp intuitions, and then come back with knowledge. Reflect on this knowledge; see it through the eyes of love and you will find Lady Wisdom. This is the transformative power that the knights were searching for in the Grail.

There is a rhythm and a personal form to every woman's menstrual cycle. If each of us can become conscious of our own rhythms, we can gain the knowledge of our sensual and feeling life that will help us reclaim our personal power as woman-in-herself, and not as daughters of the patriarchy. Much of our power lies hidden in the realm of the Unconscious.

As we know, the menstrual cycle is four-fold like the moon's phases. And just as most women's menstrual cycle averages out to about 28 days, the moon's cycle from new moon to new moon is 29.53 days.[15] Even the name menstrual cycle comes from the Latin MENS/moon and MENSIS/month. The idea of measure is connected to these words, and the measurement of time by the return of the Moon reflects the measured effects of a woman's monthly cycle on the people around her. In turn, the ebb and flow of feminine consciousness gives time a qualitative texture, periodic and rhythmic, waxing and waning, opened or closed. It mixes fullness and leanness, light and dark, and a woman experiences this "in the blood tides of her menstrual cycle and its attendant psychological effects."[16]

There is a basic rhythm that is measured by the Moon and the menstrual cycle. There is the waxing and waning of the two crescent phases, the building up (or out) and the drawing down (or in). Then there are the two poles of the full and new Moon, or in the menstrual cycle, ovulation and menstruation. Ovulation, when the ripe egg is shed into the fallopian tube, is the more culturally accepted side of the cycle, for literal fertility and childbearing are honored in a woman of the patriarchy. In the same way, women gladly accept the possibility of full Moon consciousness in their lives.

> At ovulation, a woman's body is receptive and fertile. She may feel then an emotional expansiveness, an abundance of sexual energy, a new potency in her creative ideas and insights.... .If she is related to what is happening to her body and psyche, this time of the month can give her increased confidence and new certainty in her own capacities. Because this sense of herself is rooted in psychosomatic reality, it does not lead to inflation or a drive for power, but to stabilization, and a real sense of her own strength. [17]

The other end of the pole, the blood flow itself, is viewed less favorably by society. Menstruation, symbolized by the dark of the Moon, is the time when the thick, built-up lining of the womb is shed and its wall becomes thin and exquisitely sensitive, like a wound. This can often be a time of pain and separation, and some women still view it as a bother. Nevertheless, it is a time to get in touch with a deeper and more fundamental layer of ourselves, when we touch ground with our instinctual nature. It is an in-gathering of psychic energy, a time when the Unconscious is especially constellated and open to us. This makes it a time "in which the imaginative and interpretive energies are released in body language and symbolic form."[18]

This is a time when a woman can become a shamaness; it is a time when we feel the need to dream and meditate, to withdraw to the other world, to go deep within. At such a time, we can go through the crack in the world and re-emerge with new riches for our lives and our world. Many women dream powerful dreams during this time. Today's women who have PMS often have terrifying dreams during this time, and yet who is to say that these dreams do not reflect a negative sense of self which takes on bodily symptoms during this part of the cycle.

In ancient cultures, women went away to be by themselves during their menstrual period, for this time was considered dangerous and powerful. This was true of ancient Semites as well as Native American women. The women went off by themselves during their moon-time, and dreamed dreams for the tribe. In some tribes and cultures, they were forced to go off for fear that they would *contaminate* the men, the food, the ceremonies. But in most situations, the women chose to separate themselves to explore the feminine mysteries and to bring back to their people the power of their dreams and journeys to the spirit world. We know that when women live and work together, their menstrual cycles come into sync. If nothing else, a group of women got away from the normal life of the tribe for a time each month!

What a better way to deal with this issue, actually honoring the transformative time of the cycle. What would happen if we legislated time off for our periods and we had the luxury of going within unhampered by worry or work. The Dark Goddess and the Christian Black Madonna were equally venerated for their healing powers, especially during this time in a woman's cycle, because it is this cycle which creates life.

Psychologically, this cycle which creates the physical possibility of life also symbolizes the potential for continual change and creative development in our life. Women have the immeasurable advantage of a monthly rebirth of our ego, a monthly renewal of energy and instinctual power in the body that helps us meet life in a more immediate, conscious and soul-full way. Consciously attuning to the Moon's cycles can put us in touch with the great healing and transformative powers of this Goddess. Each month as the Moon tracks through its cycle, we can go through the process of Virgin, Mother and Crone-experiencing, choosing and understanding life. And then rest and get recharged before another phase begins.

Remember my dream about the wounded lion and the great wave? All the elements of the regenerative powers of the Moon are there if we know how to look for them. The dream suggests that there is a wound to my instinctual nature that developed during my childhood. It was a wound of self-confidence and creativity (the Lion). Many people in my generation have experienced these wounds. It should be noted that the baby-boomers have the planet Pluto in the sign of Leo, the Lion. Astrologically it means that our task is to discover the wound to our *royal* nature and awaken the greater passions of the heart. Our generation has to discover that our creativity is meant for the greater good of all, not just ourselves. It is our task to heal the passion of matter. The lion is regarded as the King of the Beasts and so came to symbolize our natural passions and desires. The lion is associated with pride, and emotionality, and healthy, aggressive impulses. In the most profound sense, kingship/queenship is connected with the capacity to wrestle with the passions, for no one can govern or serve as an example to others who has not first governed her/his own impulses. The lion is also very much associated with the Goddess, who ruled the natural world of instinct, intuition and feeling. This lion's wound symbolizes how my generation has to grapple with our passionate nature. It is a call to go deeper into life, for only the wounded healer can heal.

In the dream as in real life, I am trying to protect my daughter from a similar wound. Knowing my wound, and not wanting to see my children wounded in the same way, gave me the courage to confront the lion (my foolhardy friend from college!). At the time of this dream, I did not fully understand the power and sacredness of my feminine, instinctual nature. My spirituality was learned from the Father and so I was cut off from my body. It was this dream that led me along the path to feminine wisdom, and helped me become conscious of a more earthy standpoint and feminine spirituality.

I am always amazed at how the symbolism in dreams is woven together! When I had this dream, I was just beginning my study of the ancient goddesses, and it was not until years later that I finally understood the full meaning of the images of the dream. After the dream shows me that I am becoming conscious of this wound to my instinctual nature, it shows me the next step in the process-how it will be healed. The triple crossroad, a form of the *world axis*, was sacred to the Greek Hecate, the Old Crone or Wise Woman. As guardian of the crossroads, where the traveler is faced with three choices, the Wise One offers the possibility of going beyond dualism, to that third possibility which Jung calls the transcendent function. By this, he means that if you can bear the tension of the opposites (hold on to two opposing ideas, feelings, energies) until a new, third way appears, this new path will be the perfect, balanced response to the situation.

Hecate's objective eye sees into the underworld of the dead and repressed, while her magic and Sight understand what is needed for new life. Hecate never lived on Mt. Olympus with the other Greek deities, but chose to live in this world, where she had great power over earth, sea and the heavens. She had many positive attributes which were discarded and repressed when we lost our understanding of the dark side of the Goddess. She has come down to us through Christianity as the Queen of the Witches and of the Dead, and we caricature her image every Halloween. She helped Demeter discover that her daughter Persephone had been ravished away by Hades. She gives us the gift of intuitive knowing and her symbol is a torch. She is the one who lights up the darkness of the Unconscious and reveals its treasures. She is an aspect of Lady Wisdom.

In the dream, it is under the protection of this wise energy that I realize I will give birth to a savior. The Sight comes over me just as the giant wave does. The savior, in one sense, is that virginal aspect of myself that is imaged in the waxing moon that appears after the wave washes over me. The regeneration, from old waning moon to new crescent, occurs with a rebirth of feminine consciousness. This rebirth is occurring on many levels in many people. We are living in a time of great upheaval and change, and the world as we know it will be vastly different in the future. Already, people are fighting injustice and corruption; more people are getting involved and learning how to stop the illogical and destructive forces that run our society. Like the Swiss people in my dream, it is time for dreamers to become practical and bring their visions into the world. The rebirth of Feminine Spirit and of our culture can only take hold if we let it root itself in our everyday lives, and we must cultivate and work with it so the seeds will grow. It is the Moon's rhythms, which we can see nightly, which bring about concrete change and growth.

I had this dream right before my period, and as you can see, it put me in touch with deep feminine wisdom. Penelope Shuttle and Peter Redgrove, who wrote *The Wise Wound,* feel that this wisdom is recoverable by any woman who turns to it.

> The strange fact about this moon knowledge… is that it is knowledge that is recoverable from age to age wherever women menstruate and wonder how their own interior changes are related to the changes of the moon and the tides. It is not like masculine knowledge, that is built up from painful generation to generation, and which can be lost utterly if the chain is broken. Women's knowledge is available to them if they will only look inwards and give themselves trust, and not be afraid to personify with (for example) goddess' names, those forces greater than their own selves that move them;

and not be afraid to learn from themselves rather than from men who abuse their "credulity" which is their openness, and their "impressionability" which is their ability to take what is happening and what is communicated to them, even by men, deep within. [19]

The Moon is the Mistress of the Waters of the Collective Unconscious

There is one last connection to make in our discussion of lunar consciousness: the connection between the Moon and the waters of the Earth. We know the Moon's orbit causes the tides, both in ourselves (composed of 80% salt water) and in the seas and oceans. In my dream, there is a connection between the Moon and the giant wave. This giant wave is a recurring motif in the dreams of many people today, and I think it symbolizes an important aspect of the psychic changes that are occurring in the Collective Unconscious.

Right now, the equinox position in the sky is shifting from the astrological sign of Pisces the Fish to the sign of Aquarius, the Waterbearer, who empties the water of life out onto us all. Jung saw Aquarius' image as a symbol of the outpouring of the images of the Collective Unconscious-an opening to the imagination which could renew our culture. Some people feel that this will be an age in which humanity will become holy, when we incarnate the Divine Spirit within our humanness, so that the "Godhead might be made manifest in Nature, and all of Nature would become the self-expression of the Godhead."[20]

The wave, though potentially destructive, can also give us the energy of the water of new life. The waters of the Earth are the most ancient creation, the closest to the primordial Spirit of creation, for everything is born of the waters, whether rivers, springs, wells, lakes or seas. The ancient Greeks imagined there was a river of live waters surrounding the Earth like a serpent swallowing its own tail. Jung felt that the ocean symbolizes the vastness of the Collective Unconscious, out of which individual ego consciousness emerges. The waters of the Collective Unconscious are stirring, and the wave, as an image of the new age, is bringing these images to us for conscious realization.

But the sea itself is formless, and the Moon is the Mistress of the Seas, for it is the magnetic pull of the Moon that creates the tides and gives form to the life of the waters.[21] One of the most precious forms that the waters give birth to is Aphrodite, the Goddess of Beauty and Love, who in turn awakens *psyche*, or soul, within each of us.

The waters of the Earth move to the rhythms of the Moon, just as our inner waters, including our feelings and emotions, are influenced by the Moon's force. In astrology, the Moon rules these inner tides, for they are the flow of psychic energy which moves us through life. Psychologically, it is our lunar, feminine consciousness, our subliminal consciousness that comes and goes which magnetizes the Unconscious and creates the images of our instinctual needs and desires. If we can tune into these images consciously, we pick up the information we need to live well and wisely.

The Moon, the ancient symbol of Feminine Spirit as *psyche* or *soul*, mediates between *spirit* [Sun] and *body* [Earth]. It is through *soul-making* that we become conscious of our individual lives; through our souls we express the Feminine Spirit here on Earth as we live out our individual destinies. If we are to become whole, we need to bring into balance the forces of the masculine and feminine energies at play in the universe. And that balance is achieved within the soul.

The path of individuation and individual creativity is a journey that each of us must take if we want to transform the way we live on this precious Earth. Like the Grail knights, we must enter the forest off the beaten track and make our own way to the initiation that awaits us deep within. As women, we have the great gift of our bodies through which we can experience the rhythmic energies of creation. When we listen to and trust our body as it responds to the energies of the Moon, we can access the transformative powers of the universe. As we once again learn to live within the Moon, we will come to understand and honor her light. The vision and consciousness of this light that manifests in dreams, fantasies and imagination, in the voices of our feelings, our intuitions and our bodies will create the balance that our culture so desperately needs.

When we take our standpoint on the Moon, it is a commitment to live consciously within the rhythms of the transformation of life, constantly changing, eternally becoming. Then we can discover a spirituality that encompasses the world we live in and the many worlds beyond.

The Unicorn: Archetype of Feminine Transformative Power

The power of the archetypes to initiate transformation comes to us through the symbols of the Collective Unconscious, which are accessed by our lunar consciousness. Of all the many images that have re-appeared within collective consciousness in the past few decades, there is one that represents the process of transformation itself, a symbol of this lunar consciousness. Our longing for renewal is reflected in the figure of the unicorn. The unicorn is another image of the earthy spirit that finds Fur Skin in the forest of her imagination, the Masculine Spirit of possibilities that is only attracted to a woman who is virginal, a woman who is whole and complete in herself.

Of all the legendary animals, the unicorn[22] speaks to our spirit of the possibility of an imagination that might be real—our desire for an imaginary being to really exist. The fact that the unicorn is once again appearing in modern dreams and fantasies, as well as in various art forms and popular artifacts, points to its role as a mediating symbol of the energy and power generated by the movement and development of the archetypes. The unicorn, combining both spirit and nature, calls on us to use our imaginations to bring about transformation in the world.

The unicorn has always inhabited the distant edges of the known world. In ancient times, there was always a mixture of fantasy and reality regarding it. It had been sighted in India, Persia, or Tibet, or some other exotic land that was particularly inaccessible. No one knew if it really existed, but everyone was willing to believe that it did. In the same way, most of us hope that there is more to life than what we see around us—a greater power than our modern consciousness will admit to. The unicorn established its place in western culture through its inclusion in the Septuagint translation of the Hebrew Bible, and through a bestiary compiled in the early centuries of Christianity. Within Christianity itself, the unicorn became more than just a magical, extraordinary being. It became a symbol of Christ, who showed us the way to transform our humanity into our divinity. This symbol initiates our search for Lady Wisdom, for only a whole person have the capacity to listen for her voice.

The unicorn is fierce and wild, and it cannot be captured by force. It will only come willingly to a virgin. In the Middle Ages, the virgin came to be associated with chastity, although now we see that a very different kind of virginity really attracts it. If the unicorn is an image of the wild, instinctual energy that comes from contact with the archetypes, the only attitude that can tame it is a strong stance of being-in-oneself. The unicorn is intimately associated with the virginal feminine because it can only work through a feminine attitude of openness and acceptance of the new thing that wants to be made conscious. This type of virginity—a completeness which is open and receptive—calls the unicorn to itself. If this is truly the case, then in the Middle Ages, that wild spirit was either held in captivity or else destroyed by patriarchal expectations. We have only to look at the famous Unicorn Hunt tapestries to see how this was accomplished. It seems that women were lead to betray this wild spirit in themselves for the sake of their lovers (or more probably, for the safety of their lives), for the tapestries depict women calling the unicorn to themselves, only to betray it. The ultimate act of betrayal of a Father's Daughter! Ironically, we can also see how the transformative spirit of Christ, which the unicorn symbolized, was itself destroyed by the rigid, one-sided masculine attitude of the Church.

We also find that the unicorn has strong erotic connotations, often appearing as the lover of the virgin, which brings us back to the original meaning of virgin being a woman who belongs to herself. As I mentioned before, the power and force of the archetypes are connected to the instincts, and when any transformation takes place, it is felt in the body. Carnal knowledge is not necessarily understood only as sexual knowledge; rather, it means the knowledge of the body. We have to integrate knowledge in our bodies before the transformation is truly complete. This is why Fur Skin must toil in her mantle of furs in the kitchen. The body never lies. Any new consciousness of necessity must shine through the body. The unicorn is a beast, and the spirit it represents is the beauty and truth of the Feminine Spirit in nature, the realm of the Goddess. The unicorn symbolizes that transformation which arises out of the very nature of our humanity. When we discovered Spirit living within us, we desire it as if it were a lover.

In the following dream, these elements are present, along with the wild, and seemingly destructive, power of the unicorn. We must remember that the power of the Unconscious is dangerous to our ego consciousness, for when it sees the necessity of change it is ruthless in bringing it about. But there is always danger to be faced, and the hero and heroine know that destruction and new life come of it. It is interesting that the dreamer begins to be afraid only after her father, who like the old king represents an old masculine attitude, appears in the dream. At this point, she loses her virginal stance and can no longer accept what is happening.

> I am outside at night, looking up at the stars. I see a very bright constellation of stars that reminds me of the unicorn's horn on my shoulder. I look closely and see a small group of stars in the bigger pattern which are also on my shoulder. As I watch, the stars seem to flow together, and as they disappear in the heavens, I feel a force, like a strong wind, go right through me.
> Whatever has happened, it disrupts things on earth. Some kind of futuristic scientific complex is especially disrupted. I am walking around, trying to find out what is happening, when I meet some people who are connected with the unicorn constellation and the disruption. Their leader is a very powerful woman. I tell her that I have the unicorn's horn on my shoulder, and ask if I am part of this conspiracy. She says that I am.
> Then I am with three people from this group, a very handsome man and two beautiful women. We are in a room full of other people, and the three of them kill everyone in the room. This does not bother me at the time, for I can feel that it is necessary. But suddenly, my father comes into the room and I start telling him about what these people did. Now I start to be afraid. I try to get them out of the house. When they leave, one of my sons locks the door, but another one unbolts it again. I tell them to stop it, and suddenly see the three people looking in the window at me. Now they look evil to me and I'm afraid. I go outside and tell them to go away. I know that they'll be back, because I really am one of them. Later, the man comes back and taunts me, trying to make me go with him. I think I try to hurt him.

This woman felt the awesome power of transformation as something to be desired. There was a beauty and truth to it that sustained her through the death of her old way of being. But at some point, an old attitude that feared the changes that her life was going through made her

199

step back into an old perspective. Now she was afraid of the very energies that she had aligned herself with earlier. Once she came to understand what was happening, she decided to do an active imagination with the dream images. Jung discovered that you could work with the images of the Unconscious by meeting them as equals; that is, the ego allows that these fantasy images are real and engages them in a conversation. This technique is similar to, but not the same as, most creative visualization techniques. In active imagination, the images arise from the *mundus imaginalis*, the imaginal realm between pure Spirit and earthly life, and ego consciousness observes and interacts with them. The images are not imposed from without, but rather arise from within. *This woman went back to the point in the dream when she hurt the man and told him that she was afraid and asked him what she needed to do. He told her that she must see his beauty and his truth and then he would be healed. She accepted his challenge and he was healed.* The wild power of transformation is destructive to old ways and habits, to the attitudes and values that need to die. It kills out of necessity, so that new life can come into being. One can only accept this necessity through seeing with the objective eyes of the Goddess. Otherwise, from the old standpoint, it is too scary!

The horn of the unicorn, which shares the qualities of the phallus, is potent as a charm for health and new life. There is a legend that the unicorn, merely by dipping its horn into the water, is able to purify and rid it of the deadly venom of the snake so that the other animals can drink of it. As mentioned earlier, the snake belongs to the ancient Goddess, representing her power and wisdom, as well as her healing. The serpent power is connected with the life energies called the kundalini, and in the West, came to be associated with the Devil and with evil. Hopefully, our relationship to this most ancient and sacred symbol will be changing in the future, so that we may have access to its healing powers.

I would like to end with an active imagination that speaks of a new realization of the power in nature which the unicorn represents. It seems that we can no longer kill, capture, or even tame the unicorn's transformative powers, as they did in the Middle Ages. Today, in our rapidly changing culture and with the development of consciousness in many new directions, we might consider letting the unicorn teach us its wisdom and show us how to handle the transformations that are coming our way. This could be the knowledge we need to turn back the tides of destruction.

I see a beautiful, strong white unicorn, running in a field, with his mane and tail flowing in the wind. I manage to go up to him and he lets me touch him. I am amazed that he gives me this honor. Then he tosses his head and runs off, only to return again in a moment. He starts circling around me, running faster and faster, closer and closer, while I stand there watching him. As he runs, he kicks up the dirt, and it starts encircling me in a tower of green earth. Yet it is like transparent green glass to me; I can see through it. Then it turns to the darkness of dirt, and soon I am enclosed in a small earthen tower. There is one hole left open, and the unicorn comes and looks in at me, offering comfort. Soon I sit down on the ground across from the opening and the unicorn, and wait.

After a while, I feel something on my forehead, and I discover that I have a horn growing out of the center of my brow. I see it touching the horn that the unicorn has put through the opening. Slowly, I feel myself turning into something else; when I look, I see that I now have the body of a unicorn. I am a black unicorn. When the transformation is complete, I stand and slash off the entire top of the tower with my horn. It falls away. The white unicorn uses his horn to slash down, ripping away the body of the tower, so that it falls away and I am free of it.

We touch horns and nuzzle. It feels wonderful in this body! Then he starts off and I know that I must follow his lead. We race across a grassy plain, separating and coming together, crisscrossing, playing and exalting in our movement. We come to a wood and he leads the way to a stream. I bend to drink, but I don't know what to do with my horn, it keeps getting in the way of my drinking! I realize that I have to learn how to live in this new body. The white unicorn doesn't have any trouble drinking, and he waits calmly while I figure out how to do it. Then he leads the way up a bank and on into the woods to a clearing.

He stops and starts sharpening his horn against a tree, and I begin to do the same, only I feel badly about scarring the tree. So I end up rubbing my horn on the Earth. But I feel that this is silly, a mere human perception of right or wrong, and so I finally go back to sharpening my horn on the tree. After this preparation, the white unicorn rears up, and I suddenly know that he is going to teach me how to fight. I don't take it very seriously until I see that he really is going to attack me! We rear and lock horns, baring teeth and using our hooves. I can't quite figure out how to use my horn-like a rapier in fencing or like a pike to thrust into something? After a while, the white unicorn stops and turns to face a giant who suddenly appears, as if out of the air. The lesson now continues with the giant. The unicorn rears up and plunges its horn into the giant's belly, rearing again to strike in the heart. With swift and clean strokes he fights, and then the giant vanishes.

Next a serpent appears, crawling on the path. I immediately think, "He will stomp on it or kill it with a flick of his horn." (I had become quite bloodthirsty by this time.) Instead, the white unicorn bends his horn to the ground, and the serpent twines itself around it. I see then that it is a cobra, and am amazed that it submits itself to having the point of the horn pierce through the top of its neck. Apparently unhurt, it settles there like a crown, looking out and all around. The white unicorn looks at me as another serpent crawls to my feet. I bend my head down to let this other snake twine itself around my horn. Since I am really a little bit afraid, I start wondering how it will do this, and if it will come too close to my face. But it crawls up to the base of my horn and winds itself around it, piercing itself, like its sister, on the point and settling down as if it were the Serpent Crown of the Pharaohs.

At this point, my consciousness takes over and I start to remember things about serpents. Were they dangerous to unicorns? Didn't both the unicorn and the serpent belong to the Goddess? I struggle and finally dismiss all these thoughts from my mind, because I want to experience something new.

I look around me-there is the white unicorn, crowned with the serpent of wisdom, and I know that I am just as beautiful in my blackness. We start off down the path through the forest and end up at the ocean. Out in the ocean, a giant wave is coming toward us. As the wave hangs over us, the white unicorn steps into the water and touches his horn to the waters. As he does this, the wave descends on itself, flowing back on itself. The unicorn turns to me and I step into the water, joining him, pushing back and dispersing the destructive power of the wave. We run lightly over the water, as the wave is pushed back onto itself and forms other, smaller waves which sink into the depths and rise up once again. The waters circle around; its power unchanged yet no longer destructive.

Then I look back to shore and see that all along the beach there are multitudes of unicorns, black and white ones standing on shore with their horns pointing into the water, helping to dissipate the destructiveness. And I am happy beyond measure to be one of these guardians; to be there on that beach to meet the great wave.

To become the unicorn is the only way to experience its power and being. A beast who embodies Feminine Spirit is a fitting symbol of the feminine powers of transformation, for it unites our earthy and heavenly natures. Wild, fierce and beautiful beyond imagining, the unicorn stands against the overwhelming powers of collective consciousness. It offers us the opportunity to use our creative powers to help transform the destructiveness of the collective forces at work in our world into the waters of a new birth.

Charge of The Goddess of Wisdom

Whenever you seek wisdom
Come together in love and trust and learn of Me
Who am Living Wisdom.
You who search the mysteries of the Earth,
the secrets of Air and Darkness,
The mysteries of blood and fire, the silence of the uttermost stars;
Come unto Me
And I shall whisper to you in the depths of midnight.
Approach me in the sanctity of silence,
And as a sign that you are free from fear,
You shall bare your soul unto Me.
For fear has no place in My nurturing mysteries,
And that which you seek of me will destroy you if you fear it.
For I am the dolmen arch beyond which
stretch the mysteries of infinity.
I am the silence before birth and after death.
I am the clouded mirror in which you scry your own soul.
I am mist in the twilight, the vast and starry sky
of midnight, shadows on the Moon.
All things come to me in the end,
And yet I am the beginning of all.
I meet you at the crossroads;
I lead you through the darkness;
My hand is the hand you will grasp in the
passage between the worlds.

To the true seeker I bring knowledge
beyond mortal comprehension.
Of you shall I demand the uttermost truth of all that you are;
And in return shall I give you all that you may be, all that I am.
For My wisdom is beyond the ages,
And knowledge of My secrets is power over self, over fear, over death.
I demand of you nothing which you cannot give,
For I am the Mother of Mysteries,
And inasmuch as you know Me,
So shall you learn to know yourself.
Anonymous

Chapter Six
Crowned With Stars: The Fire of Divine Wisdom

The night sky possesses an unparalleled power to excite the human imagination. Intimate, yet infinite. Dark, yet full of light. Near, yet unreachably far. No part of our world displays such immediately accessible patterns of order, and no part of our world remains so deeply mysterious. According to the anthropologists, our ability to count, to factor time, to measure space, to invent myths, and to do rational science are all closely bound up with our ancestral experience of the sky.[1]
—CHET RAYMO, *365 STARRY NIGHTS*

The starry heavens call to us. We know something magical lives up there! That's why we make a wish upon a Star. The stars hold the patterns of our stories, the purpose of our lives. They are the transmitters of Universal Wisdom. Now these patterns are changing, are growing, are deepening. We are in the midst of Galactic change. We are headed into deep space.

Ancient Wisdom

The night sky impresses upon us the vastness of the universe, the unknown depths of life, the awesome magnificence of creation. Even though modern scientists are exploring the heavens and bringing us closer to understanding what those heavens are made of, our individual experience of the night sky is still one of awe and worship.

We instinctively know it is the invisible realm from which all life is created. "We are stardust, we are golden" is the truth, because we are composed of the cosmic dust that forms the galaxies and the stars. Is it any wonder that we've placed Spirit up there in the heavens? And yet the heavens are also within us, and so we search for that lost bit of stardust within the material world as well.

Women exploring our spirituality have a grand passion and hunger for new ways to see and express the spiritual experience of being a woman. Our spiritual search is a search for our lost sovereignty, which is grounded in the sure knowledge that we are inter-connected with each other and the cosmos. Feminine Spirit demands wholeness, which means an equal union with the masculine principle, unlike the separation and domination of the masculine over the feminine that the old patriarchal model demands. Fur Skin's tasks are designed to help her integrate her left-brain, masculine solar consciousness with her right-brain, feminine lunar consciousness. Once that is accomplished, she has to find meaning in her life. She has to find her spiritual purpose. She has to find her relationship to the stars.

Fur Skin's shimmering dress of the stars symbolizes women's search for a new feminine spirituality, one in which we find a new spirit-image which reflects our feminine experiences. Like the starry sky which is 'dark, yet full of light' it is our spirituality which guides us through the darkness of life. It is our spiritual stories which guide our hearts and minds to build a worthy and honorable life. It is our spiritual essence which fills us with wisdom and love.

In the Father's House, we have been excluded from the western spiritual traditions whose vision of reality has consciously and unconsciously excluded women and our experiences of life. If spirituality is the conscious transformation of the ego's attitude to bring it into alignment with the deepest will of the Self, then women who wear the Star dress are dancing to experience, cultivate and express their unique Feminine Spirit. When a woman is true to herself, all her relationships and her creations express the light of truth and the touch of love.

For too long, women have been forced to hide and repress our true nature and accept the projections of men as well as patriarchally approved roles. Freed from masculine expectations, women find the inner freedom to joyfully flourish in our feminine nature. Just imagine what the world will be like when all women have the freedom to use our gifts and to express our perspectives. That time is coming. More and more women are providing strong role models for our girls. And Lady Wisdom is gestating new ideas and images of what women are capable of within the Collective Unconscious. These new archetypal images will arise as women connect to the repressed feminine realms of the Unconscious. As Wisdom's Daughters integrate these new images into our belief systems, we will have the guidance we need to leave the Father's House and establish our own.

Patriarchy, entrenched as it is in our religious beliefs, is firmly embedded within our own psyches. Patriarchy is built on racial, sexual, economic and political domination and oppression, and it has separated women from our unique spiritual gifts which are grounded in our bodies. Its vision has re-shaped the archetypal patterns within the Collective Unconscious for the past 4,000 years. Remember, we are influenced not only by our parents' beliefs as well as by our society's rules, but by the archetypal patterns we psychically inherit—the instincts that make us human. Those instincts, like Fur Skin's mantle, are now waking us up to the fact that we need to create a new story out of the ancient forms. The archetypal patterns are changing and restructuring themselves, because they no longer resonate with our modern consciousness. They've lost their feeling attachments and have become stereotypes. Wisdom's Daughters are called upon to help re-energize the archetypal patterns. While the archetypes create reality, we get to write the stories. And right now, we need wise stories, deep stories, true stories.

One important pattern being renewed is our relationship with the Divine. Instead of religious institutions mediating that relationship, people are engaging in their own spiritual practices, wanting to experience Spirit, and not just believe in it. Patriarchy dare not approve of individual spirituality, because a personal spirituality frees us from outer rules and control and empowers us to be responsible for our own relationship with the Divine. Feminine Spirit sees love and wisdom as the ground of our being, and understands that our ultimate inter-connectedness begins with the knowledge that matter is spirit, that heaven is within us.

Patriarchy, on the other hand, has imposed on us a vision of the separation and opposition of spirit and matter, disconnection from our inner Self, competition with and control of others, domination of wealth and resources and a hierarchy of values based on power and domination, sinners and saved. In patriarchal beliefs, someone is always *chosen*, making everyone else outcast. This is the story that frames the Judeo-Christian belief: being outcast from the Garden made us all, but especially women, sinners. The first great sin of murder occurs because one brother gets *chosen* by God over the other. The choosing of one makes an outcast of the other.

This is why it is so important, as well as so incredibly hard, to break the stranglehold these underlying beliefs have on us, but these beliefs are the source of our rage, our fears, our shame and our confusion. Women have been outcast while men are the *chosen ones*, and we have had to twist ourselves to fit their expectations. The great wound is that we have been outcast from our understanding of Feminine Spirit and life and instead, have been spiritually nurtured only on masculine values. This is why Fur Skin must labor so long and so hard in her mantle before she can wear the star dress. She must break out of the old, damning spiritual paradigm of the Father and discover her true relationship with Spirit. Like this brave princess and Dame Ragnell, each woman has to struggle with the enchantment we've been put under and break free from beliefs that negate our unique powers and destiny. We have to recognize ourselves before we can be recognized by the Other.

It is only by becoming virginal again, being-in-oneself, that we can hope to expand and discover our powers and gifts, and stand up to a belief system that fears power in a woman (which occurs in both men and women). As we go within and look to our inner sky that is 'dark, yet full of light' for new guiding images, we see ancient images of womanhood and the Goddess appearing in the dreams and fantasies of modern women. The stars' light being ancient, the night sky possesses such a 'power to excite the human imagination' because the wisdom that is the Goddess is intimately connected to the imagination. When we look to the stars, we look to understand who we might become.

The Queen of Heaven and a New Dispensation

The Woman clothed with the Sun manifested in other times and other cultures, as divine beings and as earthly women. The stories of the ancient goddesses evoke every aspect of this divine energy. And stories about women who embodied this energy encourage our own search for

Lady Wisdom. Symbolic language still contains these feminine energies and by working with the imagination they are still available in our lives. As Earth, Lady Wisdom is the womb and vessel of our growth into wholeness; as Moon, she is the process of our transformation-the hard work of living consciously with our Self. As Queen of Heaven, she is archetypal wholeness, the mother of all wisdom, self-mastery and redemption through illumination and transformation.

When Lady Wisdom is connected with the Stars, she symbolizes the essence of the divine pattern within each of us, the archetypal patterns which become individualized and manifested throughout our life on Earth. Our wholeness is both light and dark, and our wisdom is our experience, and the patterns which make up the story of our soul through many lifetimes mark our journey on the path of Wisdom.

There are many ancient goddesses connected with the Stars. They were each worshiped as Queen of Heaven, focusing both the vastness and nearness of the cosmos. When we connect to this heavenly Goddess, we connect to the wisdom of the cosmos. Her worship entails living out her spiritual truths and discovering the wisdom in life.

A few years ago, I fasted and meditated to incubate a dream while the planets Pluto and Jupiter where on the degree of the Galactic Center. I wanted to know if there was hope for our world in the coming days. I asked for Lady Wisdom's guidance. Then I dreamed of the stars.

> I am in a house, at least on the second floor if not higher, and a woman behind me says, "Look out the window. The Pleiades are shining." I look and see the stars of the constellation shining brightly – in a blue daytime sky! It is glorious. After watching for a while I go back into the kitchen and see my two little grandchildren playing. I help them with something then go to throw some water down the drain in the sink. When I look, the drain is just a hole and I see clouds beneath me. Then I look out another window and see a constellation of stars suddenly dissolve like fireworks.

The Queen of Heaven sent me this dream. It had a lot to say to me personally, but with star dreams, it always carries a collective message. The constellation of the Pleiades plays a big role in world mythology, concretely associated with the start and finish of the growing season, as well as symbolically associated with the start of a new world age. The dream seems to indicate that a new dispensation is available to us in this time of seemingly great darkness. This new dispensation comes to us from the crown chakra of our galaxy, for the Pleiades are believed to be the anti-Galactic Center. The Pleiades is considered to be the home of the ancestors by many ancient cultures; paradoxically, the star cluster is younger than our own solar system. This new/old archetypal pattern is being resonated within our collective unconscious and rising into consciousness. It is a sign of hope for these changing times. It is Lady Wisdom giving us the message, 'All is well. All manner of things will be well.'

Wisdom in the Judeo-Christian Religions

The Christian Bible gives us this image from *Revelation 12*: *And a great portent appeared in heaven, a Woman clothed with the Sun, with the Moon under her feet, and on her head a crown of twelve Stars.* This image of the world soul is Sophia, Lady Wisdom. Sophia is Creator, Wisdom and Teacher all in one. She appears in times of transformation and change to birth a new world. This visionary image speaks volumes when you understand symbolic language. The Moon as the measure of the natural cycle of change assures us that this feminine wisdom surges in our blood, and will surface as needed if we understand the cycles of life on Earth. The twelve stars in the vision symbolize the twelve signs of the Zodiac, highlighting the different initiations we are here on Earth to undergo. The Woman is clothed with the Sun because she incarnates light, consciousness and Feminine Spirit.

Wisdom is an important figure in Jewish tradition. The Wisdom literature in the Old Testament is concerned with the lessons and significance of our human experience and with the relationship between Creator and creation, giving all of creation significance in the divine order of the cosmos. Wisdom creates meaning out of our life's experience. In this sense, we experience wisdom through the archetypes of the Collective Unconscious, which structure our perceptions of our individual and communal life. These archetypes lay at the foundation of our instincts to marry, to have a family, to create art, to exchange goods, to educate and to govern. And while wisdom is unchanging, our understanding of wisdom can deepen. We are here on Earth to evolve, and that means we have to listen for Lady Wisdom's voice within ourselves, as well as model conscious womanhood to the world.

Since the *Woman* of *Revelation* has come to inspire both men and women, she calls us to be both a lover of wisdom and Lady Wisdom herself. When we find our Beloved we can fully experience the magical partnership between Solomon and Sheba ourselves. Solomon's desire for Lady Wisdom is the mark of a true king who chooses to marry Sovereignty, and being a true lover, he attracts the embodiment of Lady Wisdom in the Queen of Sheba. In Wisdom 7: 8-14, we hear the lover of Wisdom sing her praise.

> I esteemed her more than scepters and thrones; compared with her, I held riches as nothing. I reckoned no priceless stone to be her peer, for compared with her, all gold is a pinch of sand and beside her silver ranks as mud. I loved her more than health or beauty, preferred her to the light, since her radiance never sleeps. In her company all good things came to me, at her hands riches not to be numbered.

A lover of Lady Wisdom knows the treasure of an understanding heart. Lady Wisdom is here in the world with us, waiting for us to love her, waiting for us to incarnate her. We have to aspire to wisdom as well as tread the path of wisdom for ourselves. We are promised that Lady Wisdom herself will be our guide and our grounding. "She is a tree of life for those who hold her fast, those who cling to her live happy lives." (Proverbs 3:18)

Sophia came to be associated with Christ in early Christianity because, as feminist scholars point out, the early patriarchal Church would not tolerate a powerful female deity in their divine story. But later, the Roman Catholic Church associated the image of the *Woman clothed with the Sun* with the Virgin Mary[2], the Mother of God, in her aspect as the Immaculate Conception, referring to the belief that Mary was born without the stain of original sin, for all intents and purposes raising her to the status of Goddess. Mary has taken on all the ancient roles of the Goddess, except that of Lover, and remains a beautiful and truthful image of Feminine Spirit. In honoring the Virgin Mother, we honor a woman—it's always a woman and not a goddess—who was so in touch with Divine Spirit that she became wholly herself and realized her own divinity. Like the *Woman* of *Revelation*, Mary became a Great Mother through her ability to stand consciously in the lunar tides while she centered herself in the spiritual awareness of her womanhood. In giving birth to the World Savior, she nurtured a human man with wisdom, so that he too incarnated divinity. Just as Christ and the Buddha are examples of God-men, so Mary is an example of a Goddess-woman. The image of Mary as Virgin and Mother can encourage and empower us as we give birth to our inner savior and our outer children, and her feminine wisdom can teach us what we must do to heal ourselves, others and the world.

We are now seeing a transformation of this archetype as Mary the Mother gives way to Mary the Beloved, wife and disciple and mother, healing the wound to our physical natures. The Heavenly Mother was remembered in her Lover aspect when the troubadours of Provence sang her praises a thousand years ago. And now Lady Wisdom appears in her fullness as Virgin, as Lover, as Wise Woman. There are many books, especially from *The Nag Hammadi Library*, written about the role of Mary Magdalene in the early days of Christianity. Going beyond such popularizations of her story as *The Da Vinci Code*, we find that Mary was the most beloved disciple of Jesus, and perhaps also his wife. But what is becoming clearer every year is that this woman, who is portrayed as a prostitute by the Church, was really the foremost disciple of Christ. In the *Gospel of Philip*[3] we find: "And the consort of Christ is Mary Magdalene. The lord loved Mary Magdalene more than all his disciples, and kissed her on the mouth often…[the other disciples] said to him, why do you love her more than all of us? The savior answered: Why do I not love you like her?" Mary sets the standard. It was Mary who first discovered Jesus' resurrection and it was she who preached that Christ is found within each of us. This *Woman clothed with the Sun* was lover, disciple and teacher and co-equal to Christ. She is a role model for each of us when we understand that it was her ability to understand and nurture Christ's message, and by living it, grow into a deeper wisdom that made her his partner.

The Gnostics held this heavenly Feminine Spirit in high regard, naming her Sophia, or Lady Wisdom. Sophia is the Wisdom of God, a divine Feminine Spirit pervading all of life. She partakes of the power of the Creator, is capable of doing all things and is regarded as the mother of the gifts of wisdom and prophecy. She is creator, wisdom and teacher, wise in the ways of humanity, nature and divinity. In certain mystical traditions she is the consort of God and the lover and inspiration of the wise. Solomon, the archetypal wise man, declares his love for her: "Her have I loved and have sought her out from my youth, and have desired to take her for my spouse; and I became a lover of her beauty." Solomon, wise man that he was, knew that men need the guidance of a wise woman to temper them. And so Woman becomes Man's soul guide.

But Lady Wisdom is more often than not rejected by men as well as Father's Daughters. When men subjugated women politically and religiously, they repressed a feminine way of knowing that was the counter-balance to their most destructive energies. In rejecting women's wisdom, they rejected the Earth's wisdom. And look what happened to the world! Without the influence of feminine wisdom, western culture has plundered the world's resources to ensure a ready supply of consumers who work to pay their bills. Our culture is rife with death, famine and disease. If we ever hope to become the enlightened society our founders imagined and learn to manage and share collective resources with the rest of the world, we will all have to tread Lady Wisdom's path. And I have no doubt that women will lead the dance.

The Gnostic myth of Sophia is about the fall of Lady Wisdom into matter, her suffering and her redemption, and then the ultimate redemption of all her children. This is another story about the *passion of matter*. We ultimately must become the consciousness of the Earth. The story of Sophia is the story of humanity's struggle to evolve human consciousness.

Sophia, one of the first-born of the primal parents, Depth and Silence, is confused by longing and love for her Divine Parent, and falls into the abyss. Alone and comfortless, Sophia experiences every sort of psychic experience imaginable – passion, sorrow, fear, despair and ignorance. These experiences flow out of her and create not only the four elements of earth, air, fire and water, but also the Beings who end up creating and controlling our world. Looking at the flawed and troubled world created by her own ignorant offspring, Sophia is filled with pity for creation and resolves to assist it in any way she can. Thus she becomes the Feminine Spirit of the world, the

Anima Mundi, watching over it like a mother. Feminine wisdom, entrapped in the material world, must be rescued by the Masculine principle. Yet when her consort, Christ, comes into the world to rescue her and bring her back to the heavenly realms, Sophia finds that she cannot totally abandon this troubled world. And so she splits herself in half, part of her going to the fullness of heaven and the other part staying in touch with this lower world to aid in its redemption.[4]

Through her compassion and wisdom, Sophia bestows light on her children, like the Bodhisattva, Kwan Yin, whose name, Avalokitesvara, means "one who looks down from on high." The Gnostics believed that there was not only a man of light (Jesus) but also a woman of light (Mary Magdalene) who were co-redeemers or partners in the work of salvation. Sophia is the very image of the *Woman clothed with the Sun*, for the archetypal woman brings salvation to men and to the world, just as Christ does.

Down through the ages, mystics have meditated on Lady Wisdom. Jacob Boehme (1575-1624), a German mystic, practiced a form of theosophy, a natural knowledge of God. His meditations and visions led him to understand the workings of nature. And of Sophia. He believed that Sophia is a mirror of God's will, the visibility of God. Boehme believed that Sophia represents the creative faculty, summoning the uncreated into creation, through the power of desire and imagination. Wisdom provides the form, while God provides the matter from his eternal nature.

Jane Leade (1623-1704) was a member of a group called the Philadephians. She had visions of Sophia and held that Sophia gave you the ability to enter into 'one's own Native country and original Virginity.' Wisdom united you with your true Self. She recommended that in meditation, you *Draw into thy Centre-deep...thy Heavens within... because the Virgin...there will first appear...Dive into your own Celestiality, and see with what manner of spirits you are endued; for in them the Powers do entirely lie for transformation.'* [5] Richard Roach, the Philadephians' historian, talked about the correspondence between the female soul and the spirit of Sophia. The Philadephians believed Lady Wisdom is within women and will one day animate women with her graces and gifts. In other words, they believed that more and more women would incarnate this heavenly woman and spiritual power.

Then there was Mother Ann Lee, the founder and spiritual mother of the Shaker movement of Quakerism. She believed that the second coming was within each individual. Many of her followers believed she was associated with the *Woman clothed with the Sun*, and her role was the first born of many sisters and the true Mother of all living in the new creation.

> "the Almighty is manifested as proceeding from everlasting as the *first source* of power, and the *fountain* of all good, the *Creator* of all good beings, and is the ETERNAL FATHER: and the Holy Spirit of Wisdom, who was the *Co-Worker* with Him, from everlasting, is the ETERNAL MOTHER, the *bearing Spirit* of all the works of God.

> As God had sent his only begotten Son, so too, "God, the Eternal father and mother, sent forth into the world their beloved Daughter . . the mother-spouse in Christ, the express image and likeness of her Eternal Mother.[6]

Throughout the centuries, Sophia has lived in the hearts of wise women. Though we have often ignored and reviled her during the height of the patriarchy, she has stayed with us. Remnants of her story are found in the Cinderella (Ella=Light) fairy tales we tell our children. She is the light in nature, the wisdom of creation. And her daughters are awakening and remembering her once more.

Ancient Queens of Heaven

Earlier cultures held Wisdom in high honor, and we find her presence in the goddesses Inanna, Ishtar, and Aphrodite Urania, who are all Queens of Heaven and adorned with stars. One of the most ancient forms of this cosmic wisdom is the Egyptian goddess, Isis. Her divine story was so powerful that her worship spread throughout the Roman world at the same time as the birth of Christianity. In *The Golden Ass* by Apuleius, written over 2000 years ago by an initiate of the Mysteries of Isis, the main character is a man named Lucius, who is on his way to be initiated into the mysteries of the Goddess Isis.

His description is very personal and very loving. It is a portrait of his personal experience of this powerful goddess.

> Her hair, long and hanging in tapered ringlets, fell luxuriantly on her divine neck; a crown of varied form encircled the summit of her head, with a diversity of flowers, and in the middle of it, just over her forehead, there was a flat circlet, which resembled a mirror or rather emitted a white refulgent light, thus indicating that she was the moon. Vipers rising from the furrows of the earth, supported this on the right hand and on the left, while ears of corn projected on either side.... And then, what riveted my gaze far more than all, was her mantle of the deepest black, which shone with a glossy lustre. It was wrapped around her...while a part of the robe fell down in many folds, and gracefully floated with its little knots of fringe that edged its extremities. Glittering stars were dispersed along the embroidered extremities of the robe, and over its whole surface; and in the middle of them a moon of two weeks old breathed forth its flaming fires.... Such was the appearance of the mighty goddess.[7]

Isis' cult spread throughout the ancient world and it offered a fundamental challenge to Christianity until it was finally suppressed in the 425 A.D. Isis was the great Goddess of Egypt and she was worshiped for over 3,000 years, both in Egypt and later in much of the known world. As wife to Osiris and mother to Horus, she was the ideal of loyalty and love, wisdom and healing. And she has come down to us in modern times, through the esoteric traditions, as the Goddess of Magic and Alchemy. Her magic was aligned with the deeper natural laws of the universe. Also, from her own experience of loss, suffering and searching for her dead husband and wounded son, she became a Mistress of Healing. Many of the ancient Black Madonnas in the Christian Church are based on statues of Isis and her son Horus in her mothering, healing aspect. Often this healing came in the form of dreams and visions, such as the vision Lucius himself received on his initiation into her mysteries.

Ancient philosophers held her in high esteem, for she was the embodiment of Universal Nature, the cosmic laws of life. Statues of Isis were decorated with the Sun, Moon and Stars, as well as symbols of the

Earth. She was often depicted as partly nude, often pregnant and loosely covered with a green or black garment. As the source of all life and life processes, Isis is a profound image of the *Woman clothed with the Sun*.

Through the ages, philosophers and alchemists have sought Lady Wisdom. They envisioned her in the Tarot card of the High Priestess, seated between two great pillars, the black and the white, symbolizing the fact that nature works through polarity, and that consciousness comes from holding the tension of opposites. The ancient Druids knew of her, and modern occultists study her mysteries.

Crowned with Stars: The Archetypal Journey to Wholeness

The *Woman clothed with the Sun* is crowned with stars. The crown is a symbol of honor, victory and sovereignty, as well as of wholeness and completion. The crown sits on the top of the head and so represents the wisdom and knowledge of the crown chakra, the spiritual energy center that unites us to Divine Spirit, and is often depicted as radiant energy surrounding the head of a goddess, god or saint. The crown of stars represents this archetypal journey of the awakened soul.

The twelve stars in the vision are believed to symbolize the twelve signs of the Zodiac. Just as the solar hero has to go on the hero's journey through the twelve zodiacal signs to become whole, Lady Wisdom also offers her daughters the same possibility of wholeness.

The Zodiac, made up of the twelve constellations on the elliptic, describes the twelve archetypal journeys the human spirit experiences here on Earth. The signs represent different energies of the four elements: fire, earth, air and water and they represent three different modes of energy: cardinal/initiating, fixed/concentrating and mutable/dispersing energies.

- *Aries* is the first fire sign and its cardinal energy is that initial spark of life that drives us to discover our *self-identity*. It is original fire that comes out of nowhere, the light out of darkness. Aries is the archetypal *Virgin Huntress,* Diana and Artemis, the scout, adventurer and wild woman who tests herself against the world to find herself. Artemis was the goddess of teenage girls before they married, teaching them to listen to their instincts and be true to themselves. The Celtic Morrigan, the battle goddess, as well as the Amazons and Valkyries, are also Aries goddesses. For a woman Aries can represent the Virginal phase of adolescence. *Self-discovery* is the task. *Courage* is the virtue.

- *Taurus* is a solid, fixed earth sign, concerned with establishing our *self-worth,* our talents and our values. Taurus' archetype is *Gaia, Mother Earth* and the whole realm of matter and our relationship with it. The Spring Maiden, Maia (the Pleiad who gave her name to the month of May) and the Celtic blossom-faced goddess, Blodeuwedd, symbolize the beauty and pull of desire of this astrological month. The cow-headed Egyptian goddess Hathor oversees fertility and pleasure, and the Hindu goddess Lakshmi watches over abundance and joy. Aphrodite/ Venus, as the goddess of the body, love and connectedness, is the archetype of the wisdom of our instinctual nature symbolized by this earth sign. Changing Woman is a Native American personification of this Earth goddess. Taurus is concerned with beauty, fertility, sexuality and wealth, all the good things in life. *Self-worth* is the task. *Patience* is the virtue.

- *Gemini* is a mutable, airy mental sign, and symbolizes the Mind and how it works, with its need to understand and learn and experience. Gemini's archetype is the *Teacher*: *Minerva* the goddess of wisdom, strategy, schools and commerce and *Pallas Athena* who energizes the mind's quest for knowledge, strategy and the ability to communicate it. The Indian goddess Saraswati is the Goddess of Knowledge and all literary arts. Her name literally means *the one who flows*, which can be applied to thoughts, words, or the flow of a river. The Nine Muses are also teachers of knowledge. The Egyptian goddess Seshat, the divine measurer, is a scribe and record-keeper, the goddess of knowledge and writing as well as building and mathematics. *Communication* is the task. *Intelligence* is the virtue.

- *Cancer* is the cardinal water sign, able to feel the emotional atmosphere and quickly motivated to do something about it. Cancer symbolizes the archetype of the *Mother*, the emotional energy that nurtures souls and life and creativity. The *Moon Goddess Selene* represents this aspect of Lady Wisdom: the changing energy which engenders growth as well as the ability to feel what the other needs and be able to love and nurture beyond the ego self. The Virgin Mary is a Mother goddess, the Mediator who helps us in times of need. The Lady of the Lake is such a watery mother, as well as Cerridwen, the Welsh goddess of the cauldron of death and rebirth, the moon, inspiration, poetry, prophecy, shape-shifting. Hestia, the Goddess of the Hearth and Home also belongs to Cancer. At best, our inner Self is our true home, our secure refuge. *Unconditional love* is the task. *Devotion* is the virtue.

- *Leo* is a fixed, steady fire sign and symbolizes the self-confidence of the archetypal Queen, source of creative power, the creative artist as well as the individuated person. The Egyptian Lioness Sekhmet is the fierce sun aspect of Leo; both Guinevere and Cleopatra are the guides to Leo's vitality. Bast, the Egyptian cat-headed goddess of pleasure, joy, music, dance, health and healing, embodies the cat energy within women. The Celtic Brigit was the goddess of smiths, and healing and craftsmanship, especially metalwork, as well as a patron of learning and poetry. She is a fire goddess *who creates out of fire. Creativity* is the task. *Generosity* is the virtue.

- *Virgo* is a mutable, earth sign and symbolizes self-knowledge and healing in a mindful, practical way. *Demeter and Persephone, the divine Mother and Daughter,* are the Virgo teachers of the harvest and the seed, the fulfillment and renewal of purpose. They are the archetypal need for completion and renewal and appear as goddesses of agriculture, grain, harvest, fruits, flowers, and the fertile earth. The ancient Egyptian goddess Isis is a healer and the goddess of ritual magic, among other things. She searched for and recovered the 14 pieces of Osiris and brought him back to life. She was the Divine Mother with her son Horus. Many of the Black Madonnas of Europe, renowned for their healing miracles, were once Isis and Horus statues. *Service* is the task. *Integrity* is the virtue.

- *Libra* is a cardinal, airy, socializing sign that motivates us to accommodate of the Other, the Beloved. The archetypal energy of Marriage and Partnership is represented by *Hera,* goddess of the Full Moon, symbolizes the need to unite with another, the urge to be perfected by the Beloved or to actualize our true passions. The tale of Psyche and Eros speaks to the requirements of conscious love and partnership. The Courtesan is also an archetypal image for Libra, the woman who uses sexuality, art and intellect to partner with the Other. *Partnership* is the task. *Respect* is the virtue.

- *Scorpio* is an intense, fixed water sign, concentrating on hurtful emotions that need to be released. It deals with the energies of death and rebirth on an emotional level. But it is a watery death and a fiery rebirth. Scorpio demands that we confront the overpowering emotions that can threaten to swamp the ego. The Dragon Tiamat symbolizes the titanic struggles within our own feeling nature that show up when we are intimate with others. Scorpio's archetype is the *Death Crone, Hecate* of the Triple Crossroads, Persephone, Queen of the Underworld, or the fearsome Kali, the Hindu Great Mother of Death and Rebirth. In Russia, there is the Baba Yaga, another fearsome old hag who deals out death and rebirth. *Transformation* is the task. *Passion* is the virtue.

- *Sagittarius* is the last, mutable fire sign and represents our search for Cosmic Truth, and the archetypal energy is embodied in the *High Priestess and Wise Woman, Storyteller and Priestess.* White Buffalo Calf Woman brings a new teaching and a new ritual to the People and sets the highest value as Peace. Sagittarius asks, 'How do we honor truth in our lives?' The Egyptian goddess Maat personified Truth and Justice, Law and Order. The concept of Maat represented the divinely appointed order of things, the equilibrium of the universe within the world, the regular movements of the Stars, the Sun, the Moon, the seasons and time. *Open-mindedness* is the task. *Truth* is the virtue.

- *Capricorn* is a cardinal earth sign that symbolizes the social order we live in and our desire to contribute our talents to the world. It represents the societies we create. Lady Sovereignty symbolizes this commitment to administer the Earth's bounty for her people. A wonderful Capricorn goddess is Pallas Athena, virgin mother of Athens, the intellectual center of Greece. Athena taught her people about merciful justice and peaceful resolutions. Her wisdom fostered cultural strategy in support of

Athens' welfare, both within and without. Capricorn resonates with The Hours, who regulate time, and the Seasons, who bring forth the changes in seasons. *Responsibility* is the task. *Discipline* is the virtue.

- *Aquarius* is an idealistic, fixed air sign which is concerned with high ideals. It represents our search for freedom and equality for the group, and the archetype is *Paradise*. Star goddesses rule this sign that symbolizes the archetypal realm. Spider Woman spins the web of fate. Fata Morgana, Morgan le Fey of Avalon, works the warp and weft of our lives. The Ancient Queens of Heaven, Nut and Hathor, Isis and Aphrodite, all find their place here as well. *Freedom* is the task. *Cooperation* is the virtue.

- *Pisces*, the last, mutable water sign, is opened to the feelings of the Collective Unconscious. It is Aphrodite, born of the ocean's foam and the phallic power of the heavens, incarnating the final goal of our earthy experience-the Wisdom of Love. The Goddesses of Compassion and Mercy, Kuan Yin, Sophia, and Lady Wisdom, belong to Pisces. For centuries, Kuan Yin epitomized the great ideal of Mahayana Buddhism in her role as "bodhisattva - a being of bodhi, or enlightenment," who is destined to become a Buddha but has foregone the bliss of Nirvana with a vow to save all children of God. Pisces knows we are all in this together, and this water sign gives birth to the highest forms of Wisdom. *Compassion* is the task. *Joy* is the virtue.

Starting with Aries, the original spark of life comes into *being*. In Taurus, it takes on the many *forms* of life. In Gemini, it achieves *consciousness*. And in Cancer, it grows into an *emotional body* and soul. From Aries to Cancer, incarnation takes place. Then starting with Leo's fire, we engage in *creativity*, in Virgo we learn *service*, in Libra *partnership* and in Scorpio we undergo *renewal*. From Leo to Scorpio, we learn the lessons of the Heart, how to tame our passions. Finally, from Sagittarius to Pisces, we find our place in the cosmic order. Sagittarius teaches *cosmic law*, Capricorn strives to build viable *cultural structures* and processes to serve the group. Aquarius envisions a more perfect use of the *collective mind* and Pisces opens us to our ultimate *unity*.

The twelve stars of the *Woman's* crown speak to these astrological symbols and life paths. Each one of us has our initiation to complete, our wisdom to learn, our purpose to be contributed to the world. We each get to wear the crown of stars when we tread the path of Lady Wisdom.

Besides the Goddess crowned or adorned with the stars, there is also the image of the body of the Goddess covered with stars. Nut, the Egyptian sky goddess, was the personification of the heavens and the sky. Her body was covered with stars, and it was said she gave birth to the Sun out of her womb each morning and she swallowed him each night. She represented the great watery abyss out of which all things come and to which all things return. She was called Nut, the great Lady who gave birth to the gods.[8]

The Celtic goddess Arianrhod was another Queen of Heaven, presiding over reincarnation. Her home was Caer Arianrhod, in the constellation *Corona Borealis* or *The Northern Crown*. It is in the area of the circumpolar stars, those stars which circle the North Polar Star and never set. Here at the court of Arianrhod, she is the Goddess of the Silver Wheel of birth and rebirth, and the stern mistress of Destiny. Taliessin, the great Celtic bard, says that he remembers three periods of time spent in Arianrhod's ever-spinning castle in the Corona Borealis, where he underwent initiations, perhaps in former lives. It was believed that souls went to Caer Arianrhod between incarnations.[9]

Very often, the Goddess as Queen of Heaven was regarded as a literal star, usually the morning star and evening star, which is often the planet Venus. There are many myths and legends which connect the morning star with wisdom, and it is depicted as a place from which a savior of the people comes. Isis was associated with the star Sirius, called the Nile Star. It rose in the East just before dawn on the first day of summer, heralding the rising of the waters of the Nile.[10] For the Egyptians, this star literally stood for new life, since the Nile's yearly rising was and is the source of life for them.

These goddess-images of the starry heavens offer us the promise that the Divine Feminine is the ultimate source of a deep, rich life. The Divine Feminine offers us the wisdom of life. The starry realms hold the ancient wisdom of the cosmos, which is at the center of the mystery of the Divine Feminine.

Wisdom's Call: Understanding The Archetypal Patterns

The Arab word *al-kimia* means the art of transformation. Alchemy, besides being a forerunner of the science of chemistry, was also a spiritual undertaking in which the alchemists were trying to produce the Philosopher's Stone. This mystical substance was believed to be an essential ingredient for turning common metals into gold, as well as being the foundation for an elixir of life which would cure any disease as well as prolong life. As a spiritual discipline, alchemy was the art of transforming human consciousness. The Philosopher's Stone symbolized the key to the evolution of human consciousness from an imperfect, diseased, corruptible and ephemeral state towards a perfect, healthy, incorruptible and everlasting state. For the alchemist, the Stone symbolized his evolution from ignorance to enlightenment, as well as the hidden spiritual truth that leads to that goal.

Jung felt that alchemy was an historical forerunner of his own psychology of the Unconscious, whose goal is also the transformation of consciousness. The alchemical images are very similar to those images which appear in modern dreams that depict the production of a new center of personality in an individual.[11] Jung calls this new center the Self, which results from the process of Individuation. The alchemists, like Jung, explored the realm of the psyche, trying to understand its processes through symbolic imagery. One of their most important tasks was to liberate (or discover in themselves) the spirit in nature. Paracelsus, a famous medieval doctor and alchemist, states that the *lumen naturae*, which is the *light in nature,* comes from the *astrum,* the star in each individual. This star is innate in us, for it comes from God; in fact, it is the part of God within each of us. And it is through this light that we can come to enlightenment, for it drives us on to seek out the mysteries and wisdom of Divine Spirit.[12] This divine image within each person corresponds to the archetype of the Self.

The Self is the energetic center of psychic life, the archetype of wholeness which contains all other archetypes within it. Disconnected as we are from our essential nature, we find our wholeness through these other archetypes. The archetypes configure our experiences of life—friendship, parents, siblings, schooling, love, marriage, work, creativity, initiation, death, service, sacrifice, transformation. They hold the patterns of relationship and while they are eternal principles, they manifest differently in each age. They are in the process of changing, for at least cosmically, we are coming to the changing of the Great Age.

The archetypes operate within us unconsciously, energizing and informing our lives for good or ill. But we can become conscious of how they operate in our lives and actually work with them to co-create a new life. They speak to us in the symbolic language of our imagination, our visions, our dreams and more generally in our myths and stories. That's why it's so important to understand what stories you tell yourself. The old story is a small one, the story of how we fit into the patriarchy. We are taught to focus our work, our hopes, our talents toward the goals of patriarchy. But when we go in search of our soul, we need these Big Stories to reflect on. Once we see our lives in terms of these mythic stories and deep symbols, patriarchy loses our allegiance. When we work consciously with these energies, we step outside the ego delusions of what we believe we want and get in touch with the reality of the Self. When we align our ego with the Self, we open ourselves to our true desires, discover our wholeness, and understand our life purpose. It is easy to see the correspondence between the different archetypes and the many stars in the heavens, for each archetype holds out a bit of light and knowledge, each exerts an influence by its luminosity and numinosity.[13]

When we discussed lunar consciousness in an earlier chapter, I mentioned that at the new Moon, the lunar light shines out into the universe, and that this is a time in which the movement of psychic energy flows deep within. At this time in the monthly cycle, lunar consciousness looks at the stars within, just as the moonlight shines out toward the starry universe. We make contact with the archetypal images through lunar consciousness; when we look within we can bring back these images into our daily lives.

The alchemists had a similar view of the Moon's function. They believed the Moon, which they called Luna, is the sum and essence of the nature of the six major metals-silver, mercury, copper, iron, tin and lead -which correspond to the five planets known in the ancient world-Mercury, Venus, Mars, Jupiter and Saturn plus the Moon itself. Luna is called the "universal receptacle of all things" and "the first gateway of heaven. She gathers the powers of all the stars in herself as in a womb, so as to bestow them on sublunary creatures."[14]

The stars' energies are focused through this Moon funnel, just as the archetypes can only be known through the archetypal images of lunar consciousness, which come to us in dreams and are the stuff of stories. In astrology, the Moon represents our personality, the unconscious needs that give us security and comfort. The planets are the archetypal energies common to all of us, and it is the movement of the Moon through the sky and through our charts which resonant these complexes. If we understand how we are affected by these complexes, we can make them conscious. Our rational consciousness cannot go right to this source of wisdom-it must be mediated through the imagination. Even scientists like Descartes, Einstein, Niels Bohr and Elias Howe, the inventor of the sewing machine, were among the many creative people who got their initial idea from a dream image.[15] We behold this truth in the night sky, for we cannot see the stars in the light of day. They are only visible when the light in the sky is the Moon, not the Sun.

Our ancestors saw in the movements of the planets and the stars an image of the power of Divine Spirit. The sky meant something to them, for it symbolized the principles they felt ordered their lives and also the force behind those principles. They knew there was power in the sky and, just as the tides where pulled by the changing Moon, they found that the seasons came and went with the changes of the Sun and stars.[16] (I don't need to remind you that the Sun is our own individual star.) In predicting this orderly process, early humanity came to feel that their fate was also guided by a divine order. The mysterious night sky, with its billions of sparkling lights and the great soft light of the Moon, symbolizes another aspect of the Collective Unconscious of humanity, a guide to Spirit and to the greater purposes of life.

Star Stories and the Evolution of Consciousness

The primary myths of all cultures are imaged in the stars and constellations. *The North Star*, our Polaris, has been known by many names in different cultures-the Lodestar, the Steering Star, the Ship Star, and Stella Maris—Star of the Sea, one of the Goddess' many titles. But in all mythologies it is the point that holds the universe together-the World Axis.

Our own Big Dipper is in the constellation Ursa Major, the Great Bear. The ancient Greeks imagined two bears in the sky, the Great Bear and the Lesser Bear, our Little Dipper, as the maiden Callisto, a follower of Artemis, and her son by Zeus, Arcas. Many Native American tribes also see these same two constellations as bears, with hunters following them. The name for the brightest star in this constellation, *Dubhe*, comes from the Arabic *Thahr al Dubb Al Akbar*, meaning "the Back of the Great Bear." And in ancient Britain, this constellation was called King Arthur's home or Arthur's Chariot, and Arthur is connected to *artois*, the Bear.[17]

We are still in touch with the stars. A woman dreamed:

> My husband and I are outside, in the front area of our yard. It is daytime and the sky is particularly blue. I look up and see the Big Dipper. I think this is odd, since it is full daylight. As I look, a new star formation forms where the Big Dipper had been. It is four stars in a square, and two at the bottom end of the square like a tail, not in the corner, but in the middle of the bottom. Then the stars began to shift position in unison, becoming horizontal, and descend to my yard. They become a tent—really, a canopy—in my front yard, with the four corners where the stars are becoming the four spots where the tent is staked to the ground. There is a luminous, bright side to the canopy. I see that other neighbors have tents in their front yards too, but these are actual tents, not canopies. I know my tent is a "center for peace." We will hold a ritual or discussion under the canopy.

This woman is welcoming change into her life. The Unconscious offers her a vision of change that is not just for herself alone, but for everyone. When we see a constellation in the daytime sky it means that it is becoming conscious in the collective 'sky'. This woman is a channel for this energy. The change in the constellation means that an archetypal collective complex is changing. It becomes a square, which denotes manifestation. As I mentioned, the Big Dipper is often associated with bears, who carry warrior energy, but in service to life. The canopy represents sovereignty and power, as if this canopy covers the sacred person, marking a sacred space with power. In freemasonry, there's an image of a starry canopy that represents the heavens as a shelter and as a sacred space, a place of power. This woman is being offered the chance to change the archetype of the warrior. She is being called to be a spiritual warrior, who defends life. She is being called to her life's purpose. Her neighbors have regular tents, what we use when we go camping, when we rough it. The dream says that while others are experiencing these times as roughing it, this woman can offer them wise insights into their lives. She will open her canopy to them for nurturing and healing.

Then there is my dream of seeing the Pleiades in the daytime sky. There are many myths about the Pleiades star cluster from all over the world. Many cultures use the rising and setting of the stars of this constellation to signal the beginning and end of the seasons, to time the sowing and harvesting of food, and to know when to expect the rains. The Pleiades act as a calendar, setting times for these activities as well as festivals and ceremonies. There are also ancient references that make the Pleiades the marker for the precession of the equinoxes, which signal the changing of the astrological ages, most specifically marking the end of the 25,900 years of a Great Year. Along with the stars of the Great Bear/The Big Dipper, they are responsible for the timing and turning of the celestial wheel in the sky that determines the world's ages, including the destruction and recreation of the world. It makes sense that this star cluster is seen all over the world as the Keeper of Time, Fate and Destiny.

The Mayan calendar that came to an end in 2012 is based on the Pleiades as well as on the planet Venus. On December 21, 2012, the Winter/Summer Solstice, the conjunction of the Pleiades with the Sun at its zenith was believed to mark the return of the Mayan Plumed Serpent God, whom the Aztecs called Quetzalcoatl. It seems that both the Sun and the Pleiades will mark a special alignment with the center of our Milky Way Galaxy, a rare event that occurs every 25,800 years.[18]

Many ancient cultures believed that our ancestors came from the Pleiades. Since we know that this star cluster is younger than our own solar system, these stories must have another meaning. If we look at the galaxy as a whole, we could say that the center of the Milky Way Galaxy is the womb of the galaxy. We can also think about it as the root chakra of the galaxy. When we look across the universe we find that the Pleiades sit at the anti-Galactic center. We could call them the galaxy's crown chakra, the spiritual source of inspiration and wisdom. Whether we call them ancestors or spiritual guides, the energies of this galactic crown chakra seem to want to support life here on Earth. My dream of the Pleiades appearing in the daytime sky is similar to this woman's dream of the Big Dipper. Neither one of us knew any of this information when we had our dreams. But our relationship with Lady Wisdom opened us to receive these dreams. We each were gifted with an insight into the mysteries of the changing of the ages. We each have been touched by the mystical knowledge that these times we live in are important. As two of Wisdom's Daughters, we have to find ways to use the wisdom and knowledge given us.

Each constellation tells a story of the human condition here on earth, yet different cultures saw similar stories in these sky pictures. Through these myths we are offered the wisdom of the ancients, as well as the wisdom of the archetypes. Yet how many of us take time to go out and look at the starry heavens with any knowledge of their ancient meanings or look within to discover the meaning of our dreams?

Once, people used the stars to guide them on their way, just as sailors still use stars to guide them across the waters. Similarly, when we find ourselves in the darkness of the unconscious psyche, we need to find guiding lights to direct us. The unconscious psyche is that part of our psychic makeup which is still unknown to us, and also that part which is the vastness of the Collective Unconscious. When Jung speaks of the regression of psychic energy back to the archetype itself, he means that as we trace back our complexes to our early personal history, we reach a point where we break through our personal unconscious material—that is, we become conscious of it and integrate it into our lives or leave it behind—to the collective aspect at its center, the archetype itself. This happens when we experience the breakdown of our old habits, which keep our world in place and which give structure to our reality. As our old world view dies, and as our old personality starts to break up so that new and repressed parts of ourselves can come into life, we can directly experience the power of the archetype and let its images inform the new life within us. It is a question of chaos and form, of death and rebirth.

Just as the stars overhead help us to find out where we are and the way we have to go, the inner stars, which are the basic spiritual realities which manifest through the archetypal images, show us the way we need to bring our potentials into life. When we make direct, personal contact with the stars within through dreams, fantasies and the flow of psychic energy in our bodies, our work is to give concrete and individual expression to their power, which we do with the help of that other more directed, naming, discriminating, individualizing consciousness that we have come to associate with the solar, Masculine Spirit. The image of the *Woman clothed with the Sun* is so powerful exactly because she exemplifies this process of individualizing the spiritual life force within each person.

Understanding the Cosmic Story

The ancients used the sky as a tool, to tell time, to mark the changing seasons, to give direction, and to look into the present and the future. It was a star (or perhaps the conjunction of three or more planets) that prefigured and then led the wise men to the Christ Child. At the moment of our birth, there is also a special configuration of stars in the sky that symbolizes our unique destiny. This is the astrological blueprint of our birth charts, which shows the dynamic interplay of cosmic rhythms and energies that form the patterns of our lives. As we become more conscious of the pattern, we participate to a greater degree in the unfolding of our destiny. We can use these star charts, just as the ancients did, as one way of understanding the meaning of the divine pattern manifesting itself in us. By looking to the configuration of the planets in the birth chart, our experience can be seen as a process of becoming, a dynamic energy flow. Just as you can keep track of your dreams in connection with the Moon's cycle, you can track the energies at play in our star system and how they relate to you specifically through your birth chart.

In July 1997 *Look* Magazine's cover story was called *Astrology as a Blueprint for the Soul*; it stated that more and more people were paying attention to astrology and the sky. At that time, over 48% of Americans believed in the efficacy of astrology. Today, the younger generation use astrologers the way baby-boomers went to therapists. Astrology has a long and illustrious history. Most of the philosophers and scientists of western society were astrologers, believing that we are indeed connected, not only to each other, but to the cosmos and its natural laws.

For example Pluto symbolizes the evolutionary energy of life, the transformative energy activated in alchemy. Pluto is a symbolic representation of the archetypal patterns of death, rebirth and evolution. Pluto is the Roman name of the god Hades, the Lord of the Underworld and of hidden wealth. All the tremendous energy of the Unconscious, with its potential for destruction, for transformation and for richness of life, is symbolically focused through this planet. When Pluto moves through an astrological sign, it brings up what is old and outworn, twisted and dead so that the old forms get released and new forms are energized. On both a personal and collective level, this energy feels dark and extremely powerful. That's because our ego and our society do not like change, although evolution and change are the universal laws of life. Whenever we experience a transit of Pluto, we are forced to face what is dead in our lives, whether a relationship, a job, a belief system or a way of life. If we fight it, we feel as if we literally might die. If we open ourselves to the changes, new life comes into our lives. A few years before I ended my marriage of seventeen years, when Pluto was opposing my natal Mars (my man), I dreamed of a Plutonian figure. I had to freely choose to face him and go through the initiation of death which he offered. Although divorce is a sad and often traumatic process to go through for everyone involved, it appears that this was the only way for me to die to my old life and be reborn.

On a collective level, at this time Pluto's energy is helping to transform our societal, collective forms of government, religion, relationships, education and social structures. For the first time in 240 years, Pluto moved into the sign of Capricorn in 2008-2009. The last time Pluto was in Capricorn was before the American Revolution. Capricorn rules government, corporations, our money system and our society's values. As you well know, this aspect of our collective life has significantly changed since 2008. We are seeing the beginning of the end of patriarchy. The old powers are fighting the changes, but in the end, we will have a different society. The hardships we are going through are really the necessity to evolve our cultural institutions. Once we have completed the process of change, we will have a society that values the feminine dimensions of life along with the masculine ones.

As we accept this dark energy of death and transformation and work with it, these energies will help us evolve our lives and our society. It helps immeasurably to understand that there are archetypal structures

231

that will direct the energy flow for us. Once we stop projecting our shadow qualities upon people or countries that displease us, we will be able to let these forces work on us. If we become conscious partners in this rebirth, we'll see an easier transition in the collective culture. I sense that we linger on our fear of nuclear war and our war on terror because we have no images of a different world to take us beyond that point of destruction. Only our own psychological deaths and rebirths can give us the wisdom we need to create a healthy environment in which the whole world prospers.

The planets represent the archetypal energies, the instinctual patterns of behavior, which are the very essence of what it means to be human. But the contents of the archetypes are not predetermined, and the ideal pattern includes the lowest as well as the highest consciousness available to our species. The old myths and stories show us the archetypal wisdom, but we have to remember that these myths can be transformed as we consciously live them out. Depending on the inherent potentials at birth, as well as the environment the soul is born into, each of us works out different patterns of being human and of being in relationship. This is how we manifest the *astrum* or star within us. Every time we look up at the stars, we see that their ever-changing, yet basic, patterns shed light on our earthly existence, on each moment in ordinary time; yet the light that we see began its journey to Earth millenniums ago. This light that we see is somehow eternal, for it deals with a different sense of time. The light and the wisdom of the stars are ancient, and knowing this helps us engage in life in an eternal context.

A 45 year-old woman, who was getting in touch with her feminine nature, became disenchanted with Christianity. Her religion was very important to her, and yet she began to realize that there was no longer any life and soul in the church for her. Her main worry in leaving the church was "Where do I go from here?" This dream showed her the emptiness she felt in church, and then gave her an experience of Feminine Spirit when she left it.

> I'm at my church for Easter service. There is no altar, just rows of seats. I wonder if I should stay to play the organ, but think, "God, I haven't played it for a year and a half." When I look for the music for "Jesus Christ is Risen Today" it is not there. They only have what I consider to be one-dimensional music there.

Later I'm outside with my mother, who is blind. I'm helping her up some wide steps. It is night, and the sky instantly lights up with all these stars. I'm just overcome by this - it's the biggest thing that's ever happened to me. Somehow, my mother can see all of this, too.

I'm looking at a constellation and far away I see stars exploding like fireworks. There are wonderful showers of green, red and yellow lights. I think, "This is a star bursting." The green sparks fall to earth and we're caught in the shower. As we move away I say, "We are blessed, we are blessed." I feel a real heightened consciousness.

This woman realized that for her the church no longer energized the appropriate feeling response about the rebirth of life, through the image of the Easter service without altar or music. The missing altar indicates a lack of sacred focus. The feeling connection, the passion of true spirituality, is represented by the beauty of the song she is looking for, "Jesus Christ is Risen Today." She wants to feel rebirth. Even though she feels as if her musical ability (feeling life) is rusty, she is willing to take the chance. But there is only one-dimensional music in that church. She only finds the experience of rebirth imaged for her outside, in the night sky. As the star bursts (dies) it showers her with such feeling that she can exclaim, "We are blessed!" She stands there in a heightened consciousness with her blind mother, who is not denied this vision either.

The Transformation of Collective Consciousness

Working as a dream analyst, I can see a recurring motif of movement in the stars; either a single star bursts into many lights or there is a movement in the pattern of the stars. This dream marked a real turning point for this woman in her spirituality. It became a deep, indwelling connection and a true knowledge that she was indeed blessed. As people look within to their own inner light, the old patterns of belief (the single star or old constellation) die out and new patterns emerge. The next step in their evolution is upon them. The most outstanding part of the dream is usually the feeling of awe and connectedness that the dreamer feels as s/he is affected by this movement. It is through the power and energy of this movement within the deep psyche that people are finding the courage to listen to Lady Wisdom's voice and open themselves to their creativity and to Feminine Spirit.

There is deep change going on in the Collective Unconscious at this point in time. Our technology is changing so rapidly that there is a corresponding change in the Unconscious. As we deepen our consciousness, and learn to use both sides of the brain, our perception of our human capabilities will broaden to include those psychic, intuitive, feeling aspects which our rational culture has rejected along with the Goddess. Many years ago, I had a dream that spoke to these changes occurring in the collective. I was looking at some old star charts and comparing them to the constellations that were in the sky at the present time. I noticed that some were the same, but many constellations had changed. Interpreting this dream personally, I realized I was seeing the changes that had taken place within me over the years. But this dream felt like it had a collective meaning, since the stars are our collective guides. It showed me early on that changes were taking place in the collective psyche. And it has proven to be true.

Now we have only to look at the brutal truth of our unstable economy, our wars, the widespread environmental destruction, the greed and corruption of those in power, and the loss of cultural values to see how we have ignored or been unconscious of the forces that are moving within our society. Happily, people are awakening and stepping forward again to take responsibility for their lives and our collective life. Just as the dream star charts were changing, we are now seeing changes in our collective lives, and it would seem there are enough people to tip the balance of collective consciousness to a higher, more enlightened state. We have to renew our collective life through living out our individual values and highest collective ideals. We have to discover a more sacred, graceful, truthful and fulfilling way to live and relate to each other and to the Earth.

When we wear Fur Skin's Star dress, we open ourselves—body, soul and spirit—to the voice of Lady Wisdom. We accept our true nature as spiritual beings and co-creators of life, centered by the treasure of a golden reel, the World Axis. All beings need a center. Otherwise, the chaos rips us apart. If we reject our true nature, our spiritual nature, then the center is lost. Our culture has lost its center, and we substituted the pursuit of wealth and happiness here on Earth for our spiritual center. This is the princess's task, a task we all share in: we have to put our spiritual values back at our center and our highest ideals back in the center of our public discourse. Fur Skin has become the true Queen, and it is her inspiration and passion that will drive our collective transformation in the future.

The stars are waiting to give us their wisdom. When we strive to become conscious of the sacred context of our lives, the power of the archetypes will work through us creatively. Before moving back to the United States from Zurich, I had a dream about the stars that showed me all the changes I went through in analysis and in training at the C.G. Jung Institute, as well as the experience of living in a foreign land with young children. An older friend of mine who had died recently came to me in my dream, and told me that I had to bring those new things back to the States with me, so that they could grow in different ways. In many traditions, the stars were thought to be the spirits of the dead; those spirits who could now shine the light of their wisdom on their descendants.

> I have moved back to R.I. and find that we are living in the old curate's house in Wickford. R. is out and I go for a walk. It is night, and I look up at the stars. There is a row of constellations spread across the whole arc of the sky, all of them shining brilliantly. I recognize them: they are all the constellations I have dreamed about through my years of study.
>
> I lie down in the grass to keep the stars in sight, when suddenly I see Dorothy standing by an old wooden fence near the road. I consciously know that she is dead, but there she stands, obviously alive and definitely vibrant! There is a beautiful light surrounding her. She has come to tell me some important things about what I must do now that I am home.
>
> After we finish talking, she tells me it's time to leave. I want to stay, but as I walk away, I look back at her once more. I see that she is different now. She radiates a gentle numinous quality that makes me realize she is a representative of the Goddess.

When Wisdom's Daughters see our transformation in terms of the Divine Story, we do not become extraordinary as much as we begin to see that all life partakes of Divine Spirit. This is what Jesus meant when he said that the Kingdom of Heaven is right here amongst us. Matter and spirit are One, just as all people and species are one in the Earth's embrace. Wise daughters understand the meaning of our experience and respond to it with the innate wisdom being in touch with our inner truth elicits. Lady Wisdom invites us to develop new eyes with which to see our world, and understand our lives in the world. We need a new cosmic story that only Lady Wisdom can tell us. Letting this greater Feminine Spirit infuse our awareness gives us the courage and the ability to find out just who we are and what we might become. The path of Lady Wisdom challenges us to be our best selves, our most conscious selves, our most compassionate selves. What else makes life worth living?

Wisdom Takes Wing: The Dove of the Holy Feminine Spirit

Some of the most ancient goddess-figures we've discovered are bird-headed. The various birds of the air were her messengers, bringing her people the wisdom to live wisely and well. These sacred birds fly between Heaven and Earth, consciousness and the Unconscious. They transcend gravity. Like our imagination, they soar! Birds symbolize our soul. And so they are the guardians of the Wisdom of the Stars.

As we will explore in the next chapter, the one ancient goddess who still holds power in modern times is Aphrodite, who is also the *Woman clothed with the Sun*. Wisdom has come to be associated with Aphrodite's sacred bird, the Dove. Doves haunted every one of her temples, cooing and pursuing each other in and out of the colonnades. They are gentle birds, and publicly amorous, reminding us of the gentleness of youthful infatuation and love. Wisdom's light shines when we see each other and the world through the eyes of love. This wisdom opens us to see that the world is being newly created from moment to moment, and that it is alive with Feminine Spirit and wonder and mystery.

The Greeks saw doves as gentle messengers of love, and this image of them as messengers turns up in other traditions as well. It was a dove that brought back the olive branch to Noah after the Flood, symbolizing peace between God and humanity. Often doves symbolize the soul passing from one state of being to another. Doves are sacred to all Queens of Heaven, for they symbolize the Feminine Spirit of life and love that is humanity's heritage.

Under Christianity, Aphrodite's dove was transformed into the Holy Spirit, the third person of the Trinity. Christianity adopted the dove as a symbol of Sophia, representing 'God's Wisdom' as well as of Metis, the Wisdom of Zeus. This is the same Holy Spirit who descended on the Virgin Mary at the Annunciation, that moment of revelation when she knew that she would become the Mother of God. It is through wisdom that we become the vessels of life; it is through love that we manifest spirit. After Jesus ascended into heaven, he sent the Paraclete, the Holy Spirit, to his followers. The Holy Spirit appeared as tongues of flame over their heads, causing exaltation and joy. They were so filled with this Spirit that they spoke in many different tongues and the people who saw them thought that they were intoxicated. This Feminine Spirit is a flame, which warms all things in the fire of love, and it wants to come live in our hearts.

> He is the Spirit of physical and spiritual procreation who from now on shall make his abode in creaturely man. Since he is the Third Person of the Deity, this is as much as to say that God will be begotten in creaturely man. [19]

Carl Jung speaks here of the Holy Spirit as *he*, and yet it is unmistakably an image of the Goddess, for it is the Goddess who brings the divine into human form; it is Mary who agrees to give birth to divinity. The promise of the Holy Spirit is the continuing incarnation of the Divine, and it is in the Goddess and through her feminine consciousness that this incarnation is possible. The dove symbolizes Lady Wisdom, for only through wisdom do we awaken to ourselves in spirit. Only when we know ourselves as vessels of spirit can we give birth to the divinity within each of us. This is the *Woman's* divine child. Jesus said that the way to this is through love, love of God and Goddess, love of each other. The Holy Spirit is the wisdom of love at work in the world. And this love is both spiritual and physical, for Divine Spirit can truly only be known when we consciously live in the body.

Just as the body is the temple of spirit, so our physical world is the teacher of spirit. The Earth, the Moon, the Sun and the Stars are our teachers, in that they show us how to get in touch with the powers of life. The changing cycle of seasons teaches us that life is constantly changing, opening and closing, in flux and reflux. Birth, growth and decay and death, with rebirth coming soon on its heels are the processes that make up our human lot. The planets and stars shine out with the light of heaven, teaching us about ancient days, unimaginable stretches of time, and about the things which are immortal and timeless. Physical reality and spiritual truths reflect one another. *As Above, so Below.* They also teach us to look symbolically at our lives and our world in order to find out what it means to be human. The stars reflect the archetypes of the Collective Unconscious. They help us evolve our humanity.

For thousands of years, the rushing sound of doves' wings brought a shiver of anticipation to the body, heralding the arrival of a celestial messenger, or a saving inspiration that comes at a crucial time, or the departure of a beloved soul. Let the Dove of Peace bring the Wisdom of Love to your door.

The Wisdom of the Eagle

There are many birds who symbolize heavenly messengers but they all have one thing in common—their exceptional eye-sight. The owl, the falcon, the ibis have symbolized Lady Wisdom, but it is Eagle who embodies her power of *insight.*

Because Eagle can see both minute details as well as the whole picture, she doesn't have to spend all her time hunting. She catches her prey on the first try! And so she has time to fly to the heights, spiraling upwards to the heavens. She is at home both in the heavens and on the Earth. Many societies have taken the Eagle as their symbol, just as many gods have flown on her wings. The Thunderbird of Native American tradition controls the lightning and thunders, just as the Eagle of Zeus did. For many ancient people, the Eagle symbolized Divine Spirit, heroic nobility and awesome power.

But like Solomon, who in choosing Lady Wisdom also was given power and glory, when we work with the energy of Eagle, we have to remember that first and foremost, Eagle symbolizes Lady Wisdom. Majestic and mystical, it has symbolized the human soul's flight to the heavens after death. And like the *Woman clothed with the Sun,* it is connected with conscious wisdom, fire and the Sun. When the dragon is cast out of heaven and tries to destroy the *Woman* who is living in the desert, she is given the *wings of an eagle* so she can fly away to safety.

The guardian of heavenly Wisdom, Eagle can guide us through death into rebirth. Ask for the wings of the Eagle when the dragon of despair and unconsciousness tries to devour you. And fly free.

From this look at the realms of Earth and Moon and Stars, we can see that, although the task is hard, the rewards of reconnecting with Feminine Spirit are great. The *Woman Clothed with the Sun* combines these realms, for she is woman, Earth and body made conscious by the light of solar consciousness. She stands on the Moon, taking her standpoint from the ancient rhythms of life, allowing those rhythms to be lived consciously, allowing the dark, the Unconscious, to have its say. She is crowned with Stars, for she knows the archetypal patterns that make up our humanity, and she lives out her individual destiny so that she can give birth to the Savior she incarnated to become. We are the women who are learning from this image. We are the women whom this image wants to speak to.

Getting in touch with the rhythms of life is hard work for Father's Daughters, and we constantly fall back into an easier, familiar, goal-oriented, stressful schedule. But this is only half the picture. This is the Masculine Spirit of *doing* living within us. We also have to undertake the task of learning to *be*, of learning to listen to our instincts about what makes life worth living, of learning how to bring joy back into our lives once again. When we learn this lesson, we can start to re-learn *doing*, but this time our doing will come out of an authentic necessity of the Self. It is especially hard to go into the darkness of the unknown, for we have lost the tools and the knowledge of the type of consciousness which can get us through the dark places. Luckily, the knowledge is not irrecoverable, for it is still imaged in the world around us and within us.

Now we will find that the rhythms, though ancient beyond measure, are still new. We are different from the peoples who came before, and yet we are the same. Now that we know what we have lost, perhaps we will honor the wisdom of the Feminine Spirit all the more once it is recovered. Gratefully, we have the ancient images to look back to, and we have our imaginations to help bring these images living into our modern world. This is the mystery and the reality of our task, which will be explored next as we look at the dress of the Sun, because as Wisdom's Daughters, we will be clothed in Light.

Sekhmet, Lioness Goddess of Egypt

Before the Sun was associated with Masculine Spirit, it was imaged in Egypt as Sekhmet, the Lioness Goddess of Egypt. Sekhmet is one of the most ancient deities know to us – older than her husband-brother Ptah, or her father, Ra, the Sun god. Her name might mean "strong, might, violent" as well as describing her sacred sexuality. For the Egyptians, she personified the fierce, destroying fires of the Sun. This makes her a goddess clothed with the Sun. According to tradition, there were 4,000 names for Sekhmet, but only a few hundred have survived. Here are a few of her names and her attributes:

Sekhmet, Great one of Magic
Mother of the Gods
One who was before the Gods were
Lady of the Place of the Beginning of Time
Beautiful eye which giveth life to the two lands
Protectress of the Gods
Lady of the Scarlet-colored garment
Pure One
Awakener
Lady of Enchantments
Opener of Ways
Lady of Transformations
Lady of the many faces
Giver of Ecstasies
Satisfier of desires
Inspirer of males

Lady of the Magic Lamp
Mother of the Dead
Great one of Healing
Lady of the Waters of Life
Mistress and Lady of the Tomb
Winged one
Powerful of heart
Mother of images
Lady of Intoxications
Protectress of the divine order
The one who holds back darkness
Goddess of Love
Sekhmet, who gives Joys
Unwavering Loyal One
Beloved Teacher
Beloved Sekhmet[1]

Chapter Seven
The Dress of the Sun: The Woman Clothed with the Sun

The girl and the woman, in their new, their own unfolding, will but in passing be imitators of masculine ways, good and bad, and repeaters of masculine professions. After the uncertainty of such transitions it will become apparent that women were only going through the profusion and the vicissitude of those (often ridiculous) disguises in order to cleanse their own most characteristic nature of the distorting influences of the other sex. Women, in whom life lingers and dwells more immediately, more fruitfully and more confidently, must surely have become fundamentally riper people, more human people, than easygoing man, who is not pulled down below the surface of life by the weight of any fruit of his body, and who, presumptuous and hasty, undervalues what he thinks he loves.[2]
—R.M. RILKE

The Father's Daughter

Like Fur Skin, most women today are Father's Daughters, women who get our identity from pursuing masculine careers and aligning with masculine rules and beliefs. Women finally have the same freedom as men, but like the princess who is the object of her father's obsession women are bound to the patriarchy without even knowing it. And so our freedom is granted to us by a masculine hierarchy, which still doesn't value the Feminine Spirit of life unless it serves its purpose.

When women wear the dress of the Sun, we develop a strong ego-identity. We know what we want and we go after it. Women are finally getting to live out our astrological Sun sign, which represents our task and purpose in life, rather than limiting ourselves to just our astrological lunar energies of comfort, nurturing, security and reflection. The trouble occurs when our identity is based solely on patriarchy's perceptions of appropriateness and on masculine ideals of life. That's when we become Father's Daughters.

The Sun has been a symbol of life, enlightenment and consciousness since the dawn of time, because our physical Sun gives us life. In ancient times, the Sun was honored through a goddess such as Sekhmet, and was seen as both life-giving and death-dealing. The truth is the Sun is life-giving and death-dealing-ask anyone who lives in the desert! There is a harshness and cruelty to the Sun that we don't find in the Moon or Stars. That harshness results from not honoring the healing waters of the feminine Moon.

Now most often associated with the universal Father, the Sun has come to symbolize left-brain, masculine solar consciousness: Individuality, rationality, structure, focus, intention, discrimination, order, separateness, and hierarchy. It has come to represent the patriarchal-shaped ego most of us have developed. Unfortunately, it is an ego cut off from the Self, our inner wholeness, just as this inherited form of masculine solar consciousness cuts itself off from a more feminine lunar consciousness. It is this break that makes our masculine culture so dangerous, for without the cool, reflective light of our lunar nature, we become too one-sided and unbalanced.

So we find many women cut off from our own feminine qualities, trying to make it in the patriarchal peeking order. Just as most men are cut off from their inner life of feelings and intuitions, most women are overwhelmed with feelings and don't know what to do about it. That is until something wakes us up and we leave the Father's House. That's when we discover all the gifts and talents of Feminine Spirit waiting for us in the Unconscious. And that's when women begin to discover our true inner freedom.

In the Father's House, it is important that women's ego-consciousness is strong and we have the focus and determination to play the patriarchal game just as well as the men do. Dee Dee Myers talks from experience. She was the first woman to hold the office of

White House Press Secretary, at the center of power and yet, because she was the first woman to do so, kept outside the door of that power. Like many women in positions of public power, her wisdom was most often ignored or else it was only accepted after a long, hard battle. Women have worked hard to prove ourselves in the world, and when we do, we shine. But we still have to play by the men's rules. We are indeed all Sun worshippers!

The Dress of the Sun

When the princess asks her father, the king, to make her a dress of the Sun, she is asking to train her ego as a Father's Daughter, a woman who wants a share in the power and possibilities of the Father's kingdom. Women need to develop an ego identity that tries to fit the patriarchal bill. Dress right, think straight, stay focused on the bottom line, and leave your feelings and intuitions at home. But as the fairy tale continues, we see that the princess really wants these dresses, which symbolize the types of consciousness available to the Father, so that she can run away from his desire to own her-physically, mentally, emotionally and spiritually-and reclaim her sovereignty and her freedom. She wants to learn to understand these types of consciousness herself. As we've seen, the first step is to learn to untwist ourselves from patriarchal projections and then listen to our instincts. We have to first live in our mantle of furs, and learn to be *women who run with the wolves*, before we can really wear this golden dress properly.

Living in her mantle of furs, Fur Skin eventually understands who she really is. That gives her the right to wear the golden dress of the Sun to the new king's first ball. That's the ball where she plants her golden ring in the king's soup. She connects to him with the ring, for he symbolizes a new structure of consciousness, a new way of *doing* that supports her new way of *being*, just as he finally connects to her at the third ball by returning her ring, completing the circle and forming a new union of opposites. By working hard to discover her wounds and heal them while living in her fur mantle, Fur Skin reconnects with the Self. By wearing the golden dress, Fur acknowledges that she is whole again, and conscious of who she is. It is no longer about her ego-identity but about her Self-identity.

To wear the golden dress or to be clothed with the Sun in this way indicates that a woman has discernment; she can see the Truth. Discern means to recognize something as separate and distinct. It is the power to select what is true and right for you in a given moment. It is a power that helps us make the right choices and see clearly what it is we need. Discernment is the tool that will help us understand our psyches, face our life challenges and make our way through the darkness of unknowing. We need discernment to hone our perception and judgment so we can comprehend what is obscure and learn to see it clearly. This is especially important psychologically, for western ego-consciousness is prone to inflation by the archetypes. Without a clear connection to the Self, ego appropriates all sorts of power to itself instead of being a vessel of that power. When we have a vision or touch upon archetypal energy, we don't want to make the mistake of believing we are superhuman.

There's an objective knowing that comes from knowing who you are. And when you do, you can begin to understand what you're feeling, sensing, intuiting; you can name what it is and what it means, and then act on it. Through this beautiful golden light you can see the essential quality of a person, situation, or problem. Learning real discernment doesn't mean you won't make mistakes, but it does mean that if you do, you learn from those mistakes in a way that expands your life. The development of this ego-Self is the stage where our everyday consciousness is so connected to the Self, that we live in a state of wholeness with ourselves and with the world. We accept ourselves!

This type of Self-consciousness is a deep knowledge of who we are and not the ego-consciousness that puts on a mask to become what is expected of us. We see ourselves for who we are. We followed the dictum: Know Thyself. As each woman becomes a *Woman clothed with the Sun*, she lives in this Self-consciousness and makes choices based on intuitive knowing and feelings (for she stands on the Moon) and with a clear sense of spiritual purpose (for she is crowned with Stars). She is connected to her wholeness, just as she connects with the king by dancing with him and then leaving her golden ring in his soup. She connects and so achieves union, both with her inner animus and with her outer king. She is whole.

Why We Need To Leave the Father's House

Most women today are still Father's Daughters. We have all been betrayed by our culture (often through our mothers) into thinking that the men's world, a world of individualism, power, work, competition, objectivity and dynamism is better than a world of cooperation, compassion, nurturing, feeling, intuition and receptivity. We have bought into the myth that the outer look is more important than the inner essence. To survive and prosper, we have had to follow our culture's dictates and allow ambition and work to be more important than loving relationships and nurturing creativity, a culture that sees *doing* as vastly more important than *being*. The king in this part of the story *has* married his daughter, regardless of her wishes.

We don't even know that this is what has happened to us until something disrupts our lives and we are forced to change. The only way people change is if they get to know themselves, their light-filled talents and their darkest emotions. The dictum *Know Thyself* has always been the first step on the path to Wisdom. If we want to change the world, so that we have a healthy fruitful world to live in, we each have to do this work of reconnecting to our inner lives and understanding it. Because what you find when you look within is your Self, the archetype of wholeness, the energy that makes you YOU!

This is what the dress of the Sun brings us, the ability to know and name ourselves, which leads to opening and transforming ourselves. The Father's House has become a dark house, where we are expected to do what's expected of us without having the right to question or make demands of our own, let alone have any real power to effect fundamental change. That's why we must all, women as well as men, leave the Father's House and re-discover the power of the dresses of the Sun, Moon and Stars. We need the returning Goddess energy to lead us to Lady Wisdom.

When a woman has symbolically *married* the Father, she is psychologically imbalanced. Her needs are sacrificed to her father's ambitions and power or to his failure to achieve power. She is offered a narrow set of images to live by, images influenced by men's wounded perception of Feminine Spirit. Whether she dons the role of chief executive or politician's wife, daredevil adventurer or *femme fatal*, she has lost touch with something basic to her feminine psyche. We can see it too in the way couples relate now. Since the 60s, women feel more comfortable asserting ourselves with our men, but unfortunately, we often compete with them rather than comfort them. A loss of desire is the result. If we women remembered our feminine gifts when it comes to our men, perhaps our marriages would be healthier.

As women leave the Father's House and search for ourselves, we first go back to the land, to our Mother and to nature to re-discover our nature. There we can throw off the chains that bind us to roles that are too narrow or too hard to bear. It seems we, like the *Woman* who flees to the desert and Fur Skin living in her mantle of furs, must leave our old beliefs and assumptions behind and explore who we are as woman-in-herself. We must become virginal again. Then our doing will entail connecting with the new masculine energy she finds in the woods, in the land and within herself. This is the masculine energy that loves us for who we are as women and give us the self-confidence to stand up for ourselves and our vision of life.

Finding an Image that speaks to our Feminine Nature

As women realign themselves with the power of the Divine Feminine Spirit, we dive deeply into the mysteries of life and of love to find new answers to the problems of personal relationships and individual purpose. Our experience of life in the past 50 years has been a struggle to find our true individuality within a society that is demanding more conformity of its citizens, especially women, than ever before. Just because we have the right to vote doesn't mean we know how to be free.

This conformity takes us out of our bodies-out of our individual experience of life-and deprives us of our own inner compass. Our collective, western consciousness has cut us off from the most basic foundation of our being—our bodies. We have been trained to live in our heads and our ego-consciousness, watching computer screens or TV instead of experiencing life, and now we find that we no longer understand the urgings and promptings of the body or acknowledge the mysterious Feminine Spirit that wants to make itself known through and in the body. Our culture's stereotypes of the female body—incredibly clean, boyishly slim, impossibly young and always in shape—are the result of living in our heads. And so our bodies rebel because it is unnatural. Add to that the toxins in our food that effect the body, and we have an epidemic of obesity. Is it any wonder that when we don't listen to our bodies, we come down with mysterious, debilitating diseases? We have to awaken to a sense of ourselves as *embodied spirit* and learn to listen to our bodies again if we want to become whole. We have to live in our mantle of furs.

Women watch as our rights to make the most basic decisions about our bodies are taken away from us by patriarchal governments and attitudes. The old patriarchy wants to control women by controlling our bodies through laws that prohibit our right to choose, how we should dress or by valuing us less than men; it controls our minds by insisting that there is no meaning to our psychic feelings or to the intuitions of the body. How many women were told that there was nothing wrong with them, except maybe in their imaginations, until the medical profession finally named such diseases as Barr-Epstein or Chronic Fatigue Syndrome?

When we do not live in our bodies, we do not notice how our environment is being destroyed: when we are not living in our bodies, we repress the pain and loneliness of our lives by taking drugs. If the death of the old order is upon us, it is because it no longer fosters life. Women are being called to rediscover what the important things in life really are, and then mother them into being once again. We can make love, our ability to connect with others, the basis of this new life. First we must learn to love our own bodies, not as the source of fascination for men, but as the source of our own creative power and beauty.

If we want to focus on a new vision and perspective, we must let images guide us in learning just what Feminine Spirit is trying to teach us. There are many goddess images that can help us resonate to the power of returning Feminine Spirit. The Sumerian Inanna is the first deity in recorded history to die and be reborn. The Egyptian Isis, as well as the Celtic enchantress Morgan Le Fay, are both mistresses of magic. We might choose Hera, the archetypal energy of partnership, or Brigid the poetess. There are so many aspects of the Divine Feminine to choose from. These ancient images are awaking within us, and we must learn to embody the energies that are awakening with them, for they represent our feminine heritage that has been denied to us for countless centuries.

But since the times are calling us to follow the path of Lady Wisdom, I find there is one Goddess who speaks most strongly of our womanly bodies and passions, while at the same time connecting us to Feminine Spirit. She manifests the qualities of the *Woman clothed with the Sun,* although she is more often associated with the only other feminine image in the *Book of Revelation—the Scarlet Whore of Babylon.* Since Goddess energy can encompass paradox, it might surprise people that the goddess who symbolizes this energy of Lady Wisdom is Aphrodite, Goddess of Love, Beauty, Sexuality and Wholeness. I believe that it is Aphrodite's qualities, which unite Heaven and Earth in a sensuous, passionate way, which can lead women to a true understanding of ourselves as embodied Feminine Spirit and which will help us become the transformative *Woman.*

Aphrodite: The Once and Future Queen

Aphrodite the earth-born Kore is also sea born, as becomes an island Queen, but more than any other goddess she becomes Ourania, the Heavenly One… She is the only goddess who in passing to the upper air yet kept life and reality… .As man advanced in knowledge and in control over nature, the mystery and the godhead of things natural faded into science. Only the mystery of life, and love that begets life, remained, intimately realized and utterly unexplained; hence Aphrodite keeps her godhead to the end.[3]

Aphrodite of the Greeks, Venus of the Romans, is one of the most vibrant archetypal images of the Goddess that has come down to us from antiquity; the aspect of the ancient Goddess that was never totally forgotten, the form of the Goddess written about and romanticized down through the ages until she truly embodied 'the mystery of life, and love that begets life'. Aphrodite is the Goddess who combines the spiritual and natural worlds, spirit and body. She does this through her essence, which is love. She embodies the energy of connection, for she brings everything into relationship, from electrons to people. She is the Goddess of Love, the love that is rooted in the body and which is playful, sensual, and erotic. As Goddess of Sexuality, she engenders all physically passionate love: non-marital and marital, heterosexual and homosexual. As Goddess of Beauty, she connects us to Truth. As Goddess of Wholeness, she drives our individuation and awakens Psyche/soul within us.

As an aspect of Lady Wisdom, she is Aphrodite Ourania, Queen of Heaven, who was in the Beginning and who created all the worlds. She is that spiritual love we call compassion, the love which unites us in our humanity and makes us all One. She is the wisdom that teaches us greater consciousness, for she is our soul's initiator. Her energies fill us with longing to connect with ourselves, with others, and to create new life!

Aphrodite is the Goddess of Beauty, not just physical beauty but the beauty of life itself. She is the love of beauty which makes great art and music for the healing of our wounded spirit, for she is Love as a creative, cosmic force. Vanda Scaravelli, in her insightful book on yoga, *Awakening the Spine*, speaks of the beauty of a healthy, vital life.

> Beauty is not only in the spectacular glow of a sunset, in the delightful face of a child, in the incredible structure of a flower, in the joy of bright colors, in the shape of a sculpture, in the words of a poem, in the voice of a song, in the notes of a symphony. There is beauty also in the acknowledgment and expression of a feeling, in the logical process of thinking, in the discovery of a truth, in the realization of harmony, in the astonishment arising from observing the perfection with which a tree or a plant is put together.
>
> Beauty brings us back that state of vulnerability, innocence and abandon in which, like a child, we are taken by the hand to disclose the kingdom of wonders and marvels thus putting us in touch with Nature where the miracle of existence is renewed each day.
>
> We need beauty around us. Beauty is like a perfume impalpable but yet so very strong. Beauty is the essence of life. Its feeling pushes the artist to create, opens the heart to love, leads the brain to clarify, invites the mind to comprehend and brings the body to participate.
>
> You find yourself in Beauty, unexpectedly absorbed by Beauty.[4]

Aphrodite's beauty is this kind of divine beauty: it is a golden, laughter-loving beauty which engenders a warm, life-giving relatedness. It is a beauty which is inherently graceful and enrapturing. *"It is the warmth and truth of passion that shine through Aphrodite's nature, as sunlit gold shines through her whole appearance."*[5] It is the truth of her passion that is the healing of the passion of matter. We women are so passionate about who and what we love! And yet we often equate passion with *too-muchness* in our society. Women need to stop fearing that 'the warmth and truth of [our] passion' is wrong. There is a great strength in the purity of our passion, like the image of the Tarot card called Strength, where a woman gently closes the mouth of a lion. Our feminine strength lies in taming the lion of our passions rather than in killing it, as male heroes do, such as Hercules, who kills the lion and wears its skin as his own. These male myths indicate that it is men who feel they must overcome and kill these passions, not women. Women have a different path, for the ancient goddesses, such as Cybele and Astarte, rode on lions-they rode and channeled their passions. And of course, Sekhmet is lion-headed!

The Divine Mystery of the Body

The Greeks came to regard the ideal form of Aphrodite's divinity in the beauty of her naked body, for ancient statues show her either about to undress—revealing her mystery—or already undressed. If these forms express her essence, then it is the realm of body that reveals her mystery. There is a radiant charm in her loveliness which draws us into relationship, because the truth of her being is *embodied*. As the archetypal essence of love and sexuality, her heavenly nature clothes her instinctual, earthy nature, thereby uniting both realms in harmony. She asks us to love our bodies, knowing that they are truly the temple of spirit here on Earth.

It appears that the new feminine figure emerging in the dreams of modern individuals is one of passion, energy and authority. This Goddess energy is coming into consciousness and showing us something about Feminine Spirit, which invariably connects us to our repressed instinctual nature. Fur Skin's task is to live within the mantle of her instinctual nature until she can express it through her unique individuality. Then she becomes the most beautiful woman ever seen on earth.

Aphrodite is primarily a goddess who can show us how to see our instinctual nature as a blessing, something we need feel no guilt about, but rather joy and gladness that Spirit would choose to manifest in this way. In myth, Aphrodite rules over the realms of Earth, Moon (through her rulership of the sea), and the Stars, and her body is clothed in nothing more than the golden radiance of the Sun. She can offer us a deeper understanding of the images which will connect us to the new archetypal energy wanting to manifest in our times, showing us what a conscious woman can be and what feminine consciousness consists of.

Jung says that the archetype consists of two different aspects: its emotional affect, and its image, which gives order to the affect or feeling tone. The new force emerging from the Collective Unconscious is often felt first in unfocused affect; if there is no image connected to it, these feelings will unconsciously directing our actions. For example, in the 60's our newfound sexual freedom, after centuries of sexual repression, brought about a release of feeling, but the image of that sexual freedom had no positive symbol to flow into, except for the prostitute, which brings up the virgin-whore split in our western psyches.

We still have not reclaimed the image of the sacred prostitute which gave women the power and respect due her own sexual nature. Pornography, which is a growing pastime for many men because it is easily available on the Internet, is another example of Aphrodite's love and sexuality operating unconsciously and in a distorted way in the collective culture. Pornography feeds on our need to connect and experience sexual union, while at the same time disconnecting us from our sexuality as well as from each other. This is what happens when the old masculine dominant cuts Aphrodite's energy off from its spiritual roots. The patriarchy has demanded that women be either chaste or wanton, mother or mistress, virgin or whore. The old king wants to marry his daughter and use the energy and power of sexuality to feed his power rather than respecting and opening to the divine purpose of sexuality, which is balance, harmony, connectedness and peace. To restore the balance, we have to come into conscious relationship with our sexuality if we want to find the true meaning of this primal force of life.

If we look at some of the phenomena manifesting in our collective culture, we can see the close connection they have to Aphrodite's special concerns. From the realm of personal relationships to the awakening to our collective responsibilities to the starving and dying peoples of the planet, we are being posed questions about love and responsibility. From the destruction of nature to the loss of important values in our culture, we are dealing with the ideals of Beauty and Truth. With overpopulation burdening the planet's capacity to feed us all, women and men are being deprived of their rights to engage in their sexuality by the bigoted morality of western patriarchal religions.

These are only some of Aphrodite's concerns that have been forgotten, distorted and repressed by our society, and so they move within us unconsciously. Because our masculine, rational world-view refused to acknowledge the ideal of beauty, we have created an ugly world, one in which Aphrodite's ideals of beauty are ignored. While women are the unconscious carriers of that value, for women are still seen as the mediators of beauty, nothing else is, as if beauty is not the fullest expression of the truths of life and love.

Because she is ignored, Aphrodite pursues us ruthlessly; because she can only manifest unconsciously, we misunderstand this sacred energy, and so we are controlled by unrelated passion, terrible longing, unbridled sexuality and a collective stereotype of beauty. In this unconscious state, she becomes the Scarlet Whore who fornicates with all sorts of men and powers. When love and beauty are twisted by power and domination, they eventually make us ill.

Aphrodite's erotic persuasion, her unashamed enjoyment of lovemaking for its own sake, erupted in the sexual permissiveness of the '60's. In very concrete ways, women finally regained control over our own bodies after centuries of restrictions. This is our truest and most basic break with the patriarchy, for we are beginning to take back control of our bodies and our sexuality. But what was unconsciously lived out in the sixties has to be consciously understood in the 21st Century. Aphrodite's love and sexuality manifested in the flower children of the hippie movement and their ideals of free love. Now these energies have to be related to consciously and rooted in the soil of the realities of a changing world, a world where13-year-old girls give blow jobs to groups of boys, where our celebrities dress like hookers and gangsters and our children emulate them, and where sexual pandering goes on over the Internet. We need to restore the sacred to our human sexuality.

Aphrodite's companions are the Muses of music, dance and poetry, and much of our popular music recounts the joys, passions, and sorrows of love, for it is through art that we connect (Aphrodite's power) with our feeling life. Her sacred priestesses were skilled not only in the arts of sexual love but in all the arts that make for civilization-writing, poetry, history, philosophy, music, art, dance. Throughout the ages, the Courtesan exemplified this ideal: a woman who enjoyed her sexuality, who was known for her intelligence and who was skilled in the arts. This is the promise of Fur Skin's transformation: women who are conscious of our freedom to become whoever we desire to be, rather than what others want us to be. Knowledge and creativity in the Arts can also teach the art of living and loving. Isn't it a sign of ignorance that the American Congress keeps cutting funds for the Endowment for the Arts, denying the healing and teaching aspects of the arts for our culture?

And then, there is our over-concern with beauty: since it is valueless in our industrial society, where the bottom line is money, we become even more focused on outer image rather than inner truth, beauty and love. We are an image-conscious society whose focus is on the outer images of beauty—beautiful people, beautiful faces, beautiful hair, beautiful bodies, clothes, and places to visit. We concentrate on these outer forms (which come and go with amazing regularity) because we have lost the ability to find our own inner truth and beauty. We compare ourselves to collective ideals which are manipulated by computer graphics which give a distorted ideal of beauty; ideals which bombard us from magazines, television and the movies, rather than to the true images of beauty which this goddess can reveal to us and in us.

Images of beauty affect our relationship to our bodies. Because we are unaware of Aphrodite's inherent love and obedience to the *anima mundi,* the Feminine Spirit in nature, her anger at being ignored (she killed Hippolytus for thinking that he was immune to her powers of love) translates into misused energies which help create many of the psychosomatic illnesses of our times. The need to be loved and to love, freely and easily in our bodies, has been repressed and twisted in most people. Americans watched a reality television show where women had plastic surgery to change from *the ugly duckling into the beautiful swan.* Is this an advertisement for the power of plastic surgery to change your life? Or is it an example of the collective fantasy that our technology will save us from the pain and process of life itself? We look for a total makeover in the wrong places, for the makeover is really a need for an inner rebirth, a wake-up call to our sensibilities, allowing our essential self to create the life we've always wanted to live.

Addictions and eating disorders run rampant in our culture, reflecting this repression of our instinctual nature. We are killing ourselves through lack of love for the Earth, our bodies and our Selves. We are so un-attuned to our bodies that we eat poisoned food without any thoughts or qualms. We need to redeem the body through the graciousness of a loving spirit. And to help us, we need to re-establish our ancient relationship to the Earth. In letting our bodies feel the life of the planet and the life of its people, both the pain and the joy, we can make conscious choices about how we collectively want to live our lives. But we will never achieve the promise of 'life, liberty and the pursuit of happiness' until we understand not only our moral obligations but also our relationship to Truth, Beauty and Love, the gifts of Feminine Spirit. Then we can find our true beauty, which in turn will create more beauty. Our cultural images of beauty distort the real meaning of Aphrodite's beauty, for it is Aphrodite's essential connection with her own feminine nature which makes her beauty so wondrous, not a certain look that comes out of men's fantasies.

Collectively, the repression of our Aphroditian nature is reflected, along with all our other addictions, in the epidemic number of anorexic young women and overweight people in our culture. In western culture, women have come to be defined by our bodies, even though those bodies were condemned as sinful not so long ago, and that body image is the result of male fantasies of beauty. Young women do awful things to their bodies to make them conform to collective standards of beauty. Seven year olds worry about going on a diet. But this is not Aphrodite's concept of beauty, as we shall see.

It is true that the wounding of our natures becomes the source of its healing, and just as it is Aphrodite who wounds us, so it is she who can heal us. Overeating replaces other sensual pleasures, and disregards the need of our bodies to give and receive love and pleasure, as well as being a form of rebellion against an empty stereotype of beauty. Aphrodite's passion is transferred onto the illicit pleasure of overeating and overindulging, overloading our body's capacity to process what we take in. In truth, this is really a disregard of desire and passion. Overindulgence puts our senses to sleep, so that we can no longer experience the joy of living itself.

Aphrodite's laughter-loving, passionate involvement in life and love is missing from our lives, and our addictions become its substitute. We stuff ourselves to *taste* love, to understand and know what love is. The anorexic denies the roundness and fullness of the female body, compulsively impelled by an ideal of boyish beauty to reject her feminine nature. She refuses to even taste love, for she cannot bring herself to love the earthiness of her body. In all eating disorders, there seems to be a split between the instinctual need for nourishment and our cultural ways of nourishing. Our culture has lost the ability to nurture life, and we no longer know how to listen to our body's messages. Wisdom can only come if we know how to *taste of life,* for eating can either bring forgetfulness or remembrance.

As women come to understand how our bodies work and what we need to do to sustain them at their optimal level, we will engage our senses so that eating becomes a pleasure rather than an obsession. As we learn to open ourselves to the textures and tastes of food, to their colors and smells, to the satisfaction of eating with all our senses, even the smell of a fully ripe melon, the subtle flavor of herbs, the sight of how we arrange food on our plate and the conversation we share at dinner will all contribute to our nourishment. Eating is not about denying our desires. We need to re-learn how to enjoy our food through the whole range of our sensuality.

Wearing our mantle of furs necessitates that we learn about our bodies and stop listening to a cultural norm that is based on men. It means becoming virginal again, so that we know that we are different than men. Aphrodite's energy needs to come from that virginal place within each woman, so that our choices are made freely from our own inner nature. We need to reclaim our own bodies to become virginal again. Our actions follow our thoughts, and these thoughts reorganize the body at the cellular level. As old cells die, old thoughts and patterns also die. We have the ability to constantly re-create ourselves. So what will we imagine for ourselves? If we do not use this creative energy to put our talents and abilities to work in the world, then this creative energy will back up and create dis-ease in the body.

Three Dynamic States of Virginity

There are three virgin goddesses in Greek mythology who are said to be immune to Aphrodite's charms: Hestia, Athena and Artemis. Remembering that these myths come from a patriarchal viewpoint which splits the Great Goddess into many aspects, what does this say about where and when Aphrodite's power gets focused inwardly, in relating to the Self? Recall what we said about the old meaning of the word virgin: *to belong to oneself, to know oneself and be open to the mystery of Self.* As we will see later, Aphrodite is herself virginal, for while she will unite with a god or a man, she always does it on her own terms and is never ashamed of her actions and decisions. Perhaps these goddesses do not succumb to Aphrodite's charms because they are the energies which form her own virginity.

Artemis, the Virgin Huntress

The Greek Artemis is very much the Maiden aspect of the triple Goddess. She has a bond through the body with Aphrodite. Both are called *Mistress of the Animals*, though Artemis is the Divine Huntress, who cares for, yet also kills the animals of the forest. Aphrodite's power as *Mistress of the Animals* is that she causes the beasts to follow their own nature and come together in joy and pleasure. In the Native American traditions, the animal spirits in each of us help us understand our instinctual nature. Aphrodite helps them fulfill their function in life. Artemis cares for the animals but she also kills them—she supplies the Olympians with their meat at table. In one sense, Artemis is like the adolescent girl who is self-centered or self-conscious; when we are at this age we either ride our instincts or squash them in embarrassment.

The Divine Huntress goes after something she wants, either to supply the king's table with nourishment or to undertake a task. It is Artemis' energy that urges us to shape up and get healthy and take ownership of our body. When the princess demands that a piece of fur from every animal in the kingdom make up her mantle, she wants to reconnect to her animal instincts. The Maiden stands at the edge of the mystery of the unknown; she shows courage, for she does not know what will come. Unfortunately, the patriarchal Artemis can also be unrelated to her own depths-there is a distancing symbolized in the fact that Artemis uses a bow and arrow; killing from afar is a form of objectivity. Her virginity can become cold and harsh, as when she kills her lover and friend, Callisto, for being seduced by Zeus, and there is the danger that the instinctual wisdom of the body will be disregarded for the pure pleasure of strength and control of the body.

This was the case with a young woman who overdid her workout with weightlifting. She felt that weightlifting gave her a sense of power that she never felt in the outside world. But she was, at the time of the dream, beginning to feel that maybe she was overdoing it. She dreamed:

> This older woman I know from the Y has my cat Spice in her stomach. I try for months to get him out and finally I do. He's very skinny and his left eye is missing. I feel horrible and I take care of him until he finally gets better.

The older woman from the Y was someone the dreamer really knew, someone who was beginning to feel empowered by working out at the gym. But in the dream she symbolizes an energy which has gone overboard, and in trying to *digest* this special cat nearly kills it. Cats often symbolize our most independent domesticated instinct, our sexuality, as well as our specifically feminine playfulness. Trying too hard to get into shape destroys the left, feminine eye of the unconscious. The dream showed this woman that her cat-like nature was being destroyed by her over-emphasis on weightlifting, and it helped her to focus on the ways she nourishes her instinctual feminine nature, such as listening to the symbolic consciousness of the dream state.

Artemis demands concreteness whereas Aphrodite plays with many levels of reality. Young women get lost in an *all or nothing* attitude about love and life. Artemis' virginity, her expression of being one-in-herself, is an important stage of development for a woman and for the feminine; it is a closing off of oneself from outside influences to re-discover one's inner reality. But it also can take you so far that you become untouchable and unapproachable, as Actaeon found out when he chanced upon Artemis at her bath. In her unspeakable rage, she turned him into a stag and his own hounds devoured him. Artemis can help women clear a space for themselves in the world, as for instance when women want to go off to a secluded beach to swim and sunbathe by themselves. Often men will come along and feel they have a right to gawk or to initiate conversation. A woman in touch with Artemis will be able to stop that man in his tracks by her look and her actions. Z. Budapest, the Wiccan feminist, refused to speak to men for five whole years while living in Los Angeles! Now that's Artemis at her strongest.

To go off into that uninhibited and uninhabited wilderness that is Artemis' domain is an important step in reclaiming our own feminine standpoint, but it is not necessarily appropriate to make it our only state of being. The ancient Goddess included this aspect but also went beyond her. To understand the fullness of Feminine Spirit, it is necessary to develop Artemis' virginal energy in order to understand and participate in Aphrodite's opened and renewable virginity. Aphrodite is the next stage of development-that of transformative woman.

Pallas Athena the Strategist and Wisdom-Keeper

Pallas Athena is the second goddess who cannot be swayed by Aphrodite's charms. Athena is the archetypal Father's Daughter, having no mother, sprung full-grown from her father Zeus' head after Zeus swallowed her mother, Metis, Goddess of Wisdom. In Greek mythology and cult, Athena is for the man and the masculine in all things. She was worshipped second only to Zeus in Greece, and she seemed to bring her energy to bear on developing the culture and welfare of Athens, her city. Before she was turned into a Father's Daughter, however, she was a Goddess of Wisdom, daughter of the African goddess, Metis. Like the princess, she used her clear-sightedness and strategy to protect herself from her father Zeus by taking on his attributes and going him one better!

Athena represents true leadership and loyalty to a cause. She is that part of our virginity that is given to a creative project or to political action, to our ideals and purpose. She uses her strength of body and mind for the good of all, and her powers of reasoning and of resolving conflicts without violence make her the mediator who can turn even the Furies into the Benevolent Ones. Athena represents the energy women need to be clear-sighted about our future, and even ambitious for its success. Hers is the wisdom of discernment. She is the politician, the lawyer, the doctor, who enjoys meeting men on their terms and going them one better. She is that striving in each of us for new goals, new creativity, new ideas. She protects us with her mighty shield; she makes us bold and whispers strategy in our ears; she inspires creative craftsmanship to meld beauty of form to usefulness.[6] Her wisdom and her creativity are also manifested in Aphrodite's connection with the Arts and culture, and perhaps it is Athena's inventiveness which adds to Aphrodite's charms. Athena's connection to the masculine is echoed in Aphrodite's ability to relate to all men without losing her sense of herself.

Hestia the Hearth of Life

The third virgin goddess who has no need of Aphrodite's charms is the goddess Hestia, or the Roman Vesta. As Artemis was an aspect of the Maiden, and Athena was the virgin Mother of the city-state of Athens, so Hestia can be seen as the virgin Wise Woman of the trinity. Hestia is an image of the eternal fire of life, an objective cosmic force which really needs nothing more than her own flame. She was worshipped first among the gods around the hearth fire, which was considered the central point of the city. It is fire from heaven which helped humanity create culture and cook food; a fiery passion which sparks change, for fire is an elemental power which is whole unto itself. Fur Skin uses Hestia's energy while she toils in the king's kitchen. Hestia has no need of relatedness, and yet within the context of human culture, she and her fire form the circle of life which holds the tribe together. Her very power weaves relationship. She too is part of Aphrodite's virginity, for the power of Aphrodite's passion is the warmth of her lovingness as well as the searing flame of her powers of transformation.

The patriarchal stories of these three virgin goddesses keep them in bondage to the masculine; their virginity belongs to the masculine culture. This has led women to misunderstand these powers. Using and abusing our bodies can lead to becoming an Amazon. The Amazons were a tribe of fierce, women warriors who despised men. They supposedly burned away their right breasts, to allow themselves greater ease in shooting and throwing. Symbolically, this kind of attitude represses a part of our feminine nature which is both nurturing and beautiful, and it devalues its own feminine strength and independence in trying to be like men. The Feminine Spirit in women gives us strength without the necessity of becoming masculine, or of deforming our body's nature. To deny the body we have, to refuse to see and find the real strength of the feminine which stands by feelings and passion and nature, is to glorify a masculine consciousness which rejects the power of these feminine attributes. The virginity these goddesses offer women must be reclaimed, and when this happens, we can see how they are the foundation of Aphrodite's virginity in the midst of the central mystery of relationship.

Aphrodite's Power Is Embodied Love

Woman's nature is strength and endurance, beauty and passion, mystery and light, giving and receiving. Aphrodite is all of these things as the divinity of the body which is the temple of spirit. Born full-grown from the watery abyss of the Collective Unconscious, Aphrodite images the fullness of feminine being, the divine power of love, desire and passion, fully present and available to human nature. She is the cosmic force of love which generates not only children but the give and take and fullness of physical love. She can root us in the mystery of our humanity, and bring us to the knowledge of our place in the cosmos. The Cyprian sage Zenon taught Aphrodite's philosophy: *"Mankind and the universe were bound together in the system of fate..."* for he felt that the end of human existence was life lived in accordance with nature.[7]

Women are now entering into a stage of human development in which we will be called upon to live out this power of love which is so much a part of our nature, and hopefully it will be honored by men and by society. This will take strength and endurance, because we will be (and already are) called idealists when we ask that others try to come to a peaceful and loving understanding of a situation. (Consider that one of Aphrodite's lovers was Ares, the Greek god of War, and that one of their children was a daughter, sweet Harmony.) This will be a mighty and often painful labor, because the pull of unconsciousness and the tyranny of the old order, the dragon of *Revelation*, will try to stop us from our task of teaching the lessons of love and transformation. This is nothing new, and yet, it is the birth of a genuine new order—a new consciousness in which women and men will share equally in the creative tasks of life.

The Judgment Of Paris: Embodied Love

> The evil goddess of Discord, Eris... determined to make trouble... .At an important marriage, that of King Peleus and the sea nymph Thetis, to which she alone of all the divinities was not invited, she threw into the banqueting hall a golden apple marked 'For the Fairest'. Of course all the goddesses wanted it, but in the end the choice was narrowed down to three: Aphrodite, Hera and Pallas Athena. They asked Zeus to judge between them, but very wisely he refused to have anything to do with the matter. He told them to go to Mount Ida, near Troy, where the young prince Paris, also called Alexander, was keeping his father's sheep... .
>
> His amazement can be imagined when there appeared before him the wondrous forms of the three great goddesses... .Hera promised to make him Lord of Europe and Asia; Athena, that he would lead the Trojans to victory against the Greeks and lay Greece in ruins; Aphrodite, that the fairest woman in all the world should be his... .He gave Aphrodite the golden apple.[8]

The name of Troy is remembered for the war fought over Helen, that 'fairest woman in the world' whom Aphrodite promised to Paris. This is a story that has shaped our western cultural identity. Down through the ages, we have longed for, and truly feared, the power of this kind of love. We have told stories to help us understand it. Paris and Helen, Lancelot and Guinevere, Tristan and Iseult. These stories of great love and passion invariably tell us that great love brings with it great destruction. And the western psyche has still to resolve this problem. What we have to realize is that this love constellates the hatred and fear of the patriarchal mind bent on power and control, for true love burns away the illusions of ownership and possession, and sets people free. What would have been the fruits of this kind of love if Helen's choice of Paris had been honored?

It is interesting to see that, in the *Iliad*, Homer seems to reduce Aphrodite to an effeminate Goddess of Love, minimizing her powers, making her merely the daughter of Zeus and Dione, rather than of Ouranos' sea-tossed genitals. In this great story of war, Aphrodite is often mocked by the other gods and goddesses, but this seems to hide the deeper fact that Aphrodite is the most potent of all the divinities, thereby inciting Zeus' need to humiliate her.[9] If you look at Homer's great works, they both revolve around the question of the right relationship to Feminine Spirit. If the wrath of Achilles is an echo of the wrath of Agamemnon and Menalaus, then Homer condemns them all for going to war over the possession of a woman. And Ulysses must contend with the power of the Feminine before he can reclaim his wife, his home and his family. Aphrodite, being made to look powerless and foolish, is in reality the power of love which drives these heroes to their destiny. The gods are well advised to fear her powers, for she offers another dimension to life which is opposed to their masculine ideas of order and power.

> From her comes that all-powerful yearning which can forget the whole world for the sake of the one beloved; that can shatter honorable bonds and break sacred faith only to melt into oneness with her.[10]

Aphrodite is so powerful because she connects us to our deepest yearnings and desires, those very instincts and desires which we have tried to control or repress for fear of the chaos which it brings to the collective order. We fear our bodies as much as we fear death, and so we cannot give ourselves over to love. Very often our sexual desires and fantasies symbolize our deep need for union with the Divine. And if we let it, our deep union with the Divine can open us to our senses so that the world becomes holy. As we have cut ourselves off from our sexual needs, we have also cut ourselves off from a basic connection to Feminine Spirit, so that in reclaiming our sexuality, we come that much closer to Divine Spirit.

As we saw in the fairy tale, Fur Skin came to a consciousness of Feminine Spirit by wearing her mantle of furs. After living as a Father's Daughter, being nurtured by the father's high ideals, she dons the mantle of the body and through the senses comes into relationship with life and the world. Now her ideals and her desires must find a union of opposites, so that when she appears in the three dresses, her new consciousness is revealed. In opening ourselves to this Goddess who connects us to our desire to love the world and the Other, we learn to live out who and what we are. This is what we all search for, the journey we are all on. We have to reconnect with our instincts, both literally in the body and imaginally through the archetypal images, to give birth to the Feminine Spirit of life in all that we know and all that we do.

In the story, Paris not only picks the most beautiful goddess, he chooses the most true and relevant form of the divine feminine. Through the fame of the Trojan War, Aphrodite has survived down to our own age as the most compelling image of beauty and the power of love. Hera represents the feminine as a half-ness desiring the completion of the masculine, for she is called the Perfect One and Zeus is call the Perfector.[11] Hera was originally the goddess of the Moon, especially the full Moon, and so she represents the reflective feminine half of consciousness as it relates to masculine solar consciousness. Athena is the patriarchal feminine ideal, the feminine that is untouchable, not of the Earth, and yet always helpful to men and the patriarchy. It is only Aphrodite, as the wholeness of feminine being, who relates to the Other, whether male or female, out of desire and the joy of union. While Hera offers Paris the pride, glory and power of rulership and Athena offers him victory and honors in battle, Aphrodite offers him herself, in the shape of Helen. Like Solomon, Paris chooses to love Lady Wisdom. Complete and powerful in herself, she alone can offer herself to us.

Searching for Aphrodite

So just who is this Goddess who has come down to us through stories and myths as the embodiment of Woman? In her earlier forms, Aphrodite shares the qualities of other Great Goddess figures of the ancient world. In her earliest form, she was represented as a cone, and later as a female figure with prominent breasts, belly and/or buttocks, and vagina. As such, she was the great Goddess of fertility and maternal powers. But she is also descended from the Queens of Heaven, love and fertility. She shares qualities with the Sumerian Inanna, the Babylonian Ishtar, the Phoenicians Astarte, the Philistine Atargatis and Ashtoreth, and Egyptian Isis, yet she is uniquely herself. She is a bridge between these ancient goddesses and the modern world, for she is the form of the Goddess that the West celebrated in art, song and story through the Middle Ages and the Renaissance.

Aphrodite has also come down to us from ancient times through astrological symbolism. She represents the planet Venus, both the morning and the evening star in many cultures. In an astrology chart, Venus represents what we value as well as what we connect to; how we love others as well as how we love ourselves; where we exhibit creative imagination; where we might become an intermediary between the divine and the human. Venus poses the questions, "What do I value, what do I love?" and proceeds to get us in touch with the passion for that beloved thing.[12] Most appropriately, the astrological symbol of Venus has become the sign for *Woman*. The symbol stands for the circle of Spirit united to the cross of matter through love[13] and is a symbol of the Incarnation, for love fills all of creation with Spirit. It is an image of the power of cohesion, attraction and synthesis which are prominent elements of feminine consciousness. Feminine spirituality is of the Earth and of life, immediate and present in the moment.

Aphrodite/Venus rules three signs in the Zodiac; therefore she is connected with three seasons of the year. She rules both the time of flowering and harvest, as well as the source of all life. Venus rules the sign of Taurus, the time of Beltane in May when Spring flowers begin to blossom. It is when new life takes hold and flowers in all the diversity that nature can imagine. Venus in Taurus wants to feel heaven on Earth through her senses, giving meaning and value to life through the body and through sexuality. Venus in Taurus is interested in the polarities of life, the attraction of male and female, the tension of opposites which gives rise to transformative solutions. She makes us search for what we value.

Venus also rules the sign of Libra in October, the harvest time, the time of community and fruitfulness, when there is a balance between light and dark, between masculine and feminine. She is interested in social relationships; not just love relationships but the whole sphere of proper relationships between all peoples and nations. And so she rules diplomacy and all forms of art. She says each of us must examine what Beauty and Truth mean to us and consciously live it out. Venus in Libra wants each of us to have our own aesthetic, for beauty opens us to Feminine Spirit.

Venus is considered to be exulted in Pisces, which is the sign of the Collective Unconscious, the vast ocean of life where our individuality is dissolved in Divine Spirit and yet also re-born, for in this sign Aphrodite is born again out of the waves. Venus in Pisces gives us the compassion and wisdom that only empathy and an understanding heart can give. Venus in Pisces is romantic and imaginative and creative here because she is once again connected to the great realm of the Collective Unconscious, the source of all the archetypal patterns, the *beingness* of humanity.

Aphrodite's Birth

Although there are different versions of Aphrodite's genealogy[14] the principle story of her birth connects her origins with the cosmic myth of Heaven and Earth. It is Hesiod's story, related in Chapter Four, of how Ouranos, the god of the sky, spread himself lovingly over his wife Gaia, the Earth, at dusk; at that moment of his embrace, he was castrated by their son, Cronos. His blood fell on Gaia, and she gave birth to the Erinyes, the Giants, and to the ash-tree nymphs. Kronos, meanwhile, threw his father's genitals behind him into the waves of the sea and they

> Were carried for a long time on the waves.
> White foam surrounded the immortal flesh,
> And in it grew a girl. At first it touched
> On holy Cythera, from there it came
> To Cyprus, circled by the waves. And there
> The goddess came forth, lovely, much revered,
> And grass grew up beneath her delicate feet.
> Her name is Aphrodite among men
> And gods, because she grew up in the foam,
> And Cytherea, for She reached that land,
> And Cyprogenes from the stormy place
> Where she was born and Philommedes from
> The genitals by which she was conceived.
> Eros is her companion; fair Desire
> Followed her from the first, both at her birth
> And when she joined the company of the gods.[15]

This beautiful account of Aphrodite's sea birth is an image of the Goddess who is rising up out of the Unconscious as we disengage from the patriarchy within ourselves and in the culture at large. We cannot wipe out the last four thousand years of patriarchal consciousness; we must see how a new feminine attitude organically grows out of this development.

The image of Aphrodite rising up out of the waters is one of beauty and grace. How could it be otherwise, when we think of the beauty of the Mediterranean's blue waters? But if Aphrodite was born in the beginnings of the world, it was a very different ocean that she grew in. The primeval seas were alien and cold places, full of monstrous beings, first fruits of creation. Remember my recurring dream from childhood?

> I am in a bathysphere, a round pod with windows, exploring the ocean's depths. But it is an ancient place, billions of years ago. And cold. Cold and alien for a human being. I feel alone. Out in the waters swim giant monstrous fish, bigger than whales.

The thing I remember most about the dream is how completely alien those waters were. There was such a deep coldness and loneliness to that ocean like the coldness of outer space. Symbolically, these were the waters of the deep Collective Unconscious. The coldness of Ouranos' deep heavens was reflected in the coldness of those seas. The deep oceans are still alien places. You just have to go for a swim in the cold, wild waters to feel their strangeness. This vast realm gives birth to Aphrodite! This is a source of great wonder about this Goddess. For out of the cold, alien aloneness of both the heavens and the deep oceans of Earth was born the sweetness and beauty and grace of human connectedness, of sexuality and love and compassion. Out of the cold, inhuman depths comes the best of our humanity, the movement of grace and love and beauty which creates soul within us. Aphrodite is the fire of all life, both human and extra-human, within our world: the prime mover, the elementary cause of evolution and consciousness. The urge to connect, to bond together, to create and to merge are all her gifts, as well as her laws. Even subatomic particles obey these laws.

Mythically, Ouranos is the prototype of the heavenly Father. Astrology offers us a symbolic understanding of how this particular sky god differs from other father gods. The planet Uranus/Ouranos symbolizes the highest of all energies, the Divine Mind, the force of divine revelation which gives insights into the cosmic laws relating humanity to the universe. This energy operates in the realm of the Archetypes. Uranus urges us to find our individuality, our freedom and our awakened consciousness. As the night sky, Ouranos represents the stars and constellations which symbolize the archetypes and pure Spirit. This intuition or revelation tries to encompass the greatest possibilities, expanding the limits and boundaries of our knowledge of the universe and of our deepest selves. The fact that intuition, by its very nature, is a process very difficult to grasp, does not mean that it is an unconscious process.

> The intuitive function is represented in consciousness by an attitude of expectancy, by vision and penetration... intuition is not mere perception or vision, but an active, creative process that puts into the object just as much as it takes out. [16]

The energy symbolized by Ouranos is this intuitive knowing, this expectancy of potential within people and objects. In astrology, Uranus is called the Awakener, because he awakens individuals and the collective into a larger consciousness. He is the urge to break up the old structures; he is also the urge for freedom, change, originality and individuation. He is the source of our experience of the archetypal realms and cosmic consciousness. Chronos/Saturn is the Lord of this world, the Lord of Boundaries, the Lord of Time, who squeezes us into our own narrow view of reality. Astrologically, he is the great Initiator and Teacher, The Dweller at the Threshold; his is the power that tests and tries our souls until we are strong enough to break out of our self-imposed bondage and go free. He is the energy that gives us our own authority over our lives if we are conscious and responsible enough to want it.[17] For it is easier to give away our authority to the state, or the church, or the culture than it is to be the author of our own lives. To aid us in claiming this authority, he initiates a transformation of the Uranian spirit, mingling its potency and creative potential in the seas of the Collective Unconscious. What emerges from the tension of these two gods is the blessing of Aphrodite.

When revelation, imaged here as the potency of Ouranos, mixes in the elemental watery depths of the Unconscious, it is transformed into the essential mystery and beauty of our human nature. A girl is born of the foam of this union, and it is she who embodies divine Feminine Wisdom. She connects us, through our passions, to who we might become. Unfortunately, we distrust our passions, fearing they will bring us destruction, just as the love of Paris and Helen brought destruction to Troy. This is the patriarchy at its worst, for in cutting us off from our passions, it keeps us tame and unable to find our own standpoint, for how can we have a standpoint except for the one based on our truest Self? Aphrodite's birth symbolizes a way in which we can "bring alive again, or make conscious, the world of the heavens."[18]

There is an intuitive, sensitive, experiential, bodily feminine consciousness which expresses itself through the archetype of Aphrodite. It springs from this birth within women and men who are willing to turn to the Unconscious for direction and wisdom. The Unconscious can teach us about our lost heritage when we respect and value it. And it can lead us out of our participation in a patriarchal way of thinking, which is so pervasive in our culture, into true freedom of thought and creativity. It can help us become free women and men.

A woman working in analysis was becoming disenchanted with the Christian Church in which she had been very involved. Her work with her dreams connected her to her own inner life, and she began to find a new spirituality which she saw in terms of her feminine being. In the following dream, she saw that she had left behind the images of the Church and had found her personal connection to Feminine Spirit.

> I am mending things, unusual things like slippers and leather belts. While I'm working, B. (her parish priest and good friend) comes into the room in his 'priest outfit' but without his jacket. We sit together outside, and I am seeing the value of what he has given me as my Feminine Spiritual advisor. He says, "Someday we'll be friends again."
>
> He tells me that his wife has seen the pictures he gave me that were in my house, two pictures of Mary. One is of Mary holding baby Jesus; the other is of Mary, pregnant and holding a sword. B. says that his wife felt that they weren't suitable for me, so he wants to give me something else.
>
> He holds something up, but I don't feel any connection to it. Then he opens a book and I see a beautiful picture of a woman, coming out of the water, wearing a red shift. There are other women in the water, washing.

The woman coming out of the water was described as dark-haired, smiling, very attractive, even radiant. The dreamer feels connected to her. (This is one of Aphrodite's traits, for she is the great connector.) Later, the dreamer did an active imagination in order to understand who this woman in the picture was. The dreamer saw her down by the water once again. She was laughing and she splashed water at the dreamer. She cried out, "Joy, joy in living!" Her name is *Joy in Living*, and she is an invitation into life. This woman's dream is just one of many images of the Goddess that people are discovering within their psyches, but all of the images are similar in describing the passion, energy and radiant beauty of this feminine being. She is alluring, and people want to be connected to her, for it seems that we have lost the capacity for joy in the modern world. The images and attributes that belong to Aphrodite can begin to show us how we might find her within ourselves, and with her, 'joy in living'.

Great Goddess of Sacred Sexuality and Love

The Song of Songs, which is Solomon's.
O that he would kiss me with the kisses of his mouth!
For your love is better than wine,
your anointing oils are fragrant,

...

I am very dark, but comely,
O daughters of Jerusalem,

...

While the king was on his couch,
my nard gave forth its fragrance.
My beloved is to me a bag of myrrh,
that lies between my breasts.

...

Behold, you are beautiful, my love;
behold, you are beautiful;
your eyes are doves.

...

You have ravished my heart, my sister, my bride,
you have ravished my heart with a glance of your eyes,
with one jewel of your necklace.
How sweet is your love, my sister, my bride!
how much better is your love than wine,

and the fragrance of your oils than any spice!
Your lips distil nectar, my bride;
honey and milk are under your tongue;.

. . .

"Who is this that looks forth like the dawn,
fair as the moon, bright as the sun,
terrible as an army with banners?"

. . .

I am my beloved's,
and his desire is for me.
Come, my beloved,
let us go forth into the fields
…There I will give you my love.[19]

The Song of Songs, a beautiful love poem from the Jewish Bible, contains some of the most sensual and passionate images of love to be found in western culture, describing physical as well as spiritual passion. It supposedly expresses the very physical love and desire of King Solomon and his bride, the Queen of Sheba. This ancient love story speaks of a wise king who is visited by a beautiful queen, who comes to test his wisdom with her own. And her wisdom is considerable! She is the queen of a prosperous land hidden in the Arabian Peninsula, controlling trade routes and self-sufficient in agriculture. More often than not, queens ruled Sheba, and were considered the high priestesses of the land. For in Sheba, they worshipped the Sun, the Moon, the Stars and the planets, and used their knowledge of the natural world of earth, water, wind and fire to Sheba's benefit. Their civilization was one of wealth, beauty, balance, intelligence and grace.[20] When the exotic Queen of Sheba tests Solomon's wisdom, she is so impressed that she opens her heart to him and becomes one of his wives. He gives her a son and later she and her child return to Sheba. She left him with *The Song of Songs*.

Another interpretation of King Solomon's dark and lovely bride, 'the Shulamite' is that she is Lady Wisdom, she whom he desired all the days of his life. *'Set me as a seal upon your heart, as a seal upon your arm; for love is strong as death… Many waters cannot quench love, neither can floods drown it.'* The mystery of Solomon's song is this: that Love and Wisdom are one and the same, just as physical love and spiritual love are both holy.

The Song of Songs is also considered one of the most mystical expressions of God's love for his people, in both Jewish and Christian thought. It is traditionally read before Friday evening, the beginning of the Jewish Sabbath. The Sabbath is called the Sabbath-Bride, and is identified with the *Shekhinah* who, in the mystical Jewish tradition of the Kabbalah, is the feminine aspect of God. God marries his bride Israel each Sabbath. Yet on the deepest level, it is the masculine and feminine aspects of God which are united. And in human terms, it is the inner marriage of God and the soul. The people participate in this sacred marriage on a physical as well as spiritual level, for it is required of Torah scholars that they have marital intercourse with their wives on Friday nights.[21] In essence, this means that the Sabbath is spent in the aftermath of love-making, with no other distractions allowed except devotion to the Lord. The wondrous feeling that comes after the sexual act is the basis of striving for a connection with God.

This blending of the instinctual and spiritual is Aphrodite's gift. The very words of *The Song of Songs* describe her attributes of beauty and connectedness. As we gaze at her statues, her naked body calls us to see and know the mystery of her divinity, the union of Divine Spirit with our corporeality: the Spirit whose abode is the human body. Hers is a spirit that can heal all divisions, and it is she who can heal the virgin/whore split within the western psyche if we truly understand her power. Hers is the power to unite with the Divine or with the Other in strength and individuality, for her power is love. And we know the labor involved in love, which makes us strong.

We have to remember that the Christian Church, from its earliest beginnings, viewed sex as inherently evil. The early Church fathers felt that chastity was the only means of finding sanctity, and many of them were obsessed with the notion that sexuality was the cause of our fall into original sin. Medieval theologians felt that sex caused the damnation of the human race, and that women, being the cause of carnal lust, were soulless and the ultimate source of damnation! (They never blamed men for being unable to restrain themselves from raping and pillaging women and children.) The Church set out to destroy paganism and the cults of the ancient Goddess, which viewed sexuality, as well as women, with reverence and honor, and which included fertility rites, and so women were seen as the source of all evil. The Church condemned Eve as the source of our fall from grace when she taught Adam about sex. The Protestants were even worse in their view of sexuality and women, for they preached that men should beat their wives and not take pleasure in the sexual act. The Church's legacy of sexual inhibitions and repression gave rise to the sexual revolution in the '60's, and we are still dealing with inappropriate sexuality in terms of sexual permissiveness and pornography that is out of control. When we react to something, we are still bound to it. It is only when we really free ourselves that we can find a new balance.

We need to make sacred sexuality the norm. For too long it has not been so, and we are still experiencing the dysfunction of our sexual history. Most women have to go through bad relationships before achieving inner freedom, because as souls, we have had to learn to be free after many lifetimes of sexual inequality and domination, as well as having the genetic memory of submission passed down to us through our family lines. We still need to heal our sexuality.

In Raine Eisler's book, *Sacred Pleasure; Sex, Myth and the Politics of the Body*[22], she says that it is important to understand that the way society uses pain or pleasure to motivate human behavior determines how it evolves. Our traditional Christian imagery sacralizes pain rather than pleasure, especially in choosing Christ Crucified rather than the Risen Christ as their central god-image. Women's bodies and sexuality have been demonized by Christianity and therefore rigidly controlled. We end up with a society where there is mistrust between men and women because of this longstanding religious mistrust and control over our sexual relationships.

Ms. Eisler also speaks about two different models of sexuality, the dominator model and the partnership model. In the dominator model, men dominate women through fear and force. They equate sexuality with pain and domination, i.e., pornography, and block the natural bonding that the giving and receiving of sexual pleasure brings. In dominator sexuality, men and masculine consciousness are ranked higher than women and feminine consciousness. Spirit is more important than nature. Our social structure is predominantly hierarchical and authoritarian. The primary functions of sex are procreation and male sexual release. The highest power is the power to dominate and destroy.

The partnership model is based on equality between men and women, and the bonding through sexual pleasure is held sacred. Females and males are equally valued and feminine values such as nurturance and non-violence are given primacy. Both transcendence

273

and immanence are equally valued. The social structure is generally more egalitarian, with difference (religion, gender, race, sexual preference) not automatically associated with superior or inferior social/economic status. Mutual respect and freedom of choice are important. Sex is seen as a bonding between people through the give and take of mutual pleasure. Love is recognized as the highest expression of the evolution of life on our planet, as well as the universal unifying power.[23]

The feminine partnership model is based on love and connectedness. This is the model that Aphrodite advocates between lovers. Even when she mates with Ares, the God of War, she does it on her terms, not his. There is an old saying that *women have to make love to men to take the war out of them*. When we are truly free, we can do just that. In so many troubled relationships, husbands often want to begin the healing process by making love with their wives. Meanwhile, wives get upset because we don't want to make love until our problems are resolved. I wonder if men have a dim memory of the time when they could go to the sacred prostitutes of the Goddess and be healed of the psychological wounds of war. Perhaps when we women remember our sexual healing power, we will stop turning our men away from the marriage bed and from being healed. But first, we must heal ourselves. This is where our spiritual warrior nature comes in. We have to be brave to fully love. It is time to replace the dominator model of relationship and sexuality with the partnership model. If we can reclaim our capacity for sexual pleasure and love, there is hope that we can turn this world around. We need to re-learn the ancient arts of sacred lovemaking.

Aphrodite's Sexuality

Aphrodite emerges from the sea radiant in her feminine sexuality. She does not need a lover, whether man or woman, to awaken or confirm this knowledge for her. She owns her body and knows she is a sexual being. Aphrodite is opposed to those thinkers who would do away with the bodily differences that have kept women second-class citizens for millennia; who would say there is no inherent difference between women and men. Politically and economically men and women must be equal. But our equality cannot be based on sameness, for it does away with the unique vision and understanding of life that manifests through our bodily differences. Our equality must be based on the fact of our differences, for we are created male and female.

274

The Taoist concept of yin and yang speaks of how these two primal energies intermingle in all of creation, how each of us contain both male and female. As we recognize and honor the bodily differences of men and women, we begin to get a true picture of the total meaning of our humanity. The two sexes are miraculous and mysterious. To disregard our bodily differences does away with a consciousness of images, for our bodies *image* femininity and masculinity in the world. We need to get beyond the stereotypes to the reality of our bodies, and when we do, we will begin to understand the mysteries they manifest.

Aphrodite loves our differences, for she is the dynamic that connects the opposites and brings about transformation. In ancient Greece, she was paired with Ares the warrior just as they were known in Rome as Venus and Mars. *Love and War. Make love, not war.* And perhaps the most true—*only love can contain war.* Only love knows how to take the war out of men, only love and compassion can give rise to true peace. Aphrodite's love for Ares is long-standing; even when her husband Hephaestus traps them in an unbreakable chain as they lie in bed together, Aphrodite feels no shame. Perhaps in claiming a connection to the warrior energy of Ares, who as the Roman Mars was concerned with *grappling hand to hand* with an opponent, Aphrodite shows us that it takes the courage and passion of a warrior to engage in sexual love, because it is through our sexuality that we open ourselves to the Other and grapple with that Other. We connect on the most basic levels, and in the battlefield of love, we learn that sometimes surrender can be more pleasurable and ecstatic than victory. And yet in surrendering to love and passion, we come to know and appreciate *otherness.* Love seeks to unite us with all unknowns, bringing its light to each darkness It is through love that we stretch ourselves and become something more, do something more.

Aphrodite can cause the gods to fall in love with mortals, bringing together these two different types of beings, who give birth to *divine mixtures*—heroes, beauties, magicians, sorceresses, kings, gods. It is through her magic that love and life connect heaven and Earth. The instrument of this magic was a garment called *Aphrodite's Golden Girdle*, a band of fabric wound around her body at the second chakra, the energy center of our emotional life and creativity, through which love and desire could bewitch god and mortal alike. This magical garment is a consciousness which gives us an irresistible charm. It is the laughter-loving, joyous, golden consciousness which sees through the eyes of love and sexual desire. It is a consciousness that dares to connect with life. We will never know what new solutions to our personal as well as global problems we can come up with through the power of love and connectedness until we take a leap of faith and try. As we have seen in the past decades, war does not offer us the solutions we need to heal our wounds.

Aphrodite herself is not immune to her own power, which besides joy and pleasure are the emotions of loss and sorrow, for she suffers a terrible longing for many mortals, especially Adonis, who is the Greek version of the Sumerian demi-god, Tammuz.

One day, the wife of King Cinyras the Cyprian, foolishly boasted that her daughter Smyrna was more beautiful than Aphrodite. The goddess avenged this by making Smyrna fall in love with her father. She went to his bed one dark night when he got too drunk to realize what he was doing. When he discovered that he was the father of his daughter's unborn child, he chased her from his palace. He overtook her and raised his sword to kill her, but Aphrodite turned her into a myrrh-tree which his sword cut in half. Out tumbled the infant Adonis.

Now Aphrodite repented for the mischief she had made and took the child and concealed him in a chest, which she entrusted to Persephone, Queen of the Dead. She told her to put the chest away in a dark place. But Persephone was curious and opened the chest and found Adonis inside. He was so lovely that she lifted him out and brought him up in her own palace. When the news reached Aphrodite, she returned at once to claim him. But Persephone would not consent to this, for she had already made Adonis her lover. She appealed to Zeus, but he would have nothing to do with the dispute, for he knew that Aphrodite also wanted him as a lover. So the Muse Calliope was made the judge and she decreed that for one third of the year, Adonis would be with Persephone, one third of the time with Aphrodite, and one third was reserved for himself. But Adonis gave over his time to Aphrodite, and they begrudged his time with Persephone. Persephone in anger told

Ares of Aphrodite's love for Adonis and the god of war became jealous. He disguised himself as a wild boar and rushed at Adonis while he was hunting and gored him to death before Aphrodite's eyes. Anemones sprang from his blood. Adonis' soul went to Persephone's realm, but Aphrodite got Zeus to promise that Adonis would return to her each summer. And he did.[24]

This is the ancient myth of the dying and rising god, the myth of Isis and Osiris, and in a different form, of Mary and Jesus. It is considered a vegetation myth, as well as a myth about the disposing of a sacred king by his successor, for the boar is sacred to the ancient Goddess in her death aspect. The Goddess gives life as well as takes it, and we must come to understand and accept that love too must die. Adonis is killed when faced with the savage and deadly aspects of love. Adonis represents those love affairs which don't have the depth to last, those passionate three-week flings, and even those multiple marriages which end in divorce. In ancient Greece, women planted Adonis gardens in high summer, seeds planted in shallow dirt which grew quickly and died just as quickly. They threw the faded flowers into the sea, weeping and lamenting for lost love.

This is the proper attitude for this quick, passionate type of loving, for Adonis dies young, never reaching maturity. We need to experience this kind of loving and cry for its passing, but we must not hold onto it, for the experience isn't supposed to last. We need to teach our young people that every lover teaches us more about ourselves, and once we discover that our lovers cannot deal with some part of ourselves, it is time to let them go. We learn love through such sexual encounters, and we have to learn not to fear the loss. For love will come again. And so Adonis can be taken on another, imaginal level. Adonis is the willingness to sacrifice for love, so that life can continue and love can come again. In the Greek myth, although Aphrodite mourns for her lover Adonis, she also feels a great joy, for he has willingly sacrificed himself for love. This is the love that she longs for.

Divine Love wants to connect to our humanity. Aphrodite herself feels a terrible longing for the mortal, Anchises, and immediately sets out to win him, bathing and adorning herself before hurrying to find him on Mount Ida.

Zeus wanted to humiliate Aphrodite by making her fall in love with a mortal. This was the handsome Anchises, King of the Dardanians. One night he was asleep in his herdsman's hut on Mount Ida, when Aphrodite visited him in the guise of a mortal princess, clad in a dazzling red robe.

… And she came to Ida with its many springs, the mother of animals. She went right up the mountain to the sheepfolds. Behind her moved gray wolves, fawning on her, and bright-eyed lions, bears and quick, insatiable panthers. When she saw them she felt joy in her heart, and she put longing in their breasts, and immediately they all went into the shade of the valley in twos to sleep with each other.

… the goddess filled his heart with a sweet longing. And love seized Anchises, and he spoke these words:

…No one, no god, no mortal man will stop me right here and now from making love to you immediately. Even if the great Archer Apollo himself should fire groaning arrows from his silver bow - why I would even consent to disappear into the house of Hades after mounting your bed, lady, you who look so much like a goddess.[25]

Aphrodite convinces Anchises that she is a mortal maiden so that he will not be terrified at the thought of making love to a goddess. Afterwards, she reveals her divinity to him and tells him that she will bear him a son, Aeneas, the great hero who later became the founder of Rome. This Goddess is quite willing to bear mortal children.

Just as she sets longing in the heart of Anchises, Aphrodite also delights in setting longing in the hearts of the animals that follow her. This story shows her role as Mistress of Animals. Just as she takes joy in the sight of the animals, she makes them take joy in each other. Psychologically, we can imagine these are the animal spirits within us: the emotions, instincts, psychic energy and imagination that mediate our sexuality to ego-consciousness. This is our chemistry kicking into gear. This kind of love activates the mantle of fur.

Aphrodite's activity within us is the capacity to *imagine* passion as well as to be overcome by it. The dove, the white winged bird of the *Mistress of Animals*, especially symbolizes this capacity to reunite nature and imagination.[26] We can experience and know simultaneously; we have the ability to see images in the depths of our nature, so that as we experience our desire nature we become conscious of the nature of our desires.

Because this is a knowledge that comes from within each one of us, there is a feeling of subjectivity about the love Aphrodite represents. She works through the heart. Sappho, the great Greek poetess of Lesbos, embodies in her poetry this subjectivity, describing personal feelings with great power. Her poetry most often deals with Aphrodite and the themes of love, and she is inspired by the feelings aroused by love: yearning, desolation, jealousy and rapture. Sappho has a personal relationship to her goddess, and she is not afraid to ask for her help in gaining someone's affections.

Hymn to Aphrodite
… Oh Queen, don't break me with suffering and sorrow
But come here now if ever before in the past
You heard my cries from afar and marked them
… And you asked, Blessed one, with a smile on your immortal face,
What ailed me this time, why did I call you again?
And what did I most want for myself in my wild heart.

"Whom shall I persuade this time into the harness of your love?"
Sappho, who's wronging you?…
Come to me now, too; set me loose from this agony.
Fulfill everything my heart longs for. Be my comrade.[27]

Aphrodite's love persuades; it is irresistible. Yet, it is multi-dimensional, for the emotions and feelings of love are many. Between the light, laughter-loving side of love and its dark, wildly passionate side, there are many moods-sorrow, longing, despair, jealousy, hope and hate-a whole range of emotions to be explored and understood. She writes about a consciousness of feelings, a knowing from the heart, so that our feeling judgments can be valued as deeply as our rational ones. When we cultivate the dark, underworld goddess' *eye of death* we begin to see that the darker passions too are full of light. The sorrows of love, as well as the joys of love, bring us to a deeper consciousness of who we are and what we might become.

Love is the intensity of feeling in the moment, the moment made eternal. It is not so much a transient thing as that it is most alive in the immediacy of the moment. So if the same love is not there from moment to moment, its' absence signifies a need to sink more deeply into the mystery of love. The darkness of love, like the darkness of the Moon, sets up an unconscious longing, which calls us to a transformation. This is the *Dark Night of the Soul* which mystics, such as St. John of the Cross, speak of in terms of longing and love. When our love seems most betrayed, we must seek within ourselves for our most true love, the Beloved of the Soul. Mystics know that we must pass through a *cloud of unknowing* to come upon the true light of love.

> Upon a darkened night
> The Flame of love was burning in my breast
> And by a lantern bright
> I fled my house while all in quiet rest.
>
> …
>
> Oh night thou was my guide
> Oh night more loving than the rising sun
> Oh night that joined the lover
> To the beloved one
> Transforming each of them into the other.[28]

The Feminine Spirit within each person calls us to self-knowledge, through both the light and the dark experiences of life. Is there any better way to explore our wholeness than through love's joys and sorrows? The mystery of life can best be met in the spirit of love. This is what I learned from my dream.

I am on a plane and I notice that the name on my ticket is Star. We land in Egypt and I get off the plane because I want to see the Sphinx. I know that it is next to the airport. I walk away from the airport, expecting to see the desert and the big stone image. Instead, I see coming down the road toward me a beautiful baby Sphinx, about the size of a three year old child. It is golden all over and has small wings on its back. It comes right up to me and starts playing and dancing around me. We play together for a time, and then I get on my knees to say goodbye. It comes over and hugs me. As we embrace, I see the two men whom I love standing off to one side of us.

Aphrodite and Wholeness

Aphrodite is called *Philommedes*, which means *member-loving*, because she is born from the sky god's severed member. She is called Lover of Genitals, the archetypal feminine who loves the phallic potency of the masculine. She is a symbol of feminine wholeness, for she does not envy the male—she loves him and willingly unites with anyone who excites her desire. The intensity of her loving and relating exists for its own sake, for the pleasure and fulfillment of both partners. In the free giving and receiving and returning of love, she becomes the center of all creativity. There is a beautiful movie about the famous Venetian courtesan and poetess, Veronica Franco, called *Dangerous Beauty*. This film is a tribute to Aphrodite and the courtesans of Europe, who inspired and created much of western art, literature and culture since the Renaissance. If you want to see a woman who is clothed in the sun of her own creativity and individuality, see this movie!

In ancient times, when patriarchy was just gaining power and the religion of the Goddess and her relationship to fertility and sexuality was still consciously valued, there were sacred prostitutes, priestesses of the Goddess, who would make love to men as a sacred act of worship, a way of connecting men to the power of the Goddess. As the patriarchy took over power from the earlier matriarchy, men still recognized and honored the power of these sacred prostitutes, and there were still priestesses who performed the *hieros gamos*, or sacred marriage, between the king and the Goddess of the land. These women later became the courtesans of ancient Greece. Courtesans enjoyed great personal freedom and economic power, while the wives and female children of men were often treated little better than slaves. These *hetaira*, called *companions to men* were not viewed as common prostitutes, but were often in the center of the political and as well as the social life of Athens, as were her later counterparts in Venice and Paris. The most famous woman in 5th Century Athens was the *hetaira* Aspasia, who lived with the great Athenian political leader, Pericles. Plutarch claimed that

Aspasia was clever and politically astute, and noted that Socrates would bring his students to hear her speak, for she was a teacher of rhetoric, even though she also ran a school for courtesans.[29]

During the Renaissance, the courtesans of Venice, called Honest Courtesans, were as famous for their literary talents as for their sexual artistry, and for the next few centuries, courtesans enjoyed more power and independence, especially economic freedom, than any other women in Western Europe. The courtesans of Europe have left their mark on our architectural, literary and artistic heritage.[30] The courtesan became the ideal incarnation of the Goddess Aphrodite, a woman who belonged to herself, who often enjoyed the same freedom and social benefits as men, who was the intellectual equal of men, and who was as adept at the arts of music, poetry and dance as she was at the art of lovemaking. While the courtesan's place and power depended on men's need for female companionship, the courtesan certainly is the exemplar of the powerful influence women can have on men if we own our wholeness.

Aphrodite's sacred prostitutes and courtesans embodied this ideal of free and whole femininity. These sacred priestesses represented the Goddess to strangers coming to worship at her temple. They made the Goddess physically present to the worshipper, and her power was immediately felt in the awareness of sensation and feeling that lovemaking bestows. Since their sexuality was offered to the Goddess, it became a sacred and conscious part of life. They not only learned the arts of sexual ecstasy, but they used the civilizing arts of music, dance and poetry to open men to the unseen mysteries of the feeling realms, causing men to glimpse unknown possibilities in themselves and in the world. The ancient virtues of these courtesans are Timing, Beauty, Cheek, Brilliance, Gaiety, Grace and Charm. We modern women could learn a lot about getting men to value and complement our standpoint if we practiced these ancient arts.

Women will find our wholeness when our sexuality is as full and as deep as our minds have become. The centuries of shame and sin that Christianity has projected onto sexuality must be healed and transformed, for sexuality cannot be anything other than spiritual when it becomes the union of body *and* spirit. Before we can engage in true union between two people, we must first bring about a union of body and spirit within ourselves. We must *be* somebody if we are to love somebody. Aphrodite can lead us to this kind of feminine individuation.

When Aphrodite's energy works through our bodies, the enchantment, grace, beauty, wit and love of the Goddess can form the bond of relationship between ourselves and the world, drawing out the spirit in the Other, making them see their own beauty and truth. Aphrodite Hetaira is the Goddess of bonds between friends as well as between lovers. She is embodied love and so she is there for everyone who desires her.

> The bewitching one is eager to surrender; the image of loveliness voluntarily bends towards the love stricken with an undisguised yearning which is itself irresistible.[31]

Through a consciousness that grows out of a discrimination of feelings, using intuition, sensations and imagination, we can discover new dimensions of reality. At first, we seem to dissolve in this new feeling realm as we experience the break-up of old, worn-out patterns and perceptions of ourselves and of the world. Each time we emerge from Aphrodite's bath, we are transformed, and our virginity is restored to us. That virginity is our wholeness, for we are both male and female. Aphrodite, that most feminine of goddesses, was sometimes worshipped as a god *Aphroditos*. Because she was born of her father's genitals, she holds the secret of masculine potency within herself. And with the god Hermes, she gives birth to Hermaphrodite, the androgynous being.

> Shining in golden purity, Aphrodite, the male-female wholeness, makes pale every sort of partialness. She is present when wholeness emerges from the halves and when the resolved opposites become the indissoluble goldenness of life.[32]

The Woman Clothed with the Sun

More than ever before, we need to understand what it means to love and to be in relationship. All the old patterns of relationship are changing. Patriarchal marriage was based on ownership and masculine authority. Now that pattern is breaking up and we have to discover new ways to be in equal partnership. The ancient Celts had many different forms of marriage: some lasted for a year and a day; some lasted a lifetime; some lasted through many lifetimes. The

Celts were wise enough to allow for other loves, so a married person could have an official lover. Perhaps this is echoed in the legends of the Arthur, Lancelot and Guinevere triangle.

Today, women and men are searching for the perfect love. Unfortunately, most of us haven't found it yet. We have divorced our way through life, never satisfied with the partner in our lives. And yet when we have no partner, we long for one. Caught up in this paradox, we need to remember that love is sacred work. There might not be a perfect match out there for any of us, but there is the possibility of great love in our lives if we decide to work at learning to love ourselves. Love is sacred, and if we want it in our lives, we have to make it our goal, and treat the people we love with honor and respect, if we want to be treated with respect. When women are true to our own natures, which is love and beauty and sexual honesty, our men will give us the love and honor we deserve.

> You're my religion, you're my church
> You're the Holy Grail at the end of my search.
> Have I been down on my knees for long enough?
> I've been searching the planet to find
> Sacred Love…
> All the saints and angels and the stars up above
> They all bowed down to the flower of creation
> Every man every woman
> Every race every nation
> It all comes down to this
> Sacred Love.[33]

Aphrodite is the archetypal energy of connection, of union. She connects us to ourselves, teaching us to trust the body's feelings and instincts; while through our desires, she connects us to what we want and to where our talents lie. She connects us to our values, helping us live our truth. Aphrodite connects us to the world and to people. She connects us to the world of nature as well as the world of art and learning. She connects us to the people who are important to our lives. She teaches us, if we have learned to love and trust ourselves, to read and understand people, and she also teaches us to empathize with them. Aphrodite connects us to Spirit. She shows us the spirit in nature, both the Earth's nature and our human nature. She opens us to the feeling and the idea that we are all ultimately connected and she does it through our compassion and our imagination. She teaches us that we are one humanity and one world.

Aphrodite gives us many gifts: relationship, love, compassion, art, meaning, peak experiences, sensuality, magic, charisma, passion, wholeness, creativity, generosity, wisdom, transformation, independence, vulnerability. She is behind our soul-full engagement in life which manifests the golden qualities of the Sun.

Aphrodite is the Goddess embodiment of the *Woman clothed with the Sun*. When a woman knows herself and loves herself, she can wear the golden dress of the Sun, for she knows her true worth. In these transformative years, women have to reclaim a positive and responsible relationship to our bodies and to our sexual natures. Our spiritual nature takes on human nature so that we could learn the lessons of life, which is to become co-creators of life in partnership with the Divine Spirit of life. Those lessons are lessons of pleasure and fulfillment as well as lessons of consciousness and responsibility. Aphrodite can connect us to our purpose, if we are willing to playfully do her work.

As women leave the Father's House, we do not leave behind the masculine knowledge we have learned. We are setting out to discover our own feminine wisdom so that we can transform ourselves. As we live in our mantle of furs, we begin to develop a sense of our Self, our inner wholeness. We need to wear the golden dress before we can really understand the moonlit dress, because we need the ability to discriminate and understand what the Unconscious is telling us, because we can get overwhelmed by its contents. There are dangers in the Unconscious that only a deep sense of Self can deflect. We also need to have a clear vision of our beliefs so that when we wear the starry dress, we have our own unique relationship with the Divine.

The gift that women receive when we leave the Father's House is the possibility of becoming a *Woman clothed with the Sun*, who is opened to taking her *stand on the Moon*, and who is so connected to the Divine that she is *crowned with stars*. When women accept this gift and this purpose, we will finally give birth to the Savior, who is the Being we are all becoming.

285

How do you like being a Father's Daughter?
Now think of Aphrodite, her free and easy sexuality, her beauty and goldenness. Find the Aphrodite-in-you and let her play!

Conscious Woman

Someday there will be girls and women whose name will no longer signify merely an opposite of the masculine but something in itself, something that makes one think not of any complement and limit, but only of life and existence: the feminine human being.

This advance will (at first much against the will of the outstripped men) change the love experience, which is now full of error, will alter it from the ground up, reshape it into a relation that is meant to be from one human being to another, no longer of man to woman. And this more human love (that will fulfill itself, infinitely considerate and gentle in binding and releasing) will resemble that which we are preparing with struggle and toil, that love that consists in this, that two solitudes protect and border and salute each other.

Letters to a Young Poet, R.M. Rilke[1]

Chapter Eight
The New Birth

Now we are seeing a dim reflection in a mirror;
but then we shall be seeing face to face.
The knowledge that I have now is imperfect;
but then I shall know as fully as I am known.
—*CORINTHIANS: CH. 13, V. 12.*

Seeing Through a Glass Darkly

Our civilization is in the process of transformation. We are becoming new human beings, global humans. The whole community of life—nature, animals, humans—must prosper if we are to survive and thrive. There is no way around it. We must change. We must evolve. While we live under seemingly constant terrorist threats, if we can believe the U.S. Pentagon, the more challenging threat is climate change. World-wide pollution and overpopulation are reaching critical mass. Our world economy, which is collapsing, is based on the paradigm of perpetual war and conspicuous consumption which creates the widening gap between the wealthy and the poor. AIDS is wide-spread and old diseases are making a comeback. Women are still the victims of male violence and neglect, with over 2.4 million women and girls kidnapped into slavery, and over a 100 million women dead and missing from neglect.

All of the terrors of the *Book of Revelation* are present in our world. We cannot pull the covers over our heads and pretend that everything will be fine. But we also do not have to let the patriarchy's *new world order* run by multi-national corporations be our only option for the future, especially because it is not our best option. We cannot wait for a savior to rescue us. We have to save ourselves. We have to become conscious. We must take responsibility for our world.

But we will never get the balance right if women do not recognize and assume our native powers and talents, not as daughters of the patriarchy, but as an awakened *psyche/soul*, conscious daughters of Lady Wisdom. As we reject the dominator model of relationship and work at a partnership model, all our relationships, personal and planetary, will prosper. We all need to learn what it feels like to live this way, so that we feel secure enough to allow equality between partners. If our intimate relationships are based on the partnership model, we won't be afraid to attempt a partnership relationship with those people and nations who disagree with us. We will know how to trust the mediating presence of Love.

Why is it so hard to imagine the Judeo-Christian West and the Islamic Middle East sitting down together to figure out a way to create a global society that reflects a mixture of our values and creates life, liberty and the pursuit of happiness for all the world, not just America? America used to be the model for freedom around the world. It is time for America and the West to grow up and take responsibility for our actions. But when our governments or religious-political groups insist on the dominator model-our way or the highway (on both sides)-this vision of partnership is denied and invalidated. As women clothed with the Sun, we must bring this partnership model consciously into our intimate relationships, so the political body begins to feel comfortable with it. Like Scheherazade, we must enchant men into giving up their killing rage and accept the possibilities of love. Until we do, there will be no true peace on earth, or between the sexes.

The *Woman clothed with the Sun* is an image of the Divine Feminine that can teach us Wisdom. As we begin to work with this Goddess image, it is like seeing *a dim reflection in a mirror*, trying to understand who this archetypal *Woman* is and what she is trying to teach us. The first step in knowing her is to take on her image, to use our imaginations to feel what it is like to be *clothed with the Sun, to take our standpoint on the natural rhythms of the Moon, and to be crowned by the spiritual light of the Stars.* We have to know when to wear each of Fur Skin's three dresses and be flexible enough to change which one we are wearing when it is called for.

When Carl Jung proposed that there is a consciousness in and of the Unconscious, he characterized it as feminine, because it is Spirit's ways of knowing that have been repressed and lost to our rational, western ego-consciousness. This feminine consciousness is imaginal in nature, because the language it speaks in is the symbolic language of images-the images of our dreams, of our fantasies, and of our primary, feeling experiences.

Our ancient mythologies and fairy tales speak to us in this imaginal language, teaching us their wisdom through the understanding of the heart. This language speaks to us of the uttermost realities, the deepest truths about the way we live and die. The images are a living language, which breathes life and energy into our own lives. They are the stories which teach us our humanity. So to understand this *Woman*, we have to imagine that we *are her* to become her.

We modern women search for our heart's desire when we search out the images and stories of the Goddess, letting them work their magic on our hearts and our minds. We can no longer split up the image of the comforting and comfortable girl-next-door from that of the courageous heroine; the image of the smart businesswoman from the mother; the image of the intellectual from the femme fatale; the image of the virgin from the whore. Women have two distinct sides: one is mysterious, cool and distant as the Moon, imaged as Isis Veiled; one is opened, warm and comforting as the Sun, imaged as Isis Unveiled. These images can be united within each of us. We just have to find ways to let them live themselves out in us. In using our imaginations, the way we did as children, these archetypal images can speak to us, and open us up to Divine Spirit in the world all around us, making us newly aware, in very concrete ways, that there are other dimensions of reality of which we are a part.

The dynamic of transformation is at the very heart of the mystery of Feminine Spirit. That is why it is so important for women to reclaim our ancient knowledge and powers, because our world needs to undergo a transformation. And women have to lead the way. Women exemplify this in our bodies, which undergo major transformations at adolescence, pregnancy and menopause, as well as the monthly bodily transformation of the menstruation cycle. Women's lush bodies image creation and destruction and transformation. The ability to create and nourish new life, as well as the acceptance of the necessity of a blood sacrifice of the old to make way for the new, are both part of this bodily rhythm. Each month, women renew our virginity with the shedding of the old lining of the womb, making our bodies once more ready for the conception of new life. At the same time, women can psychologically reclaim our virginity, our *being-in-one-self*, which calls forth the mystery of the unknown. Unfortunately, our fear of the unknown often keeps us blinded to the fact that with the death of the old comes the transformation into new life. If women can learn to let go of this patriarchal fear of change and death and accept the unknown, we can teach these lessons to our children and to our men. These lessons are about exploring the potentialities of our body, our psyche, our imagination and our spirit. What new wonders will come of this exploration? Whatever they are, we must pursue them with knowledge and wisdom and love, for these enduring soul qualities lead us to the truth of our humanity.

Because women's deep bodily wisdom has been ignored and denied within the culture at large, we have also lost our personal connection to this wisdom. Like men, we would rather live in our thoughts than in our hearts. But times are changing, and women are reclaiming our ancient wisdom. Just as Fur Skin labored in her furry mantle, women are toiling to become conscious of our instinctual nature, which is the ground of our being. The work of becoming conscious of the purpose and meaning of our feminine bodies can lead women to participate consciously in the psychic and spiritual transformation that comes through an understanding of our own human nature. Like the *Woman clothed with the Sun*, we can live consciously in our human bodies, *knowing them for the temple of Spirit that they were meant to be*. When we heal our relationship with our bodies and begin to live more instinctively as well as spiritually, in the future we will find ways to consciously control conception, illness, aging and even death by how we use the power of our imaginations and our intentions.

Women's bodies contain, as well as symbolize, the creative power of transformation in our ability to conceive, gestate, give birth to and nourish life. Feminine Spirit also knows how to allow life to pass over into other states and forms. These are the psychic possibilities of

Feminine Spirit, just as the Masculine Spirit is one of initiating change, of fertilizing power, of penetrating deeper into the mysteries of life. Penetration, fertilization, opening up, taking in, conceiving, gestating, giving birth and nourishing are psychic functions in both men and women. Women have learned about Masculine Spirit through the ages, becoming daughters of the Father. Now it is time to reclaim our feminine gifts and Feminine Spirit and bring them into equal balance with the masculine. It is the spiritual essence of the feminine to initiate openness and receptivity to the penetrating, fertilizing Masculine Spirit. Nothing new can be conceived without this openness, surrender and receptivity. It takes that masculine potency down to the depths of creative power in a spiral dance of balanced relationships.

The Feminine Spirit knows when balance must be restored. Both Inanna, and Psyche descend into the underworld to reclaim the neglected feminine aspects that rule from the Unconscious, thereby initiating a new process of death and rebirth. The Christian savior, Jesus Christ, makes that same descent to reclaim and renew the laws of Spirit by submitting to his own death, while King Arthur and his warriors traveled in his ship Prydwen to reclaim the Celtic treasures from the Caers of death when they go harrowing in Annwn. The descent is the necessary path to shed old attitudes and stand in our primal nature. It is the hero and heroine journey, for after the descent there is always a return to the upper world with the treasures we have reclaimed, and a rebirth to a new sense of ourselves and of our responsibilities to our people. Our responsibilities now are to make sure that our grandchildren to the seventh generation will have a safe and viable world to live in.

What We Imagine, We Can Create

This is the time of worlds colliding
This is the time for kingdoms falling
This is the time of worlds dividing
Time to heed your call.
Send your love into the future
Send your precious love into some distant time
And fix that wounded planet with the love of your healing
Send your love
Send your love.[2]

Once women remember and reclaim these powers of Feminine Spirit, living through its transformative mystery ourselves, we can initiate the transformation of the collective consciousness, bringing to birth a new consciousness of individual destiny and responsibility, as well as a renewal of the culture. This is how we can send our love into the future, by fully living in the *now*. This new vision comes from the wings of the eagle that are bestowed on the *Woman*, wings that are given to us once we see that we have a spiritual heritage that calls us to create heaven here on Earth. We can see this already happening, as more and more people turn to the search for Wisdom, for understanding and for meaning.

As we begin the new millennium, we must be sure that the old *powers-that-be* do not try to absorb this new Feminine Spirit into the old order, like the king's desire to marry Fur Skin. This is the dragon of unconsciousness who waits to devour the *Woman*'s child. We wear the fur mantle until such time as we can also wear the dresses of the Sun, the Moon and the Stars in front of everyone. Each woman must pick her own King, if she is truly to become Queen, and not be coerced into a marriage of convenience with the powers-that-be. Women want to be granted sovereignty during this time of cultural transition. Just as Scheherazade faced the destructiveness of the sultan and brought about his transformation, so we too must face the destructiveness of our times with our new vision and new story, and transform it into a new awareness and a new, fuller life.

This new paradigm being birthed is based on the union of spirit and matter; centering our lives on honoring both in nature and within each other. We can fully live our stories by honoring the beauty and mystery of night as well as the vision and productivity of day; by giving thanks to Brother Wind and Sister Water, Brother Fire and Sister Earth. In waking to the magic of each new dawn, we will find our energy renewed. And each new sunset will take back our excess energy to be renewed in the night. Honoring Feminine Spirit amidst the fullness of our earthly life is not only possible, but necessary. It is our calling and great destiny, for if we don't do it, who will?

Women need to share our new wisdom of transformation with men. Like Aphrodite, who grew out of the foam surrounding the phallus of Ouranos as it floated in the ocean, this new revelation comes from heaven and mixes with the waters of the Collective Unconscious to create their union: Love! Aphrodite calls us to understand and accept our sexuality; Aphrodite brings us to a new awareness of the dynamics of relationship that will strengthen the bonds between men and women. In the image of the Goddess Aphrodite, we see how the power of Lady Wisdom—love, beauty, sacred sexuality and unity—can be the foundation of all our relationships.

This consciousness that comes through all acts of love is a larger awareness and understanding of how we are all one. Sexual union makes us open ourselves to another, deepen ourselves with another, understand ourselves through another. Women have to relearn the ancient arts of lovemaking, seduction and enchantment. This is not about manipulation or servitude, however. If women come to lovemaking knowing our own power, we can become Aphrodite's priestesses for our lovers. Then love can give us the strength to be open and vulnerable to each other and to all of life's experiences. As women come to understand the power and creative possibilities of this power to transform, as we feel it at work within our own souls, we will be able to awaken this feminine power within men. Men will want this tremendous transformative love, instead of being afraid of it. It is our great gift to them, just as their gift to us has been the knowledge of our individuality, which is the greatest gift of the Masculine Spirit. With a true mutual sharing between women and men will come a new masculine creativity that is in tune with this new Feminine Spirit.

Once we contact the transformative power of the feminine within ourselves, we begin to perceive and concretely experience the reality of other dimensions of life, an imaginal consciousness which can open us to the many tremendous possibilities that are encoded and yet still unused in our DNA. Our task is soul-making, the task of awakening our souls through love and desire. As the world comes alive around us, and we know that we are a unity of body, soul and spirit, life will take on these many dimensions, and our true connection with others and with the world at large will become evident. As we come to know ourselves, we will learn to accept the desires and yearnings that this Feminine Spirit engenders in us, and find ways to creatively express them. Whereas before we were cut off from our instinctual natures, we will now learn to express the passions and desires of our feminine sexuality in conscious ways. Like Sir Gawain, we must give sovereignty to the Feminine Spirit of life. This means making love, beauty, playfulness, artistic creativity, courtesy, connectedness, and the wisdom of the Earth priorities.

Where before we were trained to obey like good daughters of the father and follow conventional standards set up for us by church and state, we must now listen to the inner voice of the Feminine Spirit, discriminating between right and wrong according to our own consciences, based in our ideals, for we must never forget that we are all one, and what we do to another person, animal or the Earth herself, we truly do to ourselves. As we become individuals, we learn to take responsibility for our own lives, choosing to follow our own destinies. Free will, the gift of Spirit to humanity, means freely choosing to do what must be done. Then indeed the gifts of Spirit will be poured out upon our humanity.

We need to use all three types of consciousness—masculine, feminine and spiritual—to be truly free. In terms of the world, women need to re-shape the culture, away from our concern with economics to a more creative, life-giving culture that values differences and honors the Earth. We do this through a re-birth of our spiritual consciousness, seeing God and Goddess in all things, honoring the Earth, our personal lives, others, our creativity and our compassion. We are here on Earth to learn the lessons of Aphrodite, born of the starry heavens and the waters of the Earth. She is God's Sophia fallen to Earth; she wants us to see the world and each other through the eyes of Love and Wisdom.

As we come to know ourselves, we will begin to see the Goddess face to face. This seeing will enable us to incarnate her Spirit in our individual ways. No two women will need to be alike, nor look alike, to manifest her beauty. Each woman, in discovering which gifts the Goddess has given her, will manifest what *woman* is and what she can become. *Someday there will be girls and women whose name will no longer signify merely an opposite of the masculine but something in itself, something that makes one think not of any complement and limit, but only of life.*

Our bards—the poets, musicians and storytellers—are already singing about their experience of this new woman. They give us a picture of real women who are totally accepted, with love and not a little confusion, because her lover sees the Goddess in her-the warm and sweet love, the hard truth of the *eye of death*, the innate intelligence and skill, and the turbulent passions and feelings of our longings. Woman

295

becomes a man's grounding, like Mother Earth herself. And he can come to accept the unexpected as part of it all.

Woman is a word that will come to mean many things: Woman will be seen in many images. But the connecting thread of all these images, all these words, all these textures, will be the open, loving, passionate, transformational character of each woman. It will be the golden beauty of life which surrounds a woman- wisdom won by stubborn and day-long toil which adorns and clothes her. The divine image will shine out from her, and people will once again see the beauty of Lady Wisdom on Earth, in the form of her daughters. This transformed consciousness is our next evolutionary leap; it is goal of an awakened humanity, for otherwise we would not have stories that speak of it.

Creating Heaven on Earth

Feminine Spirit says *Yes! Life is sacred.* The world and matter are also spirit. Feminine Spirit denies the patriarchal dogma that says this world is only Maya, illusion, sin and guilt, and that better things await us in a more spiritual realm. Feminine Spirit says that this world is the testing ground of Spirit; it is the place where the Divine manifests in matter. This is a consciousness that can heal the hurts and wounds of the world, *heal the passion of matter*, yet it can only be gained by individual struggle and understanding.

The image of Lady Wisdom, the *Woman clothed with the Sun,* calls us to our destiny as women. The Goddess has returned from the Underworld, and she wants to remind women that we are her daughters. In the *Book of Revelation*, this *Woman* gives birth to the Divine Child, the New Aeon which will establish the City of Peace. Each of us needs to give our love and our creativity to this enterprise, for this is the heroine's task in finding her destiny. Otherwise, our mother the Earth will suffer even more, as will all the life on Earth.

I offer up a dream of paradise re-gained, a gift and a promise from the Unconscious to all of us.

I am walking down to a perfect, crystal clear lake, surrounded by green grass and vibrant trees. The lake is set in a beautiful park. The warm golden sun shines in a deep blue sky. I see animals wandering around - lion, unicorn, wolf, bear - as well as ducks and birds playing in the lake. These, and other animals, are all magnificent and quite friendly, and I am at peace with myself and with them.

Soon I notice three tall beings walking toward me. They have human bodies with the heads of birds: the one in the middle is a magnificent white-feathered hawk, while the two on either side of him have the heads of the sacred Ibis. As they come up to me a voice speaks from the very air: "Behold the new rulers of Paradise. They will replace the old god."

The three beings stop in front of me. The Hawk-headed god looks deeply into my eyes and I feel his power. It is the power of creative life. But it is over-whelming to me, hard to bear. I look beyond them and off to the left, and through a grove of trees, I see a big white marble temple. I know that a woman I want to see is there, and I want to go to her and get away from these powerful beings.

Suddenly remembering that I can fly in my dreams, I slowly rise up and form the wish to go to the temple. Instead I keep floating straight up until I grab hold of a tree branch and climb into the tree. I sit in the tree. Waiting.

Paradise is so often imagined as a Garden or a special island, home of the gods and goddesses as well as the reward of the human soul. The Native Americans, as well as the Celtic peoples, tell of the Blessed Isles to the West, where there is neither want nor hunger nor sorrow nor death, but pleasant fields, abundant food and beauty and truth abounding. *The Isle of Avalon. The Court of Joy. The Orchard of the Rose.* These are all images of the Goddess; images of nature, both Earth's nature and human nature, made holy and whole. This Garden differs from the Garden of Eden "to the extent that primitive innocence differs from the purified innocence of Wisdom and Experience."[3]

The new gods are triune-natured: their bird-heads denote spiritual beings imaged in animal nature united with human bodies. Some of the earliest statues of the Goddess have such bird-heads. It is an animal—human—divine mixture, combining body, mind and spirit. The hawk and the ibis are birds of wisdom. This hawk-headed being is the Egyptian god Horus, who is associated with the Sun, which is our solar system's individual star; the Sun symbolizing the meaning and purpose of our solar system—our place in the cosmic scheme of things. Did you know that "the name Jerusalem or *Urusalem* may be resolved into Eros *al em*, the City of Eros or Horus, our Lord the Sun?"[4] This god calls on us to take up our spiritual power, our nobility of spirit, our royal nature as human beings. He calls us to live soulfully, just as Christ does. And like Horus, whose mother is Isis, this royal nature is based on and gets its power from Feminine Spirit, the powers of Love and Life and Mystery.

The Ibis is another bird which represents the soul's perseverance and aspiration, and is sacred to Thoth, the Egyptian God of Wisdom. These gods call on us to show our true face, our soul and our spirit; they call on us to take a stand for our truth; they call us to action! They are fitting gods for the future, for if we cannot live in the presence of Lady Wisdom, then how can we ever become responsible adults? When the god-image is one of Christ-consciousness, we are called upon to open to cosmic consciousness, to find our destinies, to live in balance with each other and the world, and to penetrate into the mysteries of life.

In the dream, I was not prepared to stand face to face with the power of these new gods, and so I looked first to find the Goddess in her temple. But instead I ended up sitting in the tree, waiting for the right moment to take up my individual destiny, just like Fur Skin sleeping in a tree in her mantle of furs. I had to go back to the Earth and to my most essential Self and wait upon the action of the Self. We all have to. Paradise shows itself to us in a dream or vision, and we are awed by its beauty; yet it awaits the day when we have the strength to bear it. Until that time, we must tell ourselves stories which will prepare us to meet our tasks with love, wisdom, passion, grace, and laughter, which are Aphrodite's gifts to us all.

When a woman imaginally steps into the role of the *Woman clothed with the Sun*, she activates the archetypal power of this ancient symbol, allowing its energy to reverberate through her life and her choices. In aligning herself with this transformational image, a woman reclaims the divine purpose of her life. This story of the *end times* in the *Book of Revelation* is one man's vision of a great change in consciousness, and the need to align ourselves with Spirit's will. But it is not the only vision. It's time women began to *en-vision* the cosmic story of our times.

Pulling Back the Veil

This image of the *Woman clothed with the Sun* says that a new revelation—a drawing aside of the veil in front of divinity—is upon us and this revelation is not about suffering and destruction, but about the new life that comes from the acceptance of death and re-birth. Feminine Spirit wants to create the possibility of new conditions here on Earth and within humanity. Women who are clothed with the Sun, who take our standpoint on the Moon and who are crowned with Stars want to give birth to the possibility of a new consciousness, and to the belief that we don't have to destroy ourselves to change. Women have to take on the challenge of changing our own lives as examples of change. Wisdom's Daughters can heal their relationship with men and help them accept their own connection to Lady Wisdom. Wisdom's Daughters can inspire our sons and daughters to grow up consciously and responsibly.

It's time to look at the world and take on the challenges it presents us with. The challenge might be to start an arts program for troubled teens after school or to get Washington to restore funding for the Endowment for the Arts. We might be called to get involved on a local level to find ways to preserve the purity of our drinking water or fight for better air standards on the national level. We might be called upon to govern, while not engaging in politics. We need to change the way corporations work and how the people in those corporations can share in the profits. We need to advance the role of alternative healing in our lives and take on the responsibility of our own health, which includes making sure our environmental laws are strictly enforced. We need new standards for educating our young, teaching them how their bodies work, the importance of equal and loving relationships, the true powers of the mind and the magic of the imagination. There are so many ways women's vision can heal the world. It is time to just go out and do it!

Lady Wisdom invites us all to sit down at the Round Table of life, where all are equal, to find solutions to the world's problems. Women can come up with some very amazing solutions to many of our world's problems if our institutions would respect and acknowledge our vision. Because they still hold so much power, we have to get men to listen to our deep wisdom and believe in us. Women will probably have to enchant, seduce, inspire, convert and challenge men one at a time to open up to their own feeling life and find Lady Wisdom within themselves. But never doubt that men need to see her in us first! When men learn to trust that women's intuitive ways of knowing do produce real results, when they can also balance their feeling and intuitive side with their rational, concrete reality, then we might begin to find the peace that we all crave.

Humanity may never totally recover Paradise, but if women take on our power to give birth to a new way of being, a balanced equality between Goddess and God, Lady Wisdom and Christ, women and men, dark and light, feminine and masculine, intuition and sensation, feeling and logic, there is the very real hope that the creativity, power and love of the Divine Spirit will not forsake us.

This image of Lady Wisdom as *the Woman clothed with the Sun, standing on the Moon and crowned with twelve Stars* was given to us in the midst of a dark and troubling story, and we need to listen to her if we want to get through this dark and troubled time in our history. The *Woman clothed with the Sun* mirrors our eternal *becoming*. She is set within the context of the cosmos—clothed with the Sun, standing on the Moon, crowned with Stars—and she, like the universe, is engaged in the birthing process. If women look to her as a source of our being, as the Feminine Spirit incarnate in the universe, then perhaps we can reclaim our place in the cosmic story. By seeing ourselves in the mirror of her Being, we can become, as Rilke so rightly saw, the feminine human being, the guardian of the mysteries of birth, death and transformation.

If we want to make sure that the people we love and the world that we live in have the possibility to live, evolve and grow in a positive direction, we could do worse than to turn to Lady Wisdom. She knows us even better than we know ourselves. And that makes all things possible.

For more information on how to become a daughter of Lady Wisdom, go to the Lady Wisdom Chronicles at: http://ladywisdomchronicles. blogspot.com/

About The Author

Cathy Lynn Pagano, M.A is a Counseling Psychologist and Empowerment Coach, and studied Jungian dream analysis at the C.G. Jung Institut-Zurich. She has worked on the process of leaving the Father's House and following Lady Wisdom for over 30 years. As an evolutionary astrologer, she helps her clients understand the Cosmic Story—the energies at play in our solar system. As a Wisdom Coach, she helps her clients access their own inner wisdom. Cathy is an initiated priestess of Sekhmet and leads Wisdom Salons to learn the lessons of Lady Wisdom.

You can find out more about Cathy and her work at her websites: www.wisdom-of-astrology.com, www.imaginecoachingservices.com, and www.starofthebards.com.

Cathy writes four blogs.
Her astrology blog @ http://wisdom-of-astrology.blogspot.com/
Her dream blog @ http://wisdom-of-dreams.blogspot.com/
Her movie blog @ http://thebardsgrove.blogspot.com/
Her Wisdom blog @ http://ladywisdomchronicles.blogspot.com/

You can read her bi-monthly astrology reports online at www.opednews.com and www.astro.com

And you can go to her Wisdom Salon fan page on Facebook at: https://www.facebook.com/pages/Wisdom-Salon-Astrology-Jungian-Psychology-and-Empowerment-Coaching

If you enjoyed *Wisdom's Daughters*, look for the *Wisdom's Daughters Workbook: The Dance of Goddess & God: Further Steps Down the Path of Wisdom*

Footnotes

INTRODUCTION

All Bible references are taken from the <u>Revised Standard Version of The Holy Bible </u>(Camden, N.J.: Thomas Nelson & Sons, 1946.)

CHAPTER ONE

1. Dee Dee Myers, Why Women Should Rule the World, (New York: Harper, 2008), p.240.
2. Liberating Psyche in the Aftermath of 911. Talk by Randy Morris to the C.G. Jung Society, Seattle, Antioch University, Seattle Washington. December 11, 2001.
3. There are many books and Internet sites about the Hopi Prophecies. See http://www.welcomehome.org/rainbow/prophecy/hopi1.html
4. Jose Arguelles, first among many, has written extensively on the Mayan Calendar. http://www.theawakeningshift.com/2010/02/27/mayan-calendar-jose-arguelles-the-dreamspell-calendar/
5. Gregg Braden, Fractal Time, The Secret of 2012 and a New World Age, (Carlsbad, CA: Hay House Inc, 2009). http://www.greggbraden.com/interviews-and-articles/
6. Ray Grasse, Signs of the Times: Unlocking the Symbolic Language of World Events (Charlottesville, VA: Hampton Roads Publishing Company, Inc., 2002).
7. C.S. Lewis, Out of the Silent Planet (New York: Macmillan Publishing Co., 1965).

8. See PBS.org for a series on Frontline called Apocalypse.

9. There is No Tomorrow, article by Bill Moyers, January 30, 2005 on AlterNet.

10. Matthew Fox, The Coming of the Cosmic Christ (San Francisco: Harper and Row, Publishers, 1988), p. 138.

11. John J. Delaney, Ed., A Woman Clothed With the Sun (Garden City, N.Y.: Image Books, 1960), p. 77.

12. Geoffrey Ashe, The Virgin: Mary's Cult and the Re-Emergence of the Goddess, (London: Arkana Books, 1988), p.161.

13. Joseph Campbell and Bill Moyers, The Power of Myth (New York: Doubleday, 1988), p. 5.

14. Fox, Cosmic Christ, p. 18.

CHAPTER TWO

1. Richard F. Burton and Jack Zipes, Ed., Arabian Nights (New York: Penguin Books, 1991), pp. 2-14.

2. Leonard Shlain, The Alphabet versus The Goddess (New York: Viking, 1998).

3. Ibid. p. 3.

4. Robert E. Ornstein, The Psychology of Consciousness (New York: Penguin Books, 1972), 3.

5. Diane Ackerman, The Alchemy of Mind, (New York: Scribner, 2004), pp. 154-155.

6. Liz Greene, The Puppet Master (London, England: Arkana, 1987), p. 51

7. Ray, Paul H.; Sherry Ruth Anderson, The Cultural Creatives: How 50 Million People Are Changing the World (New York: Harmony Books, 2000).

8. Matthew Fox, The Coming of the Cosmic Christ (San Francisco: Harper and Row, Publishers, 1988), p. 19.

9. William Irwin Thompson, Ed., GAIA; A Way of Knowing (Great Barrington, MA: Lindisfarne Press, 1987), p. 8.

10. Jane Roberts, A Seth Book: The Nature of Personal Reality (New York: Prentice Hall Press, 1974), pp. 64-65.

11. Quoted in Jean-Yves LeLoup, The Gospel of Mary Magdalene (Vermont: Inner Traditions, 2002) p. 14.

12. The compact Edition of the Oxford English Dictionary (Oxford: Oxford University Press,1971).

13. James Hillman, Re-Visioning Psychology (New York: Harper & Row, 1975), p. xi.

14. Michael J. Caduto and Joseph Bruchac, Keepers of the Earth (Golden, Colorado: Fulcrum, Inc., 1988), pp. 3-4.

15. George MacDonald, The Gifts of the Child Christ (Grand Rapjids, Michigan: William B. Eerdmans Publishing Company, 1973), p. 27.

16. Jolande Jacobi, Complex, Archetype, Symbol, trans. Ralph Manheim (Princeton, N.J.: Princeton University Press, 1959), pp. 48-49.

17. C. G. Jung, "The Structure and Dynamics of the Psyche" in The Structure and Dynamics of the Psyche (CW 8, 1969), par. 417, p. 213.

18. C. G. Jung, Collected Works, XVIII, p.371.

19. Stephen Mitchell, Ed. & Trans., The Selected Poetry of Rainer Maria Rilke (New York: Vintage Books, 1980), p. 135.

20. Coleman Barks, Ed. & Trans., One-Handed Basket Weaving: Rumi, (Athens, Georgia: Maypop, 1991), p. 29.

CHAPTER THREE

All symbolic interpretations are taken from J.C. Cooper, An Illustrated Encyclopaedia of Traditional Symbols (London: Thames and Hudson, 1978).

1. Quoted in Caitlin Matthews, Arthur and the Sovereignty of Britain, (London, England: Arkana, 1989), pp. 250-252.

2. See Jung's works on alchemy, esp. C.G. Jung Alchemical Studies (CW 13, 1967); Psychology and Alchemy (CW 12, 1968); and Mysterium Coniunctionis (CW 14, 1970).

3. M. Fox, Cosmic Christ, p. 19.

4. George MacDonald, The Gifts of the Child Christ, p. 25.

5. There are many fairy tales concerned with this theme. The one Fur Skin is based on is the tale, Allerleirauh found in the Grimm's Brothers, The Complete Grimm's Fairy Tales (London: Routledge & Kegan Paul, 1975).

6. Marie-Louise von Franz, An Introduction to the Interpretation of Fairytales (Dallas: Spring Publications, 1982), p. 1.

7. Ibid., p. 1.

8. Harold Bayley, The Lost Language of Symbolism (London: Ernest Benn Limited, 1968), p. 167.

9. Fox, Cosmic Christ, p.

10. Bayley, Lost Language, p. 192.

11. There are many myths and tales describing the descent of and to the goddess. The oldest known myth is that of the Sumerian goddess, Inanna, the Queen of Heaven. Inanna decides to go into the underworld, and at each gate of the underworld, she must remove one piece of her magnificent clothing. Her dark sister, Ereshkigal, kills her and hangs her corpse on a peg for three days. Finally she is restored to life, and she reclaims her garments as she returns through the seven gates. Inanna then sends her consort, Dumuzi, to take her place in the underworld, for he was the only one who did not mourn for her. See Sylvia Brinton Perera, Descent to the Goddess (Toronto: Inner City Books, 1981) for a psychological study of this myth.

12. Edward C. Whitmont, The Symbolic Quest (Princeton, N.J.: Princeton University Press, 1969), p. 214.

13. See Karl Kerenyi, Athene, trans. Murry Stein (Zurich: Spring Publications, 1978).

14. Edward F. Edinger, The Creation of Consciousness (Toronto: Inner City Books, 1984), p. 23.

15. Sukie Colegrave, The Spirit of the Valley (London: Virago Ltd., 1979), p. 63.

16. Edward C. Whitmont, Return of the Goddess (New York: Crossroad, 1982), p. 140.

17. Colegrave, Spirit, pp. 96-104.

18. C.G. Jung, "On the Nature of the Psyche" in The Structure and Dynamics of the Psyche (CW 8, 1969), par. 389-390, pp. 192-194.

19. Ibid., par. 390-392, pp. 193-195.

20. Quoted in Storytellers: The Paintings of Susan Seddon Boulet, ed. Michael Babcock from Edward S. Curtis' The North American Indian (1907) (Rohnert Park, CA.: Pomegranate Calendars & Books, 1996).

21. Rosina-Fawzia Al-Rawi, trans. by Monique Arav, Grandmother's Secrets (Brooklyn, NY: Interlink Books, 1999), pp. 57-58.

22. C.G. Jung, "Definitions" in Psychological Types (CW 6, 1971), par. 763-764, p. 450.

23. Jung, "Religious Ideas in Alchemy" in Psychology and Alchemy (CW 12, 1968), par. 334, p. 230.

24. Nor Hall, The Moon and the Virgin (New York: Harper & Row, 1980), pp. 109-133.

25. Quoted in Marie-Louise von Franz, Shadow and Evil in Fairy Tales (New York: Spring Publications, 1974), pp. 38-39.

26. See Tom Brown, Jr. and William Jon Watkins, The Tracker (New York: Berkley Publishing Corp., 1978); and Brown and William Owen, The Search (New York: Berkley Publishing Corp., 1980). These two books are about a young man who grew up in the woods of New Jersey, and was taught the ways of the earth by an old Apache Indian.

27. Fox, Cosmic Christ, p. 53.

28. See two articles on Hestia, the Greek Goddess of the Hearth. Koltuv, B.B. "Hestia/Vesta" in Quadrant-The Journal of the C.G. Jung Foundation for Analytical Psychology, Winter 1977, pp. 57-63; and Stephanie A. Demetrakopoulos, "Hestia, Goddess of the Hearth" in Spring - An Annual of Archetypal Psychology and Jungian Thought 1979 (Irving, Texas: spring Publications, 1979) pp. 55-76.

29. Jean Baker Miller, Towards a New Psychology of Women (Boston: Beacon Press, 1976), on the problems of women finding their own grounding.

30. Maria-Gabriele Wosien, Sacred Dance: Encounter with the Gods (London: Thames and Hudson, 1974).

31. Al-Rawi, Grandmother's Secrets , p. 56.

32. Ibid. p. 33.

33. Ibid.

34. Ibid. p. 55.

CHAPTER FOUR

1. Heinrich Zimmer, The King and the Corpse, ed. by Joseph Campbell (Princeton, N.J.: Princeton University Press, 1956), pp. 89-95.

2. Chief Seattle's Speech, http://www.barefootsworld.net/seattle.html

3. Caitlin & John Matthews, Ladies of the Lake, (London: the Aquarius Press, 1992) pp. 213-214.
4. Shirley Nicholson, The Goddess Re-Awakening, (Wheaton, Ill.: The Theosophical Publishing House, 1994) p. 74-75
5. Charles Boer, trans., Homeric Hymns (Dallas, Texas: Spring Publications, 1970), p. 1.
6. T.C. McLuhan, compiler, Touch the Earth: A Self-Portrait of Indian Existence (London: Abacus, 1980), p. 6.
7. Ibid., p. 107.
8. K. Kerenyi, The Gods of the Greeks, trans. Norman Cameron, (London: Thames and Hudson Ltd., 1979), pp. 20-22.
9. Patricia Berry, "What's the Matter with Mother?" in Echo's Subtle Body, (Dallas, Texas: Spring Publications, 1982), p 2.
10. Ursula Le Guin, The Earthsea Trilogy: The Farthest Shore (New York: Penguin Books, 1979), pp. 422-423.
11. Erich Neumann, The Great Mother, trans. Ralph Manheim (Princeton, N.J.: Princeton University Press, 1970), p. 150.
12. Carlos Castaneda, Journey to Ixtlan (New York: Simon and Schuster, 1972), pp. 54-55.
13. Women Who Run With The Wolves, pp, 3-4.
14. Al-Rawi, Grandmother's Secrets, p. 57.
15. Ibid. pp. 54-55.
16. Ibid. pp. 54, 58-59.
17. Kerenyi, Gods, pp. 46-48.
18. Hall, Moon and the Virgin, p. 45.

CHAPTER FIVE

1. Joseph Jacobs, Indian Fairy Tales, http://www.sacred-texts.com/hin/ift/ift28.htm.
2. Rosemary Ellen Guiley, Moonscapes (New York: Prentice Hall Press, 1991), p. 75.
3. Marina Warner, Alone of All Her Sex: The Myth and Cult of the Virgin Mary (New York: Vintage Books, 1983), p. 258.
4. More English Fairy Tales, ed. Joseph Jacobs, (New York: Schocken Books, 1968) pp. 102-108.
5. Maria Leach, ed., Funk and Wagnalls Standard Dictionary of Folklore, Mythology and Legend (New York: Funk & Wagnalls, 1972), p. 363. Many legends speak of the man in

the moon as someone being punished; some say that he is Judas, exiled for his betrayal of Christ. Other stories say that he is a man who went out on the Sabbath to gather sticks, and in punishment was put on the moon, while certain Native American stories say that the man is there as punishment for incest. It seems that being in the house of the Goddess is punishment for men! And yet, this isn't completely true, for there were civilizations which worshipped the moon as a god. In the ancient Middle East, *Sin* was the moon god of the Sumerians, Babylonians and Assyrians. He was the father of the goddess Ishtar, who ruled the moon and Venus. He was a wise god, who advised the other gods. The same is true of the Egyptian god, *Thoth*, who was worshipped in the form of an ibis, and who was the god of writing, time-keeping, wisdom and magic, as well as all the arts and sciences. But it is Ishtar and Isis who were the Mistresses of moon magic and who were worshipped as such in the ancient world.

6. Demetra George, Finding Our Way Through The Dark, (San Diego, CA: ACS, 1994). A great book about the meaning of the lunar cycle.

7. Erich Neumann, "On the Moon and Matriarchal Consciousness," trans. Hildegard Nagel in Fathers and Mothers, ed. Patricia Berry (Zurich: Spring Publications, 1973), p. 42.

8. See Barbara G. Walker, The Crone: Woman of Age, Wisdom, and Power (San Francisco: Harper & Row, Pub., 1985) for a detailed study of the place of older women in Western civilization.

9. See M. Esther Harding, Woman's Mysteries (New York: G.P. Putnam's Sons, 1971) for the history of the moon's images and for an understanding of the ancient idea of virginity.

10. Hall, Moon and Virgin, p. 11.

11. See Sylvia Brinton Perera, Descent to the Goddess (Toronto: Inner City Books, 1984), Chapter 2 on "The Objectivity of the Eyes of Death."

12. Penelope Shuttle & Peter Redgrove, The Wise Wound: Menstruation and Everywoman (New York: Penguin Books, 1978), p. 14.

13. Emma Jung & Marie-Louise von Franz, The Grail Legend, trans. Andrea Dykes (New York: G.P. Putnam's Sons, 1970).

14. Carlos Castaneda, The Second Ring of Power (New York: Pocket Books, 1980), p. 164.

15. Shuttle & Redgrove, Wise Wound, p. 134.

16. Ibid., Ch. 2, "The Menstrual Epidemic," pp. 42-94.

17. Ann Belford Ulanov, The Feminine (Evanston, Ill.: Northwestern University Press, 1971), p. 175.

18. Ibid., p. 176.

19. Shuttle & Redgrove, Wise Wound, p. 218.

20. Dion Fortune, The Sea Priestess (York Beach, Maine: Samuel Weiser, Inc., 1978), pp. 315-316.

21. Ibid., p. 122.

22. See Nancy Hathaway, The Unicorn (New York: Penguin Books, 1980); Rudiger Robert Beer, Unicorn: Myth and Reality (New York: Mason/Charter, 1977); Odell Shepard, The Lore of the Unicorn (New York: Avenel Books, 1982).

CHAPTER SIX

1. Chet Raymo, 360 Starry Nights (New Jersey: Prentice-Hall, Inc., 1982), p. ix.

2. Warner, Alone of All Her Sex, p. 256.

3. Stephan A. Hoeller, Jung and the Lost Gospels: Insights into The Dead Sea Scrolls and the Nag Hammadi Library (Wheaton, Ill: Quest Books, 1989), pp. 105-11.

4. Caitlin Matthews, Sophia, Goddess of Wisdom, (London: Grafton Books, 1991). pp. 154-155.

5. Ibid., 273.

6. Ibid., pp. 275- 276.

7. Jack Lindsay, trans., Apuleius:The Golden Ass, (Bloomington, Ind.: Indiana University Press, 1962) pp. 236-237.

8. E.A. Wallis Budge, The Gods of the Egyptians, Vol. 2 (New York: Dover Publications, Inc., 1969), pp. 100-105.

9. Caitlin and John Matthews, The Western Way, Vol. 1. (London: Arkana, 1986), p. 77.

10. Raymo, 365 Starry Nights, p. 23.

11. See C. G. Jung's Collected Works on *Alchemy*.

12. Carl G. Jung, "On the Nature of the Psyche" in The Structure

and Dynamics of the Psyche, Vol. 8 of the Collected Works of C. G. Jung, trans. R. F. C. Hull, (Princeton, N.J.: Princeton University Press, 1969), par. 389-390, pp. 192-194.

13. Ibid., par. 392, p. 195.

14. C. G. Jung, Mysterium Coniunctionis, Vol. 14 of the Collected Works, trans. R.F.C. Hull, (Princeton, N.J.: Princeton University Press, 1970), p. 130, footnote 177.

15. Jeremy Taylor, Dream Work (New York: Paulist Press, 1983), pp. 6-8.

16. E. C. Krupp, Echoes of the Ancient Skies (New York: Harper & Row, 1983), p. 2.

17. See Raymo, 365 Starry Nights, p. 10.

18. Munya Andrews, The Seven Sisters of the Pleiades, (Melbourne, Australia: Spinifex Press, 2004). p.320-48.

19. 32. C.G. Jung, "Answer to Job" in Psychology and Religion: West and East, (CW 11, 1969), par. 692, p. 431.

CHAPTER SEVEN

1. Robert Masters, The Goddess Sekhmet: The Way of the Five Bodies (NY: Amity House, 1988), pp. 56-65.

2. John J.L. Mood, Rilke on Love and Other Difficulties, (Toronto, Canada: WW Norton & Company, 1975), pp. 36-37.

3. Jane Ellen Harrison, Prolegomena to the Study of Greek Religion (New York: Meridian Books, 1957), p. 314.

4. Vanda Scaravelli, Awakening the Spine (UK: Labyrinth Publishing Ltd., 1991), p. 97.

5. Karl Kereny, Goddesses of Sun and Moon, trans. Murray Stein (Irving, Texas: Spring Publications, 1979), p. 53.

6. Zsuzsanna E. Budapest, The Grandmother of Time (San Francisco: Harper & Row, Pub., 1989), pp. 133-135.

7. The Woman's Encyclopaedia of Myths and Secrets, ed. Barbara Walker (San Francisco: Harper & Row, Pub., 1983), p. 45.

8. Edith Hamilton, Mythology (New York: Mentor Books, 1942), p. 179.

9. Paul Friedrich, The Meaning of Aphrodite (Chicago: The University of Chicago Press, 1978), p. 62.

10. Walter F. Otto, The Homeric Gods, trans. Moses Hadas (Norfold, England: Thames & Hudson Ltd., 1954), p. 98.

11. Karl Kerenyi, Zeus and Hera, trans. Christopher Holme (Princeton, N.J.: Princeton University Press, 1975), p. 98.

12. Caroline Casey, in a lecture given at Ceres Center in Providence, RI in October, 1983, "The Astrological Significance of the Planet Venus."

13. Isabel M. Hickey, Astrology: A Cosmic Science (Watertown, MA.: Fellowship House, 1970), p. 30.

14. There are other versions of Aphrodite's genelogy. Trying to make her fit in with the rest of the Olympian dynasty, Homer says that she is the child of Zeus and a shadowy goddess called Dione, whose name means the feminine form of Zeus. There is also a Syrian version of her water birth, originally associated with her forerunner, Atargatis, in which an egg falls from the sky into the river Euphrates. Fishes roll it to the bank, doves sit on it to warm it, and finally Venus emerges from it. See Geoffrey Grigson, The Goddess Of Love (London: Quartet Books, 1976), p. 33.

15. Hesiod and Theognis, trans. Dorothea Wender (Middlesex, England: Penguin Books, 1973), p. 29.

16. Quoted in Liz Greene, Relating: An Astrological Guide to Living with Others on a Small Planet (New York: Samuel Weiser, Inc., 1978), p. 78.

17. Hickey, Astrology, pp. 33-36.

18. Greene, Relating, p. 45.

19. Revised Standard Version of the Holy Bible, "The Song of Songs" (Camden, N.J.: Thomas Nelson & Sons, 1952).

20. Barbara Black Koltuv, Ph.D., Solomon & Sheba (York Beach, Maine: Nicolas-Hays, Inc., 1993), pp. 17-31.

21. Gershom G. Scholem, On the Kabbalah and Its Symbolism, trans. R. Manheim (New York: Schocken Books, Inc., 1965), pp. 138-145.

22. Riane Eisler, Sacred Pleasure: Sex, Myth, and the Politics of the Body, (New York: HarperCollins Publishers, 1995.)

23. Ibid., pp. 403-405.

24. 26. Robert Graves, The Greek Myths, Vol. 1 (Baltimore, MD.: Penguin Books, 1955), pp. 69-72.

25. 27. Boer, Homeric Hymns, pp. 72-75.
26. 28. James Hillman, "Silver and the White Earth" in Spring 1981, pp. 44-49.
27. 29. Quoted in Friedrich, Meaning of Aphrodite, p. 124.
28. Verses to *The Dark Night of the Soul* from Loreena McKennitt, The Mirror and the Mask CD (Ontario: Quinlan Road Ltd., 1994).
29. Sarah B. Pomeroy, Goddesses, Whores, Wives, and Slaves: Women in Classical Antiquity. (New York: Schocken Books, 1975), p. 89.
30. Susan Griffin, The Book of the Courtesans, (New York: Broadway Books, 2001).
31. Otto, Homeric Gods, p. 102.
32. Kerenyi, Goddesses of the Sun and Moon, p. 59.
33. Sting, *Sacred Love,* Sacred Love CD, A & M Records, 2003.

CHAPTER EIGHT
1. Rilke on Love and Other Difficulties, pp. 28-31.
2. Sting, *Send Your Love,* Sacred Love CD, A & M Records, 2003.
3. Harold Bayley, The Lost Language of Symbolism (London: Ernest Benn Limited, 1968), p. 227.
4. Ibid., pp. 227-228.
5. Ibid., pp. 227-228.

Made in the USA
Monee, IL
13 February 2020